GAS ATTACK!

By the same author

Accidental Agent
The Thin Yellow Line
The Durham Light Infantry
See How They Ran
Fetch Felix
Against the Assegai
Storm of Steel
Bayonets in the Sun
The Long Way Round

GAS ATTACK!

Chemical Warfare 1915–18 and afterwards

by

WILLIAM MOORE

Leo Cooper
London

Hippocrene Books
New York

First published 1987 by Leo Cooper

Leo Cooper is an independent imprint of
the Heinemann Group of Publishers,
10 Upper Grosvenor Street, London W1X 9PA

LONDON   MELBOURNE   JOHANNESBURG   AUCKLAND

ISBN: 0–85052–4806

Hippocrene Books, Inc.,
171 Madison Avenue,
New York, NY 10016

ISBN: 0 87052 455 0

Photoset by Deltatype Ltd., Ellesmere Port, S. Wirral
Printed by Mackays of Chatham Ltd
Chatham, Kent

Contents

Illustrations

Maps

Drawn by Patrick Leeson

Preface

During an air raid on Tyneside early in the war a 1914–18 veteran suddenly cried 'Gas!' The sound of a rattle could be heard plainly. Bowing to experience, we hastily put on our masks and sat apprehensively until it was realized that the noise had been caused by flapping fabric on a torn barrage balloon. One or two other old soldiers in the street had made the same mistake in other shelters that night and the incident was not referred to again. Poison gas was a subject which people shied away from, especially in those days when the memory of it was still fresh in the minds of so many men.

Chemical warfare is not, however, just part of military history. It is being used today. This year, as last, doctors in Britain have identified injuries to Iranian soldiers brought to private hospitals as being mustard gas burns. A coroner has recorded a verdict that a young soldier was a poison gas victim. Yet politicians still shake their heads and frown at the mention of 'chemical warfare' as if the bombs and missiles in national armouries contain beneficial compounds instead of high explosive products of formulae and precise industrial processes.

Why should the Iraqis (the Iranians are not fighting anyone else) feel it is necessary to be reticent about using a blister agent in their defence? Why does the Soviet Union have an estimated 100,000 VKhv troops trained for CW? Why did Britain cease long ago to make such weapons?

Let us look at the background to this form of warfare.

In 1915 when gas was liberated in cloud form at Ypres there was an outcry from the Allies (and protests from some Germans) on moral grounds. The implication was that it was somehow 'unfair' to choke an enemy to death or disable him when he had no chance to defend himself.

At the same time no one seemed to see anything particularly 'immoral' about using machine guns to hose massed ranks of lumbering infantry at 2,000 yards or more, though it was eventually realized that it was criminally stupid to order troops forward in such a manner against automatic weapons. Nor was it considered 'unfair' to send two massive battle-cruisers with 12-inch guns to the Falklands to sink an outranged, inferior German squadron from which there was only a handful of survivors.

'Morality' gaps can be quickly closed and a few months after the enemy *pioniers* released *kampfgaz* at Ypres, the British 'Special Companies' were preparing for the Battle of Loos and the French *Compagnies* Z were preparing *gaz de champs* for the Champagne offensive. By early summer 1917 both sides had cylinders and shells and a chemical warfare stalemate had been reached; then the Germans used mustard gas for the first time. It took the Allies months to catch up, but they did in the end. Gas development and research continued until the Armistice and there were confident forecasts that in the 'next war' (no one doubted there was going to be one) it would play an important role.

Aerial bombs filled with vesicants, tanks dispensing deadly clouds, all were envisaged. In the event, Blue, Green and Yellow Cross shells were not fired in the Second World War, the geranium-scented 'Dew of Death' did not fall, but gas exerted an influence all the same. Like the 'fleet in being', which never sails but must always be taken into calculations by its opponents' navy, it was always there.

It is still there and no expressions of outrage will make it go away. Should the democracies restore chemical warfare to their options? As long ago as the 1920s a British committee set up to investigate the subject came to the conclusion: 'A nation unprepared for gas warfare lays itself open to sudden and irretrievable disaster.' Has anything really happened to change that assessment? Have we still something to learn from a reappraisal of the use of poison gas on the battlefields of the Western Front and its presence on the sidelines during Hitler's war?

I hope this book will give readers food for thought. In researching it I have received guidance and help from many quarters, though any opinions expressed are my own.

I would like in particular to thank Nigel Sargeant of the Army Information Service in Germany, and his friend Herr Thomas Schmidt for supplying information about Rifleman August Jager, of whom more later. The good soldier Schweik would have recognized him immediately.

Colonel 'Paddy' de Burgh of the Badley Library at the Royal
School of Artillery, and Mrs Zana Hunt, his assistant, were very kind
to me and I am extremely grateful to Major Arthur Hogben,
Custodian of the Explosive Ordnance Disposal Technical Information Centre at Chattenden for his advice on gas shell nomenclature.
The Earl of Dundonald was most encouraging and lent me negatives
of portraits of his ancestors who made a unique contribution to
chemical warfare.

Thanks to Sydney Smith, retired Northern Editor of a national
Sunday newspaper, I was able to get first-hand information as to the
training of 'CW' sappers in 1940, while another old friend, Dr Keith
Norris, cast an expert eye over the scientific content of these pages.

Others I must thank include Major Wade Russell, a serving officer
of the Royal Tank Regiment, Lieut-Colonel Nick Hornby, RA;
Brigadier Joe Starling, now Secretary of the TAVR in Western
Wessex; Colonel G.W.A. Napier of the Institution of Royal
Engineers and Miss E.D. Norris, Assistant Librarian Royal
Engineers Corps Library; Major D.B. Riches, Regimental Secretary
Royal Anglian Regiment; Colonel A.P. Gilks, HQ 9th/12th Royal
Lancers (Prince of Wales's); Lieut-Colonel 'Gus' Gilliver, Regi-
mental Secretary of the Gloucestershire Regiment; Lieut-Colonel
A.A. Fairrie, RHQ Queen's Own Highlanders (Seaforth and
Camerons); Major J. McQ. Hallam, Lancashire HQ, Royal
Regiment of Fusiliers; Peter M. Brown, of the *Lincolnshire Echo*;
Miss Tanya Spriggs, of the *Methodist Recorder*; Mr. R.E. Hooley,
archivist of Messrs Rustons and Hornby, and Mrs Kathleen Watson
and Messrs Walter Asbridge and A. Major-Stevenson of Lincoln.

In preparing and typing the manuscript my wife showed great
patience and perseverance. Finally I would like to pay tribute to the
courtesy and attention I enjoyed at the Public Record office, Kew.

Le Flaguet,
Rauville la Bigot,
January, 1987.

CHAPTER 1

The Admiral's Secret

Midnight. Flanders, Tuesday, 13 April, 1915. The sounds of war are hushed. In the shadows of no-man's-land a German inches towards the ruined village of Langemarck. He moves slowly and carefully. If seen, he is likely to be shot at by sentries on either side. He finds a gap in the barbed wire and scrapes through. Slithering over a mound, he lies still on the edge of an empty trench. He lowers himself on to the firestep and pauses until he hears footsteps, low voices. Taking a deep breath he steps forward. '*Kamerad*!'

The interrogation of Private August Jager of No 6 Company, 234th Reserve Infantry Regiment, 51st Reserve Division, was long and thorough. An officer took notes.

Jager had been content with life. As driver to a general he had warm quarters, good food and interesting work. Then he did something to upset his master and was sent back to his unit in the front line. There he reviewed the prospects, took a poor view of them and decided to desert. He carried with him interesting information.

According to Jager, all was ready for an attack in which asphyxiating gas would be used. The projectors were actually in position, four batteries of twenty 'tubes' to each infantry company. The signal for the assault was to be the firing of three red artillery flares. They were to go up on the 15th.

Special troops had been detailed to handle the 'tubes'. They had devices which would enable them to breathe oxygen during their operations. Ordinary soldiers had protective masks. Jager passed over a satchel to his captors. It contained a pad, large enough to cover the nose and mouth, which could be tied on with tapes.

'It has to be soaked first in a special solution.'

The interrogators handled it gingerly.

Jager had fallen into the hands of the French 11th 'Iron' Division, so called because of its resolute performance during the opening battles on the frontier. Its commander, General Ferry, was a good soldier and promptly passed the warning of a possible attack to the formations on his flanks as well as to his superiors. The reaction of his own chief, General Balfourier, commanding XX Corps, was not exactly what he expected. Jager's information was derided and Ferry was told he had been taken in. The deserter's tale was nonsense – '*billevesée*'!

A liaison officer from Grand Quartier Général was not only scathing but critical. Ferry had passed on his warning to the British. It was not up to mere divisional commanders to send unconfirmed reports of such a nature to Allies. The proper chain of command was through Corps headquarters. The bureaucracy of war frowned on General Ferry.

The only people to take the warning seriously were Ferry's own troops. The 4th Chasseurs, to whom Jager had surrendered, had no doubt the deserter was telling the truth. They had concocted masks of cloth filled with damp hay and had placed containers of lime in their trenches in the hope of neutralizing whatever was going to descend on them. It would be '*les chlores*', they told the Algerians who relieved them.

The Zouaves, in their dashing Second Empire uniforms, short blue waistcoat and baggy red trousers, scoffed at such stories. The Chasseurs, in the equally outdated navy blue capote, which did service for jacket and greatcoat, and their celebrated dark pantalons with the yellow stripe, shrugged their shoulders, pulled down the peaks of their battered kepis and trudged off.

Chemical warfare is ancient history. The Spartans burned faggots soaked in pitch and sulphur under the walls of Belium hoping to upset the besieged Athenians. When the Romans tried to tunnel under the walls of Abracia in 190 BC the defenders drove them out of the workings by pumping in smoke from smouldering feathers. 'Stink pots' were catapulted into mediaeval fortresses (along with plague victims) and Chinese and Malay pirates are said to have used them. But it was a Scottish sailor who first applied himself to the possibility of overcoming opponents with the aid of pungent fumes. By 1811 Thomas Cochrane had earned a high reputation as a naval officer, had captured enemy vessels and been captured (and exchanged) himself.[1]

---

[1] During the Napoleonic wars (as in earlier times) captured officers were often exchanged.

His capacity as an energetic and independent commander was widely recognized, if not always admired. Cochrane was the son of the ninth Earl of Dundonald (the title had Cavalier origins), who had spent the family fortune on agricultural and industrial research, including the manufacture of alkali. Sharing his father's scientific bent, Lord Cochrane studied methods of sulphur production while based in Sicily. He noticed that fumes escaping from the local kilns first rose with the heat, then fell to earth 'destroying all vegetation and endangering animal life to a great distance'. During the sulphur production season no human being was allowed to sleep within three miles of the kilns.

This phenomenon immediately suggested a military potential and Cochrane sent off his observations and suggestions for their implementation to the Prince Regent. 'Prinny' promptly set up a commission to study them. In 1812 the Duke of York, Admiral Lord Exmouth, the Commander-in-Chief Mediterranean, Admiral Lord Keith and Colonel William Congreve, inventor of the artillery rocket, considered what became known as the Arcanum project – arcanum being a profound secret of the type sought by alchemists. The board reported favourably as to the probable efficacy of the Cochrane plan but no decision was taken to adopt it. Cochrane was thanked for his efforts and the papers were filed away. All who knew of them were sworn to secrecy.

With such a fertile and inquisitive mind it was not unnatural that Cochrane should run foul of the Admiralty, and, for a variety of reasons, including a financial scandal within the service, he was dismissed. Undismayed, he took service abroad and led the Greek navy, as well as Chilean-Peruvian and Brazilian fleets to victory in South America's struggle for independence. Such feats could not be ignored. Their Lordships were obliged to take the greatest British admiral since Nelson back into the fold.

The tough old seadog did not give up easily. He apparently mentioned his secret to King William IV and was praised for not having sold it to a foreign power. In 1846 he resurrected the scheme and it was considered by a committee formed under the chairmanship of Major-General Sir John Fox Burgoyne, a veteran of the Peninsular War and at that time inspector-general of fortifications. A naval captain and a gunner colonel were joined on the board by Mr Michael Faraday. This eminent scientist, who had been the right-hand man of Sir Humphry Davy, inventor of the miners' safety lamp, pointed out that the wind could pose problems. He considered that the fumes would be too heavy to rise high enough to be able to affect gunners on bastions or floating batteries, defended ports being the potential targets under consideration. Mr Faraday knew what he was talking about when it came to gases – he had worked, among other projects, on the liquification of chlorine. The Arcanum papers went back to their pigeon hole.

Lord Dundonald – he had now succeeded his penniless father – proceeded to irritate a great number of his contemporaries by championing the case for steam warships. In old age his brain remained as sharp as ever and when, in 1854, during the Crimean War, the British and French armies stalled outside Sevastopol he recalled his Sicilian sulphur plan. Born before the loss of the American colonies and the French Revolution, he dug out his original notes, penned his reflections and conclusions in a fine hand,[1] and sent them off to Lord Palmerston. The Prime Minister read them with interest.

Should he wish to adopt Lord Dundonald's patent method of expelling the Russians from Sevastopol he would be obliged to use four or five hundred tons of sulphur and two thousand tons of coke.

'Experimental trials have shown that about five parts of coke effectually vaporize one part of sulphur.'

The Admiral also suggested it would be advisable to have a thousand barrels of tar on hand to create a smoke screen.

'A quantity of dry firewood, chips, shavings, straw, hay or other combustible materials . . . ought to be kept in readiness for the first favourable and steady breeze.'

Lord Dundonald was confident that the fumes would sweep over the Russian defences and, getting down to business bred from experience, suggested that the outer batteries of the port should be 'smoked, sulphured and blown up by explosion vessels.'

Palmerston seems to have been attracted by the scheme but weighed the implications carefully. He wrote to Lord Panmure, the Secretary at War, with whom he had discussed the proposal:

'I agree with you that if Dundonald [who was then 80] will go out himself to superintend and direct the execution of his scheme, we ought to accept his offer and try his plan. If it succeeds, it will, as you say, save a great number of English and French lives; if it fails in his hands, we shall be exempt from blame, and if we come in for a small share of the ridicule, we can bear it and the greater part will fall on him.'

The inevitable committee sat in secret to consider the Arcanum,

---

[1] Example produced in Churchill's *World Crisis*.

decided it was feasible but that the effects would be 'so horrible that no honourable combatant' would stoop to use such means to achieve the end in view. The plan was not adopted and instructions were given to destroy all correspondence relating to it.

This did not satisfy Dundonald. He petitioned the House of Commons for another inquiry into his 'invention' which he described as 'a simple yet irresistible means whereby ordinary implements in war might be dispensed with and speedy and successful results insured'. He claimed that his plan would enable the British to subdue Cronstadt (the fortified Baltic island covering St Petersburg) or any other stubborn fortress. The Earl's petition was ignored. He then wrote to sundry newspapers and a variety of journals pointing out that 'combustible ships' would never be able to defeat 'stone batteries firing red hot shot' and urged the Government to reconsider his secret method. The topic was raised by MPs from time to time but the Government spokesmen gave answers which, according to a Crimean War history published in 1856[1], 'implied that the scientific and military men consulted saw insurmountable obstacles to the success of the scheme, although the power employed, if really applicable, would be fearfully irresistible'.

In the end the Allies attacked Sevastopol in a manner which bears close comparison with the trench fighting of the Great War and suffered heavy casualties. Parliament and the public were left mystified as to the nature of Dundonald's secret weapon.

The possibilities of chemical warfare excited the imagination of many Victorians. One visionary, writing in the *Popular Science Review* in 1864, said, 'If science were to be allowed her full swing, if society would really allow that "all is fair in war", war might be banished from the earth as a game which neither subject nor king dare play at.'

The writer declared that a few hundred engineers, properly equipped, could render Regent's Park 'utterly uninhabitable' in an incredibly short space of time.

As the smoke of factory chimneys grew thicker over the spreading industrial towns of Europe and as new wonders emerged, feelings of unease grew among statesmen. The subject of projectiles designed solely to give out suffocating gases was discussed at the International Hague Conference in 1899. The following year a number of powers, including Germany, signed a declaration agreeing not to use such weapons. Among those who did not sign were Britain and the United

---

[1] *Chambers Pictorial History of the Russian War*, Edinburgh and London

States. A distinguished American delegate, Admiral Alfred Thayer Mahan, 60-year-old historian and Civil War veteran, said:

'The reproach of cruelty and perfidy addressed against these supposed shells was . . . equally uttered previously against fire-arms and torpedoes, although both are now employed without scruple. It is illogical and not demonstrably humane to be tender about asphyxiating men with gas when all are prepared to admit that it is allowable to blow the bottom out of an ironclad at midnight, throwing four or five hundred men into the sea to be choked by water, with scarcely the remotest chance to escape.'

Evidently he was not impressed by the legal phraseology of the drafters of the legislation. During a debate on the proposed declaration the text was held to imply that a gas shell was all right as long as the effect of the high explosive was greater than any harm which might be caused by the accompanying fumes. Shortly after this the British were accused of using gas shells in South Africa. It was also claimed as proof that vultures always died after eating horses killed by the Royal Artillery's fire, though who identified the unfortunate birds and recorded their fate was not clear. The accusations were dropped, however, after an investigation showed that the brownish-yellow clouds which had given rise to the complaint were the by-product of the shell filling, lyddite, which contained picric acid. Boer victims of the guns were held, therefore, to have been dispatched in a proper manner.

When the subject of chemical warfare was raised again at the Hague Congress of 1907 the rules attached to the 'Convention Respecting the Laws and Customs of War on Land' stated in Article 23

'It is expressly forbidden
    (a)   to employ poison or poisoned arms
    (b)   to employ arms . . . of a nature to cause unnecessary suffering.'

To this Britain formally adhered.

In the meantime the development of more powerful weapons was made possible by the improvement in the quality of steel and chemicals plus means of propulsion. 'Smokeless powder' became commonplace and automatic weapons standard equipment. Soldiers began to consider new methods for attacking the mighty fortresses which blocked traditional invasion routes. At one end of the scale massive howitzers were built to fire shells capable of penetrating steel and concrete. The Austrians excelled at this type of design, probably because of the importance of the fort in Eastern Europe, where Przemysl and Lemberg were spoken of in awe. At the other extreme, the French produced a 26mm rifle grenade. With *fusils lance-cartouches eclairantes* they proposed to attack the narrow slits and loopholes of flanking galleries and casemates.

The grenades were said to have been used in 1912 to subdue the notorious Bonnot Gang – pioneers of the use of getaway cars in bank robberies. Bonnot and his chief lieutenant had been killed when cornered by police at Choisy le Roi in April and in May gendarmes and troops caught up with the survivors. They defended their hideout at Nogent-sur-Marne vigorously, losing two dead, before, according to some accounts, tear gas grenades persuaded them to surrender. The gas – ethyl brom-acetate – did them no harm and they were soon on trial for various crimes including murder.

Within a few years ethyl brom-acetate and similar gases were to bring tears to the eyes of men imbued by much higher ideals than a bunch of bank robbers[1].

[1]A search of the archives of the Paris Prefecture of Police failed to produce any confirmation of the use of '*gaz lacrymogene*' in either encounter. Dynamite was certainly used to wreck both hideouts. As various law enforcement elements were involved – police, *gendarmerie*, the *garde mobile* – someone may have tried an unofficical gas experiment.

CHAPTER 2

A Letter to Winston

The encounter and manoeuvre battles were over. From the Swiss border, through the Vosges, along the heights of the Aisne, across the open moorland of the Somme and the coalfields of Artois, the trenches were strung until they ended in sandbag redoubts on the Belgian shore.

The two sides studied each other's earthworks and wondered how they were going to break through. Attempts to date had been costly failures. A prodigious amount of digging went on.

There was nothing particularly new about their predicament. In the 17th and 18th centuries the recognized way of capturing a fortress was to dig a series of trenches or parallels – so-called because of the way they progressed – so that the besiegers reached a point where their cannon could make a breach in the walls. Honour was then considered satisfied and the commander of the fort had the right to capitulate with the 'honours of war' and march off with drums beating and flags flying. That way lives were saved and the feelings of the vanquished spared. Where stubborn or awkward generals broke the rules and defended a breach unsuccessfully the result was apt to be a messy affair of massacre, looting and pillaging once a place was captured. Warfare became a lot bloodier in the 19th century – hence the severe losses at Sevastopol and in various American Civil War battles – but the trenches remained similar and a soldier from Marlborough's army or General Grant's would have felt quite at home in the earthworks of 1914. Gabions – wicker baskets filled with earth – were in use particularly near the Belgian coast where water lay near the surface. Sandbags – there had been a Sandbag Battery in the Crimea – were in great demand everywhere and 'bomb-proof' shelters were constructed of whatever material was available.

Even barbed wire was not exactly a novelty. *Chevaux de frises* – barriers of felled trees chained together with the branches outwards –had been used for centuries. Barbed wire itself had been used before. Baden-Powell had strung tin cans on it at Mafeking to warn of any Boer approach. He had also sited a Maxim gun to cover the obstacle.

The trenches dug by the Germans and the Allies in 1914 were merely throwbacks to earlier times. Ideally the front line was approached through communication trenches. In front of it lay disputed territory which might be fifty or hundreds of yards wide.

Keeping the enemy beyond grenade range was a belt of barbed wire strung on stout posts. As the blast of a shell was likely to travel along a straight trench and knock out the garrison, the front line was dug in a series of bays, each of which had a step on which a rifleman could stand to fire over the parapet. The firing bays were connected by deep stretches of trench known as traverses. So much for the theory. In practice some positions were simply glorified ditches which had been adapted on the spot to provide cover at some desperate moment and subsequently retained out of sheer stubbornness.

Behind the trench lines stood batteries of guns covering no-man's-land and threatening the enemy rear.

In the First Battle of Ypres the Germans, advancing in masses, recalling scenes from the Franco–Prussian War forty-four years earlier, suffered appalling losses at the hands of the regular British infantry, skilled in the use of the powerful .303 Lee-Enfield rifle. Like the flower of Britain's manhood sacrificed on the Somme in 1916, the German volunteers who fell at Ypres in 1914 were of superlative quality, so clearly heroism was not enough. Any breakthrough on the Western Front was going to need careful planning and preparation – siege operations, a breaching bombardment and the storming of the gap created. There was, however, ample room for manoeuvre on the Eastern Front, which, by virtue of its vast expanse, could not be held in the same way. Indeed there was a strong school of thought which argued that 'the war must be won in the East'. The newly-promoted Field Marshal Paul von Hindenburg and his chief aide, Major-General Erich Ludendorff, were its sponsors. As they had shattered and rounded up the Russian Second Army at Tannenberg in August, 1914, their views could not be ignored.

The problem was carefully considered by the Chief of the Great General Staff, General Erich Von Falkenhayn.[1] Much was expected of him. After the German defeat on the Marne he had been called

[1] Falkenhayn, an infantryman, had spent three years, 1900–3, in China following the Boxer Rebellion.

from the post of Prussian War Minister to take over the reins from the cultured, portly and physically unfit General Helmuth von Moltke[1], nephew of the revered victor of 1870.

While accepting that victories could be gained in the East, Falkenhayn doubted if they could be decisive: 'Napoleon's experience did not invite an imitation of his example.' He could not, however, ignore the precarious position of his Austrian allies who were in serious trouble in the Carpathians and looked like giving way. The consequences of such a reverse were completely unacceptable and finally Falkenhayn decided to reinforce Hindenburg from the central reserve in Germany and to send seven infantry divisions and a cavalry division from the Western Front to Galicia. Once the Russians had been struck a powerful blow and the morale of the Austrians had been restored, forces could be switched back to the West.

Falkenhayn was able to implement this imaginative and complex manoeuvre thanks to the excellent German rail network and the specialist troops available.

There were two regiments in the Berlin railway brigade, a third at Juterborg and there was also the Military Railroad Bureau. Movement orders were quickly drawn up to make the fullest use of the internal lines of communication.

The troop transfer was carried out under conditions of strict security. The Germans did not even inform their allies of the plan until the middle of April, 1915, when Falkenhayn telegraphed his proposal, saying, 'In view of its vital secrecy, I have not yet had it worked out by my own staff'.

Conrad von Hotzendorff, the Austrian Commander-in-Chief, was so elated by the arrival of news of impending succour that he caught the first train to Berlin and arranged to call at the War Ministry at 6 pm the following day.

The route taken by the German divisions bound for Galicia was deliberately circuitous. All soldiers' mail was censored and units were not told of their destinations until they were almost there.

In order further to deceive the Allies a strong cavalry raid was to be launched into East Prussia, while there was to be 'lively activity in the positions along the whole Western Front, combined with attacks, in so far as the modest numbers remaining there permitted'.

Falkenhayn's memoirs also contain the following revealing passage: 'One such undertaking in the area of the Fourth Army

[1] Moltke 'the Younger' died suddenly at a function in Berlin in 1916 aged 68.

before Ypres developed into a serious attack because the gas weapon, which was used for the first time on a large scale, supplied the opportunity. Its surprise effect was very great.'

In other words, modern chemical warfare – 'lively activity' – was introduced to the world almost as an afterthought. The gas attack in Falkenhayn's eyes was on a par with the diversion to be created by the squadrons trotting between the Niemen and the Baltic, lance pennants fluttering, sabres ready to spring from their scabbards and carbines lashed to their saddles.

Later he was critical of the handling of the cavalry. It had not advanced in mass. Eventually an operation had to be launched to extricate it from its difficulties.

The possible use of gas as a weapon had been considered earlier in 1914 as a filling for shells and hand bombs. The French experimented with a grenade containing a more powerful mixture of the tear gas used against the Bonnot Gang. The Germans tried to find ways of adding to the effect of an exploding shell. Front-line commanders were apt to blame the failure of their attacks on the inadequacy of conventional explosives. They required something which would enable them to overwhelm opponents who held out stubbornly in the cellars of ruined villages. In October, 1914, Falkenhayn set up a committee to study the problem. A non-poisonous irritant powder, double salts of dianisidene, was tried in standard shrapnel shells[1] but the use of some 3,000 of them in the Neuve-Chapelle sector at the end of the same month appears to have gone unnoticed by the recipients. The search continued and, thanks to the perseverance of the brothers Tappen, one, Hans, a chemist, the other, Gerhard, chief of Falkenhayn's operation branch, shells were produced filled with xylyl bromide, a liquid which on explosion gave off a vapour similar to the French tear gas.

After extensive tests on the Kummersdorf artillery ranges near Berlin, a consignment of 18,000 of these projectiles rattled over the indispensable railway system to the front between Lodz and Warsaw. These T-shells (so-named because the contents were marked T-stoff after Tappen, the chemist) were fired in large numbers against the Russian position at Bolimow. They made no more impression than those used at Neuve-Chapelle. The attack met fierce resistance and foundered. It was quickly realized that the extreme cold had affected the reaction of the chemical but by that time thousands of German soldiers had paid with their lives for this laboratory oversight.

[1] See A.M. Prentiss, *Chemicals in War*, McGraw Hill, 1937.

There was, however, every reason to believe that in a temperate climate T-shells would be more effective. The filling was boosted with another chemical (the bromacetone of the French grenade-launcher) and consignments of the new shell were sent to Flanders. Fired by 150mm howitzer batteries in the Nieuport sector, they too burst upon their targets without attracting any more attention than conventional high-explosive shells.

Commanders continued to question the viability of gas as an artillery weapon. Certainly the manufacture of the shells was complicated. A lead cylinder containing chemicals had to be fitted into the normal casing; production lines had to be set up and the whole process needed careful supervision; and this at a time when the front was short of ordinary HE shell.

The matter had caused much discussion and many people were consulted including Dr Fritz Jacob Haber, Director of the Kaiser Wilhelm Chemical Institute in Berlin. Dr Haber, a 46-year-old non-commissioned officer in the Landwehr (militia) before the war and the son of a wealthy dry-salter from Breslau, Silesia, had been appointed head of a newly-created chemical warfare section of the German war ministry and promoted captain by special warrant.

An expert on the properties and composition of ammonia, Haber considered the problem facing the High Command and came up with the suggestion that chlorine might be used as a war gas. As a potential weapon it had much to commend it. It was an acute lung irritant; it was easily compressed into a liquid which would turn into a 'gas' when released; it was more than twice as heavy as air and therefore capable of travelling some distance before dissipating into the atmosphere and, most important of all, it was readily available and made sense economically.

Germany had the most powerful chemical industry in the world. Her synthetic dye plants used large quantities of toxic materials. Great manufacturing concerns provided them – the Badische Anilin und Sodafabrik at Ludgwigshafen; the firm of Meister, Lucius and Bruning at Hochst-am-Main; the Bayer Company at Leverkusen and the Griesheim-Electron Chemische Fabrik. Commerce, not militarism, was their inspiration and they had been assiduous in their attempts to corner the market.[1]

German strength in this field was the subject of a special report[2] written in Washington by Sir Cecil Spring Rice and sent to Sir

[1] See Prentiss, pp 623–646.
[2] PRO CAB 37/127/49

Edward Grey, the Foreign Secretary, who received it on 30 April, almost a fortnight after it was despatched.

It stated that the textile industry in the United States was supposedly suffering from a shortage of 'dyestuffs' which were manufactured exclusively in Germany. The German Ambassador and a certain Mr Metz, a German-American who had met the Kaiser, had issued a manifesto that supplies would be withheld as long as American industry supplied the Allies with the means of continuing the war.

Few things better underline the hold Germany had on the international dye industry, with its stockpile of chemicals. With such massive reserves to call upon there was no danger that the use of gas would interfere with the production of conventional munitions.

Falkenhayn: 'The ordinary weapons of attack often failed completely [in trench warfare]. A weapon had, therefore, to be found which was superior to them but would not tax the limited capacity of the German war industry . . . . Such a weapon existed in gas.'

The small-scale tests carried out by Haber on the ranges convinced Falkenhayn of the viability of creating a battlefield gas cloud and he gave the order to try the real thing. The reason for the proposed attack has already been stated – to divert attention from the East. The question was: Where? And by whom?

Commanders along the whole front were consulted but enthusiasm for the new weapon was lacking. The mediaeval attitude to warfare still persisted in the European officer caste. It seems to have leapfrogged the bigoted butchery of the wars of religion and manifested inself in the continued widespread attachment to the horse.

The Kaiser's annual manoeuvres were expected to end with squadrons charging en masse to victory. An idealized portrait showed Wilhelm II in dragoon uniform wearing a magnificent eagle-crested helmet.

Contemporary German literature made much of the fact that every trooper, hussar, dragoon or uhlan, had been equipped with the lance. It was standard equipment in addition to the sabre and short-range carbine.

The equine influence was just as strong in France. Cuirassiers rode off to war in 1914 wearing breastplates which would have been à la mode at Waterloo. Their concession to the Maxim and the 'quick-firing' field gun was a cloth cover for their polished helmets and another for their shining armour.

Both French and German were addicted to the idea of thundering charges and flashing sabres. Huge oil paintings of the gory cavalry battles of 1870 – the Oldenburg Dragoons and the Garde-Lanciers at Mars-la-Tour, Gallifet's Chasseurs d'Afrique at Floing – were to be found in cavalry barracks on both sides of the Rhine.

The British cavalry, having learned much from small wars and a great deal from the Boer War, was a more practical proposition, its men trained to the standard of the regular infantry in the use of rifle and machine gun. The feeble carbine had been abandoned for the foot-soldier's proven .303 Lee-Enfield.

The British trooper was a good shot, good scout and good horse master. Nevertheless, even among the rank and file, heated arguments persisted as to the superiority of lance over sword and vice versa.

The legacy of the knight in shining armour, Prince Rupert's cavaliers and Zeithen's hussars faded slowly in Europe. Quite a number of soldiers at the top of their profession did not seem to realize that Mars's brazen chariots were being made by Krupp, Vickers, Skoda and Schneider-Creusot.

Sir Douglas Haig firmly opposed the suggestion made by the ageing Lord Roberts after the South African War that lance and sword should be kept for ceremony only. His views may be held to be those of a contemporary edition of *Cavalry Training*: 'Situations may occur when the rifle can be used with greater effect than the sword or lance, but a bold leader will find frequent opportunites for mounted attacks which produce more rapid and decisive results than can be gained by even the most skilful use of the rifle.'

He can hardly have been delighted, therefore, to learn in March, 1915, that the Earl of Dundonald was to visit his headquarters. The twelfth earl was a cavalryman with an obsession about machine guns. As Lord Cochrane he had joined the 2nd Life Guards and fought with the regiment's squadron of the Heavy Camel Corps at Abu Klea in Egypt in 1885. Later he had performed a remarkable ride across the desert to report the death of General Gordon. When commanding his regiment he had done everything possible to promote the use of automatic weapons and had invented a horse-drawn version of the Colt machine gun to accompany cavalry. During the Boer War he had employed a section of Colts in an improvised mounted brigade which, certain officers said, did well despite him. He was criticized by some for his caution in the operations to relieve Ladysmith but no one could dispute that his scouts, under unpaid acting Major Hubert Gough, got there before anyone else. Some of his contemporaries thought him as odd as some of his forebears and dubbed him 'Dundoodle'.[1]

---

[1] See H. Gough, *Soldiering On*, Barker 1954.

Came 1914 and Lord Dundonald, who in the meantime had reorganized the Canadian Militia and advanced to the rank of lieutenant-general, thought of his grandfather's plans for Sevastopol. In great secrecy he wrote to Lord Kitchener, then War Minister, giving details. Lord K, weighed down with a multitude of burdens and doubtless aware of Dundonald's eccentricities, side-stepped the issue. He suggested that as the plans had been put forward by an admiral they should be referred to the Admiralty, once more in great secrecy. Thus it was that they arrived on the desk of the First Lord, Mr Winston Churchill.

Churchill was much more sympathetically inclined than Kitchener. He had been Lord Dundonald's saddle companion at the relief of Ladysmith, the two men having galloped into the town side by side. He studied the copperplate handwriting of the illustrious Admiral Cochrane with respect and allowed his prodigious imagination full rein. He considered also a letter in which Dundonald stated that 'from the coast of Holland to Berlin . . . the wind (from the west) is far more prevalent than from the opposite or eastern section of the compass, especially . . . during November, December, January and February'.

The Earl mentioned the need for men in 'gas-proof helmets' to run the operation: 'An attack against miles of entrenchment would be made on sectional fronts by sulphur and smoke, the intervening blocks where sulphur would not be employed being smoked only, in order to blind the hostile artillery.'[1]

The practical problems involved overcame even the ingenuity of Churchill who, nevertheless, passed on the proposals to Colonel Hankey, Secretary of the Committee of Imperial Defence.

In search of further enlightenment on modern warfare, Dundonald visited the front in March, 1915. He was not to know that his arrival at Haig's headquarters would coincide with the second day of the frustrating battle of Neuve Chapelle and he was received rather coolly. Having explained that he was seeking ways of applying his forebear's plan for 'driving a garrison out of a fort by means of sulphur fumes', he was asked tartly by Sir Douglas how he was going to arrange for a favourable wind. Lord Dundonald took his leave and returned to England where Churchill made him president of the Admiralty Committee on Smoke Screens.

---

[1] Generally accepted proportions – one pound of smoke material per minute per yard of front, a crushing logistic burden.

Soon afterwards the Earl received a letter from the Admiralty stating that the idea of using 'noxious fumes' in land warfare was being dropped. Mr Churchill had agreed with his advisers that it might be inexpedient to introduce into the war an element which might justify the enemy in 'having recourse to inhuman reprisals'.

No one at this time, neither Lord Dundonald, Kitchener nor Churchill, seems to have been aware that details of the scheme had been revealed when Lord Panmure's papers were published in 1908. It is generally accepted, however, that *The Panmure Papers* are singularly dull and it is unlikely that many readers of an inquiring mind ever reached page 340 where the short account begins.

Finding a commander prepared to try out gas was not easy for Falkenhayn. Crown Prince Rupprecht of Bavaria, commanding the Sixth Army in Artois, was unequivocal in his belief that its use was unchivalrous. He also considered its introduction unsound on military grounds. If it were to prove effective, the Allies would copy it. Furthermore he was advised by meteorologists that, with the exception of a spell in the spring, the prevailing winds blew towards the German lines over the greater part of the front.

Colonel-General Karl von Einem, commanding the Third Army, wrote to his wife that not only was the gas weapon anathema to soldiers as a tool of the trade but would be counter-productive in the field of propaganda, creating a 'tremendous scandal' world-wide.

Falkenhayn's operational requirements were pressing, however, and outweighed the philosophical arguments against the use of gas. In his view, by shortening the war it might save many lives. Dr Haber used the same line in discussions with his fellow academics, and there is no reason to doubt his sincerity. Both the General and the chemist were at one in believing that German industry was so far ahead of that of the Allies that there would be no question of competition or swift retaliation.

The meteorologists were brushed aside. Falkenhayn was advised by the experts that Nature would favour them with a fair share of sympathetic breezes. Besides there was one tender spot in the enemy defences where a variety of winds might serve their purpose.

The commander of the Fourth Army, Duke Albrecht of Wurttemberg, had been on the verge of success at Ypres the previous autumn. It was clear that any renewal of the attack in Flanders would draw attention from other fronts, thus fulfilling Falkenhayn's need for a diversion. Ypres was important to the Belgians as it represented a large part of their territory still free from German occupation. Its possession touched an emotional chord with the British public as the BEF had lost heavily defending the town in October and November, 1914. To the French, who had also suffered severe casualties in the earlier battles there, the possession of the sector kept the invaders out of the Pas de Calais – and for once they were not fighting on their own soil. The strategic value of Ypres as a bastion covering the approaches to the Channel ports was evident to all.

The Fourth Army's plans for an orthodox offensive were already well advanced by the spring of 1915 and Major-General Emil Ilse, the Chief of Staff, seems to have had little difficulty in persuading his superior that Falkenhayn's offer of gas as a weapon was acceptable. If the staunchly Catholic Duke had any misgivings on moral or religious grounds they failed to triumph. The fact that the conqueror of Ypres must feature large in the history books may not have escaped the notice of the 50-year-old heir to the Wurttemburg throne.

Ilse it almost certainly was who approached the next actor in the drama – Major-General Berthold von Deimling, already known to the European Press for his part in the 'Zabern Affair'. In 1913 a row over the treatment of Alsatian recruits turned into a constitutional argument on the powers of the military and the rights of civilians. The high-handed behaviour of regimental officers stationed in parts of Alsace and Lorraine, annexed forty years earlier, was criticized. Most of the incidents – for example a crippled cobbler was struck on the head with the pommel of a sword for alleged disrespect – occurred in Deimling's military district which had its headquarters at Strasburg. The general took a very subjective view of the whole business, supported his more bellicose officers and generally pleased Falkenhayn, who was then Prussian War Minister.

Deimling and his troops, who formed XV Corps on mobilization, had been transferred to Flanders during the outflanking manoeuvres of 1914.

Militarist or not in agreeing to be the first commander to use gas, he had his doubts. Perhaps he had learned his lesson from the appalling Press coverage on both sides of the Rhine during the Zabern business.

'The mission of poisoning the enemy as one would rats affected me as it would any straightforward soldier,' he recorded. 'I was disgusted.'

However, not unlike Lord Palmerston seventy years earlier, he found reasons to compromise. 'If these poison gases were to bring about the fall of Ypres, perhaps the victory would decide the whole campaign. Faced with such a possibility it was necessary to suppress one's personal feelings. We had to go on, come what may.'

CHAPTER 3
Hell on Hill 60

Salients present irresistible attractions to generals bent on the offensive. They invite attack. Costly to hold because they are exposed to fire from flank and rear, their extended contours require more troops to defend them than a straight line. If they are overlooked so much the better. The classic means of 'pinching them out' is to strike at the base on both sides.

In the spring of 1915 the trenches protecting the moated Flemish town of Ypres ran in a rough curve from the hamlet of Steenstraat in the north to encompass the larger village of Langemarck. Then, falling short of Passchendaele, they straggled along the slopes of the Gheluvelt plateau and came to rest below the German-occupied Hill 60. The Lizerne–Ypres–Comines canal formed a chord across the bottom of 'The Salient'. From the Menin Gate in the eastern ramparts to no-man's-land was a distance of some five miles.

Beyond the canal, red brick villages and farms and barns of lath and plaster stood battered but not obliterated. Wood and copse sprouted green. Shell holes were most numerous on the modest ridges in the gently rising ground. Though there was plenty of mud about, the fields were tolerably well drained into small streams and lakes. Blackthorn hedges provided sparse cover. Undestroyed church spires made excellent aiming points for the German artillery.

At the beginning of 1915 the French occupied the whole of the Salient but, even as Falkenhayn was secretly preparing an offensive in the East, General Joseph Jacques Cesaire Joffre, the 63-year-old Commander-in-Chief, was covertly preparing to strike towards Vimy in what had been the ancient province of Artois. The British were asked to relieve two of the corps defending Ypres so that the Tenth Army, due to make the attack, could be reinforced. The Tenth was led by General Comte Louis de Maud'huy, who had distinguished himself as a corps commander on the Marne, but came under the direction of General Ferdinand Foch, head of the *Groupe Provisoire du Nord*, a loose command, including the British and Belgians.

Britain had two armies in the field in Flanders. Slotted between the French Eighth at Ypres and the Tenth in Artois were, on the right, the First under Sir Douglas Haig and, on the left, the Second commanded by Sir Horace Smith-Dorrien. Until February both had been composed of two corps of two divisions but, as fresh formations arrived over the Christmas period, they were reinforced. The 27th and 28th Divisions, formed from Regular battalions withdrawn from the Empire, made up V Corps under Sir Herbert Plumer. Having gained some experience of trench war and suffered few casualties, these highly-trained troops were a natural choice to replace the French in and around Ypres. They began a relief in the Salient at the beginning of April and in the middle of the month they were joined by the Canadian Division. The Canadians had arrived in France in February and, having undergone a mild baptism of fire on the fringe of the Neuve Chapelle battle in March, were also up to strength.

The deployment of V Corps meant that the British held an unbroken line from Cuinchy on the La Bassée Canal in the south to a point two- thirds of the way round the perimeter of the Salient. In the north French troops occupied the trenches on the left of V Corps, linking up with the Belgian Army.

The incoming British and Canadians were not exactly pleased with the condition of the sectors they took over. Water was often just below the surface and many defences consisted of piled-up sandbags, not always bullet-proof, which merely served as rests for riflemen. Few of these breastworks had protective barricades behind them, so defenders were vulnerable to shells exploding in their rear. Belts of barbed wire and machine gun posts were pronounced good but most dugouts were better at keeping out the rain than shell splinters and the sanitary arrangements were universally condemned.

The last of the Canadians moved in on 17 April which, until early evening, had been a glorious spring day and comparatively quiet. Only the occasional crump of a searching 5.9 inch howitzer, the brief chatter of a machine gun and the spasmodic crack of a sniper's rifle disturbed the peace. Observation planes droned overhead, watched enviously by the earth-bound on both sides. Still, the muddy communication trenches were drying out, the buds fattening on the wild flowers, and the numerous shops still open in Ypres did good business. By 6.30 hardly a sound disturbed a golden evening.

Half an hour later the British blew five mines under Hill 60, held by
a company of the German 172nd Infantry Regiment. The two largest
contained 2,700 lbs of gunpowder, the smallest 500 lbs of gun cotton.
Before the smoke and dust had cleared the British artillery roared into
life and Royal Engineers with parties of the 1st Royal West Kents,
2nd King's Own Scottish Borderers and the Queen Victoria's Rifles[1]
raced up the crumbling slopes to seize the smouldering craters. Hill
60 was merely the topmost point of a spoil-heap created before the
war by the digging of a railway cutting but it gave observation deep
into the British rear. Its capture was thought important enough for
the Cabinet to be informed. The Prime Minister passed on the news
to the King.[2]

Survivors of the blast were in no fit state to fight but counter-
attacks by their comrades followed fast and furious. The British
troops were forced back over the summit and reported that the enemy
was firing anything he could find at them, including gas shell. At least
that was what they believed was responsible for the pungent smell.
They were not too far out in their guess. Concerned as he was at the
loss of a vital observation post, General von Deimling was even more
anxious to regain the churned-up hillock because its unpleasant secret
might leak out. Cylinders containing chlorine had been buried in the
area for more than a month.

Once scruples had been overcome and the decision to launch a gas
attack was made, the responsible authorities wasted no time. Half of
Germany's total stock of commercial chlorine cylinders had been
requisitioned and the manufacture of another 26,000 smaller containers was started.

Military engineers were allocated and scientists recruited to form
special units which were eventually organized as Pionier Regiment
35. A certain amount of training was carried out and by the end of
February the first cylinders were in position in the XV Corps sector
on the south-eastern side of the Salient. They were placed in groups
of ten and described in signals and messages as 'F' batteries. The gas
pioneers took up residence with the infantry to await a suitable breeze
and the orders to open the valves.

The wind stayed obstinately in the same unhelpful quarter and the
popularity rating of the cylinders dug in alongside the front-line
garrison sank low. Shrapnel and splinters caused unpleasant and
dramatic emissions – the chlorine was under pressure – and unlucky
soldiers were carried away coughing and gasping. Protective pads for

[1] Territorials.
[2] PRO CAB 37/127

the infantry were not on general issue at that time.

Haber himself was gassed while helping to conduct a large-scale exercise at Beverloo in Belgium on April 2. He and another officer trotted their horses incautiously into a patch of thick fumes. Both spent some time in hospital.

As the days passed fears grew for the security of the operation. Fourth Army headquarters decided to prepare another gas attack on the opposite side of the Salient held by two of the reserve Corps – XXIII and XXVI – which had been made up to strength after suffering severely in the autumn. Cylinders were installed along a joint front extending nearly four miles. Some were new deliveries but others had to be dug up and transported with great difficulty from the XV Corps trenches. By 11 April Duke Albrecht had options on both flanks of the Salient. His influence on the wind remained nil.

Enter at this stage the bold ex-chauffeur, August Jager, unaware that he was not the first German soldier to warn of the peril. Two weeks earlier (30 March) an Intelligence bulletin of the French Tenth Army stated:

'According to prisoners taken from XV Corps, there is, along the whole front in the neighbourhood of Zillebeke, a large supply of iron cylinders, 1.4 metres long, which are stored a little in the rear of the trenches in bomb-proof shelters or even buried. They contain a gas which is intended to render the enemy unconscious or to asphyxiate him.'

The method of operating the cylinders was described, as was the protective mask and the need for a favourable wind. The dimensions of the mask exactly tallied with the sample later produced by Jager.

From the amount of information volunteered by the prisoners it is possible that they may have been disaffected Alsatians of the type insulted during the Zabern affair.

Corroborating evidence from different sources should have been at least enough to make people think that something serious was afoot. Unhappily, the statements of Jager and the German XV Corps soldiers were not readily available for comparison. The French division which had taken the prisoners near Zillebeke had been on the point of moving to Artois. Hence the report in the bulletin of the Tenth Army.

Jager's captors were themselves preparing to move, along with the rest of Balfourier's crack XX Corps. Two run-of-the-mill divisions were to take their place. The moves were all part of a masterpiece of muddled military reorganization in which the title Eighth Army disappeared and was replaced by its former description –

Détachement de l'Armée Belgique. For political reasons this all-French formation deployed on either flank of the Belgian Army, two divisions holding the Nieuport Sector next to the sea while the others were miles away at Ypres. At the head of this split command was one General Putz.

Dutifully going through the hand-over notes Balfourier had left for him, Putz seems to have been struck by the report of Jager's interrogation and ordered the deserter to be re-examined.

Doubtless seeking to please, 24-year-old Jager overdid his efforts to co-operate. He recalled too much of what he had seen and where he had been, at the wheel of his General's car. Putz studied the new report and came to the conclusion that Jager was a 'plant', an agent or volunteer primed with false facts to mislead the French and spread dismay. Young Jager must have been a very unhappy man when he was taken away after his second grilling. 'Plants' could be regarded as spies and shot. He could only hope that events would prove his story to be true.

The day forecast for the attack passed without incident on Putz's front. A plane from No. 6 Squadron, Royal Flying Corps, was sent out to search for suspicious signs on the 15th but found nothing.

Fortunately for Jager, supporting evidence for his story came the following day with a report from a Belgian spy that a Ghent factory had manufactured 20,000 'mouth protectors' (*imbibés d'un liquide approprié*) to counter the effects of 'asphyxiating gas'. The dimensions of the waterproof bag for carrying the mask and its other details were identical with the one which Jager had brought with him. Still nothing was done by the French. The British reluctantly loosed off some of their precious stock of heavy shells. No startling results were observed.

The fact that the British, with their acute ammunition problems, were prepared to expend even a few rounds on an attempt to test the gas 'tube' reports implies that the warning had reached high places.

General Smith-Dorrien had certainly been informed and confided to his diary on April 15:

'Reports have come in through agents employed by the French, and also one or two prisoners captured by the French, that the XXVI Reserve Corps has made all its plans for attacking us tonight on the front which we have taken over, partly by the 28th Division and partly by the Canadians.

'The details given by the prisoners are so voluminous and exact that I am sure they are untrue – in fact, possibly the prisoners have been allowed to be captured to spread these stories of German attacks to prevent us attacking them and to keep us on the jump.

'The prisoners described how they had arranged in their trenches batteries of enormous tubes of asphyxiating gas, a battery of sixteen of these tubes to every 40 metres, and how, at a given signal, when the wind was in the right direction, all these tubes were to be opened.'

After a 'decent pause to allow our men to become insensible' the Germans were to charge forward and mop up. Smith-Dorrien was probably referring to Jager when he talked of one prisoner who produced a packet of wool 'which at the right moment was going to be soaked in oxygen to be applied to their own noses'.

Smith-Dorrien concluded: 'One cannot take chances in a war like this, and in case there is any truth in it I have to let all commanders know.'

As V Corps would obviously suffer in the event of an enemy attack, Plumer passed on Smith-Dorrien's warning to his divisional generals, adding the debilitating rider, 'for what it is worth'. Nevertheless he ordered reserve battalions to move nearer the threatened line and the senior medical officers were instructed to prepare to receive extra casualties.

By mid-April there is no doubt that both French and British commanders were in possession of intelligence which indicated that an attack using some sort of disabling gas had been prepared. Fighting actually took place around the cylinders dug in on Hill 60 and in the *Daily Express* in the thirties an ex-sergeant claimed to have been a member of a detachment which not only saw the 'tubes' but actually reported their discovery. His notebook containing details was still in his possession, he wrote in the newspaper.

On top of everything else there was that strange phenomenon 'front-line rumour', inevitable when two armies have trenches close together. Furthermore the idea of chemical warfare in France was not entirely new. On March 17 the *London Illustrated War News* published an artist's impression of 'The German use of burning liquid as a missile in trench warfare: an attack on French trenches preceded by a fiery cataract, and a column of smoke under which the enemy advanced.' The incident was said to have taken place at Malancourt Wood, north-west of Verdun. The caption says that the Russians had reported a similar 'German trick'. In West Poland, according to an official communiqué issued in Petrograd on March 9, 'new methods of fighting, throwing boiling pitch, or some other liquid, onto our infantry as it approaches their trenches . . . causes bad burns and sets fire to the clothes of our soldiers'. After such revelations, the possibility of a gas attack was not something to be rejected out of hand.

Why then was nothing done? Why were no precautions taken?

It would be unfair to blame the generals for failing to envisage the extent of the danger. Smith-Dorrien and Plumer were men of common sense and proven moral courage; but they were not soothsayers. In their time warfare had already made unbelievable strides. Both had joined the Army even before the Cardwell reforms gave infantry regiments names instead of numbers. Smith-Dorrien had seen action against Cetewayo's Zulu warriors in 1879 and been one of the few British to escape from the massacre of redcoats[1] at Isandhlwana. Plumer, who passed from the sixth form at Eton straight into the 65th Foot[2] in 1876, saw his first battle at El Teb in Egypt in 1883 after which he wrote of active service: 'I have seen enough to last me some time.'

Both had proved successful commanders in the South African War and it is arguable that Smith-Dorrien showed himself to be the most professional and effective British leader during the retreat from Mons. Plumer, at 58 a year older than Smith-Dorrien, had not arrived in France until the beginning of 1915.

As no one on the Allied side had any knowledge of the appearance or properties of a gas cloud it was asking a great deal for elderly generals to conjure up a picture from thin air.

What is astonishing is that no one, particularly the French, to whom the initial information came direct, thought of asking a chemist's opinion. The 4th Chasseurs did not keep their theories to themselves and the reports of the crude protective arrangements made by troops, the lime and damp masks, hint at the presence of an amateur scientist in the 11th Division.

The predicament lay in the fact that chemists and scientists were certain to be civilians. Intelligence of the nature provided by Jager and other prisoners was a military secret. To pass it round might compromise security. It was a dilemma that was to cause other problems during the war.

To investigate the threat properly called for determination, time and energy. The first was lacking and the other commodities were already at a premium. Everybody was busy, too busy.

The French Tenth Army was engrossed in its plans to break through in Artois where General d'Urbal was taking over from General de Maud'huy, considered 'too emotional'. Neither of these officers were likely to find time for cool assessment of a potential situation. As for the Army Group commander, General Foch was

[1] Cetewayo had given instructions to his troops to concentrate on killing men in red coats – fortuitously Smith-Dorrien was wearing a blue patrol jacket.
[2] 1st York and Lancaster.

entirely pre-occupied with master-minding the impending offensive. An undefined, bizarre threat to Putz's indifferent corps-sized detachment miles from the coming storm centre rated a very low priority at his conferences.

The British too were busy. Having blown the top off Hill 60 they had to contend with the hornets' nest they had disturbed. It was all they could do to cling to the scorched mine craters. The clamour from '60' dominated the whole Salient, rising and falling incessantly. Its oft-reshaped slopes tended to be completely obscured by dust and the thick black smoke of howitzer shells – Coal Boxes the soldiers called them, or Jack Johnsons after the Negro world boxing champion. The bombardment of Ypres intensified. The cobbled streets were blocked with rubble from tumbled buildings, wrecked vehicles and dead horses. Little groups of terrified civilians who had decided at long last that their future lay elsewhere straggled back across the canal. A 17-inch howitzer joined stridently in the wholesale destruction. Its shells screeched and rattled overhead to plunge deep into the ground. Delayed action fuses blasted cobbles, walls, roofs, churches, chapels and people into an unconcerned blue sky.

A defiant German captured on Hill 60 forecast: 'We will be in Ypres on the 22nd.'

CHAPTER 4

The Joyful Ones

August Jager's erstwhile comrades spent 22 April most uncomfortably. The soldiers of the German XXIII and XXVI Reserve Corps were packed into their trenches cheek by jowl with the loathsome gas cylinders. Extra bandoliers had been distributed, bombs handed out, iron rations checked. Orders had arrived at midnight and they occupied their 'jumping-off' positions soon afterwards. 'Mouth protectors' were inspected by NCOs to ensure they were properly moist; scaling ladders were jammed into fire bays; knife rests (portable frames) removed to open passages through the entanglements and the gas pipes uncovered ready to be placed over the parapets.

The troops took some comfort from what their officers had told them – that the gas really would wipe out the opposition. It would be a question of simply following the cloud and, once it had dispersed, digging in on Pilckem Ridge.

As further proof of confidence, rifles were not to be loaded. It was to be a case of 'cold steel only' in the opening stages. At five o'clock in the morning, when word came round that the gas was to be released in 45 minutes' time, bayonets were fixed. The wind then died down.

An hour passed and there was no gas discharge . . . two hours . . . three.

The sun rose and the temperature with it. Waterbottles were opened as the men got thirsty. NCOs cursed extravagant drinkers for using too much too soon. Meals had to be improvised; orders passed; latrines visited. Until midday the assault troops listened to the sound of Ypres disintegrating as the 17-inch howitzer, supported by twenty of its eight-inch brethren and more than seventy of the renowned 5.9s, redistributed the ancient walls. Then a strange silence fell. A

light northerly breeze cooled the necks of the overburdened infantry.
The spiked helmets with their grey cloth covers were removed, brows
mopped, packs adjusted. The waiting went on . . . and on.

At four o'clock a purposeful stir went through the ranks. Helmets
were replaced, chin straps tightened. They would be 'going over'
within the hour.

Three red flares challenged the sky at five. A volcanic rumbling was
followed by an ear-splitting blast as the bombardment of Ypres began
again. Along the German line the pioneers applied their spanners and
the compressed chemical shot into the air.

The pipes had been extended beyond the trenches and the contents
of nearly 6,000 cylinders went hissing and whistling into no-man's-
land which quickly became lost to view from the German parapets. A
dense white cloud arose as the escaping chlorine expanded and the
moisture in the air cooled and condensed. At its base was a greenish-
yellow stain. The cloud grew higher, reaching ten, twelve, fifteen feet
and more as it drifted away from its 'liberators'. It took five[1] minutes
to release the greater part of 180,000 kilograms (168 tons); due to
some 'technical hitch' a number of batteries near Steenstraat remained
undischarged. On a front of nearly four miles the fumes slid swiftly
into and over the French trenches. Then the German field batteries,
ordered to remain silent during the discharge in case bursting shells
dispersed the gas, opened up. Howitzers began to pound new targets
in the rear. Some German soldiers ignored the 'bayonets only' order,
clambered into the open and stood blazing away with their rifles as
the cloud rolled into the distance. They could see the French fleeing
from their defences.

At 5.20 whistles shrilled and the infantry clambered into the open,
filed through gaps in the wire and formed waves which moved
steadily forward. For the most part they carried empty rifles with
bayonets fixed. The Spanish pikemen of the Duke of Alva had
advanced in much the same manner over the same fields hundreds of
years earlier.

In the German trenches pioneers wearing oxygen masks closed the
valves of the reeking iron cylinders. The genie was out of the bottle.
No one had any idea where it would come to rest.

Serious fighting was over within two hours. The French artillery
east of the canal fired for a time but soon ceased. There were only
sixteen of the famous 75mm 'quick-firers'; twenty-nine obsolete but
powerful 90mm cannon which had been brought out of retirement
provided the backbone of the defence but were quickly silenced.

[1] Some reports say ten.

The 45th Algerian Division had no particular reputation to live up to and the gas phenomenon was too much for it. Many troops took to their heels.

On their left was the 87th Territorial Division, its ranks filled with Bretons and Normans. The 87th had been fighting at Ypres since the autumn and knew the area well. The gas cloud did not hit them so hard, but when dying Algerians began to reel into their positions they made for the Yser bridges as fast as their middle-aged legs could carry them.

The 2nd Duke of Cornwall's Light Infantry, in billets just north of Ypres on the west bank of the canal, recorded:

'French stragglers from the north started coming in saying the Zouaves had been attacked with asphyxiating gas and that there had been a general retirement . . . on a wide front.'

Other troops in reserve were startled to see French transport galloping madly to the rear.

The Reverend Owen Spencer Watkins,[1] the senior Wesleyan chaplain with the BEF, was helping in the women's asylum which had been turned into a hospital and was crammed with wounded from Hill 60. A veteran of the Boer War who had also taken part in the retreat from Mons, he was puzzled by the noise of 'very heavy firing to the north' and went out of a stifling ward to scan the countryside through field glasses. He was startled to see 'figures running wildly and in confusion across the fields'. The French appeared to have broken.

'Gun-limbers passed at the gallop, fugitive Zouaves and Turcos clinging to them. In a few minutes the road in front of the asylum was choked with . . . soldiers and panic-stricken peasantry from the farms and villages round. The story they told we could not believe; we put it down to their terror-stricken imaginings – a greenish-grey cloud had swept down upon them turning yellow as it travelled, blasting everything it touched, shrivelling up the vegetation . . .

'Then there staggered into our midst French soldiers, blinded, coughing, chests heaving, faces an ugly purple colour . . . speechless with agony.'

Some survivors reported leaving trenches full of dead and dying men. Watkins commented,

'The enemy, in violation of every law of war, of civilization and of Christianity, had descended to the use of asphyxiating gases.'

Smith-Dorrien had been visiting the Hill 60 sector that afternoon and as he made his way on foot from the headquarters of the 14th

[1] Watkins survived the war and became Deputy Chaplain-General (1924–9).

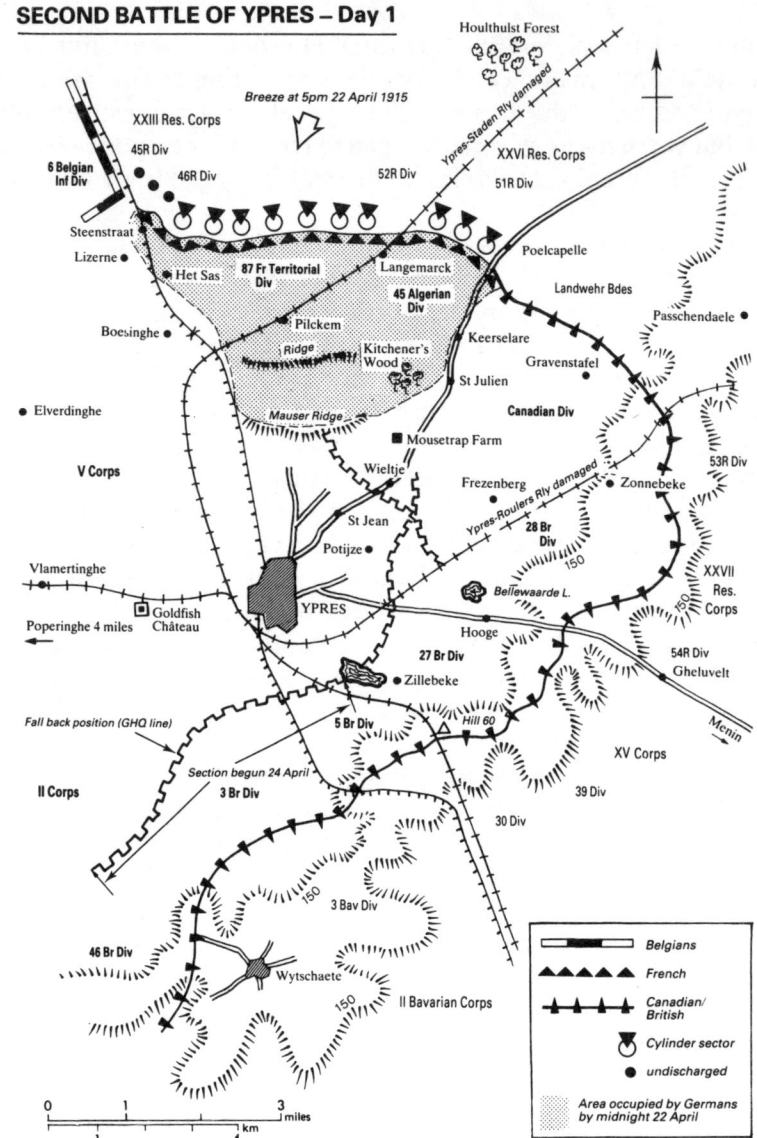

SECOND BATTLE OF YPRES – Day 1

Houlthulst Forest

Breeze at 5pm 22 April 1915

XXIII Res. Corps

45R Div

6 Belgian Inf Div

46R Div

52R Div

51R Div

XXVI Res. Corps

Ypres–Staden Rly damaged

Steenstraat

Lizerne

Het Sas

87 Fr Territorial Div

Langemarck

45 Algerian Div

Poelcapelle

Landwehr Bdes

Passchendaele

Boesinghe

Pilckem

Ridge

Kitchener's Wood

Keerselare

Gravenstafel

St Julien

Canadian Div

Elverdinghe

Mauser Ridge

V Corps

Mousetrap Farm

Wieltje

Frezenberg

Ypres–Roulers Rly damaged

Zonnebeke

53R Div

St Jean

28 Br Div

150

XXVII Res. Corps

Potijze

Vlamertinghe

Bellewaarde L.

150

Goldfish Château

YPRES

Hooge

54R Div

Gheluvelt

Poperinghe 4 miles

27 Br Div

Zillebeke

Menin

Fall back position (GHQ line)

5 Br Div

Hill 60

XV Corps

Section begun 24 April

II Corps

3 Br Div

39 Div

30 Div

150

3 Bav Div

46 Br Div

Wytschaete

150

II Bavarian Corps

0   1   3   miles

1   4   km

	Belgians
	French
	Canadian/ British
	Cylinder sector
	undischarged
	Area occupied by Germans by midnight 22 April

Brigade he became aware of a furious cannonade six miles to the north. He had a mile-long walk to reach his car and as he tramped on he noticed a pronounced and pungent smell growing stronger. At his headquarters he learned that observation planes had reported smoke rising from the French trenches as if the whole line were in flames.

General Mordacq, commanding the 90th Brigade in the 45th Division, was given the first hint of something suspicious going on by his Chief-of-Staff, in civilian life the Caid of Algiers. He reported that a reconnaissance plane had come under heavy fire for no apparent reason. Soon afterwards the Commanding Officer of the 1st Tirailleurs, Colonel Villevalleix, gasped painfully over the phone that his men had been the victims of 'asphyxiating gas'. Commandant Fabry, of the same regiment, came on another line to report: 'Everyone is dying around me . . . .I am abandoning my command post.'

Mordacq hurried to the bridge at Boesinghe where he saw: 'Territorials, Tirailleurs, Zouaves and artillerymen, without their weapons, their collars torn open, asking for water, shouting loudly and spitting blood.'

The reaction of the British troops was more of curiosity than anything else. The 2nd Buffs were in tents near the village of St Jean at the heart of the Salient. With the 3rd Middlesex they were to due to relieve a section of trenches near Zonnebeke that night. The men had heard the outbreak of firing at 'tea-time' and noticed a 'cloud of greenish vapour' in the distance. It was only when machine gun bullets came 'spattering' into the village 'which ought to have been safe enough from this sort of fire' that they realized something was wrong. Half an hour after the cloud's appearance the first 'Turcos and Zouaves' arrived and headed for Ypres 'rapidly and in a disorderly manner'.

The eye-witness recorded: 'Poor fellows . . . they simply fled as if the Devil were after them.'

The Buffs at first thought that the gas attack was of 'no consequence' and continued to make preparations for the relief they were to carry out. When their commanding officer, Lieutenant-Colonel Augustus David Geddes, was ordered to leave the battalion and take command of all troops in the vicinity, some of them began to suspect there was something serious afoot. Others were less responsive. While the stricken French were streaming past, Tommies were still to be seen standing 'nonchalantly' in the streets of St Jean, while Canadians marched 'calmly' towards their positions to the north.

About the time Smith-Dorrien was leaving Hill 60 a soldier of the

2nd Zouaves in reserve at Elverdinghe, west of the Yser, had seen 'in the distance, towards the lines, a great yellow curtain climb into the sky and travel towards Boesinghe. As dusk fell no doubt remained. The enemy was attacking. German planes, under fire from our guns, strung out signal flares in glowing clusters in the once more clear sky.'

In the gathering darkness observers saw small groups making their way across the fields carrying boxes and long poles.

'The Territorials were saving their regimental trophies and their Colours.'

Other determined Frenchmen hung on where the gas had not been so effective because of slight changes in the breeze. Machine gun and rifle fire continued to come from Langemarck Château where survivors of the African Light Infantry were living up to their reputation as the bad boys of the army. The 'Joyeux' – Joyful Ones – defied Duke Albrecht's 51st Reserve Division for some time.

Zouaves holding a farm near Boesinghe later saw a solitary Joyeux staggering towards them shouting and waving his hands. He begged for milk when he reached them, then rasped: '*Les vaches* have poisoned the lot of us.'

The Joyeux was not entirely right. Around Steenstraat, where the cylinders had not been discharged, bitter fighting was in progress and Zouaves and Territorials were struggling to contain a German bridgehead across the canal at Het Sas; but in the gas-affected area to the east, all resistance, including the defenders of Langemarck Château, had been overcome by about 6.30 pm. Not until one approached the Canadian sector could a formed body of French troops be found. The 1st Tirailleurs Algeriens and a supporting Zouave battalion had escaped the gas and were holding out. This did not stop the enemy pushing round them and threatening the rear of the 3rd Canadian Brigade.

Two platoons of the 13th Battalion (Royal Highlanders of Canada) fell to a man opposing the German advance near the ruins of Keerselare which had been well behind the line only an hour earlier. Field-guns fired over open sights while Lance-Corporal Fred Fisher kept his Colt machine gun in action to protect them after the rest of his detachment had fallen. New men took their place but Fisher[1] was killed after the artillery had withdrawn safely.

Had the German attack begun at 5.45 am as planned there is every likelihood that in daylight their troops would have pressed on into the rear of the Canadians and of the British divisions on the other face of the Salient. The ill wind that bore the fumes south had at least done the Allies the favour of arriving late.

[1] He was awarded a posthumous Victoria Cross.

CHAPTER 5

Sewing Sisters

The day before the gas attack Falkenhayn had visited Duke Albrecht's headquarters at Thielt, between Bruges and Courtrai, to express his concern about the delay in launching the offensive. He was told that all was ready and the battle would begin the next day if the winds were as forecast. Falkenhayn and Colonel Tappen, who was with him, cautioned against expecting too much.

Previously the Supreme Command had refused to allocate reserves, but the Duke was assured that if opportunities for exploitation did arise they would be made available. In any case, if Pilckem Ridge was secured the heavy artillery could be installed there to make the Salient untenable by the Allies.

Once battle had been joined, and despite the dramatic results, Duke Albrecht suffered from having adopted a compromise plan. Even before the use of gas had been suggested, General Otto Freiherr von Hugel, whose XXVI Reserve Corps had suffered so severely in the autumn, had proposed a major assault to seize Pilckem Ridge. General Hugo von Kathen of XXIII Corps,[1] which had also been mangled the previous year, had urged a thrust across the canal at the junction of the Belgians and French.

The plan implemented on the 22nd was an amalgam of both. Hugel attacked Pilckem. Kathen advanced on his flank, clearing the canal bank prior to seizing crossings on the Yser.

Neither commander had anticipated the sensational effect of the gas, though both had been at the trial when Haber strayed into the chlorine cloud. That evening, Hugel, a Wurttemburger recalled to active service, learned that his troops had pressed beyond Pilckem to

---

[1] He had replaced von Kleist, its original commander.

another ridge only two and a half miles from Ypres. Mindful of previous painful experiences in the area, he ordered them to dig in. He knew the survivors of the 1914 battles had lost much of their ardour. Though units were well up to strength, enthusiasm had dwindled during the weeks spent waiting for a suitable wind. On his flank Kathen's corps had easily cleared the canal bank but found it much harder to force crossings, especially at Steenstraat where the gas cylinders had not been opened.

Duke Albrecht and his Chief of Staff spent much of the night preparing an operation order for the next move, having cautiously sent a Landwehr brigade to dig a support line behind the troops on the conquered ridge.

The uncertainty of the Germans was as nothing compared to the confusion among their opponents. Smith-Dorrien's first official confirmation of the breach in the French line was a phone call from General Putz about 8 pm. Putz himself was ill-informed and underestimated the size of the gap by about two miles. An alarming report then arrived that the Germans were at St Julien in the immediate rear of the two Canadian brigades in the line. Reserves were hurried off and Smith-Dorrien phoned the British Commander-in-Chief, Field-Marshal Sir John French, to suggest that he ask General Foch to find troops to plug the gap.

Foch's immediate reaction was to send a staff officer to make a report on the spot. Then, with his Chief-of-Staff, Colonel Max Weygand, he began to look for reinforcements which could be allocated without interfering with the impending Artois operation. Eventually the newly-formed 153rd Division was roused in its billets behind Arras.

A rosy sky above Ypres reflected burning buildings. Soon after midnight the southern front of the Salient roared into life as Duke Albrecht launched subsidiary attacks to pin down the 27th and 28th Divisions. The fighting died down but Plumer was left with serious doubts about the wisdom of sending battalions from his own line to repair the broken French front. At the same time he was acutely aware that his men now had the enemy poised at their backs.

As the new clash flared, two battalions of Canadians, the 10th and the 16th (Canadian Scottish), stormed a wood on the slopes of Pilckem Ridge. Under the impression their attack was being made in conjunction with a French effort, they charged in a compact mass which the enemy machine gunners quickly reduced by two-thirds. The wood[1] was taken, but the Canadians found themselves alone and withdrew.

[1] Called Kitchener's Wood by the British.

Probably the most practical contribution to the Allied cause during the day was the refusal of General de Ceunick, commander of the 6th Belgian Division, to over-react. His infantry held fast on the left of the French at Steenstraat and his artillery pounded the far bank. An enemy attempt at an amphibious crossing resulted only in heaps of bodies mingled with shattered timber and boats on the eastern shore of the Yser. Tear-gas shells were reported to have been used but the Belgians said they caused only temporary discomfort.

Sir John French was an early caller at Foch's headquarters on the 23rd. He reported that the British had strung about ten battalions across the gap left by the 45th and 87th Divisions and wanted to know what his Allies intended to do. Foch assured him he had ordered up divisions to recover the lost ground. Sir John promised to co-operate in the counter-attacks.

Shortly afterwards Foch was on his way to see for himself. No one could ever accuse the dapper little artilleryman of avoiding a fight. He had even been involved in a row over the pennant on his staff car. His staff argued that as both he and Joffre commanded army groups (as well as being generalissimo, Joffre retained command of the central army group for a while) their ceremonial trappings should be the same. It was pointed out that Joffre was head of all the army groups and only the tricolour on his car could be dressed with a white riband fringed with gold. The identical streamer on Foch's car had to go and was not seen there again for three years.

Protocol and heraldry have their place in military circles but they were of no use to the soldiers locked in combat at Ypres. Yet when Foch arrived at Putz's command post he had little more to offer than his ornamental flag. The proud commander of the Groupe d'Armées du Nord could wave his arms – he was famous for his gestures – as much as he liked; he could demand the creation of a firm base from which to launch counter-attacks; he could insist that these assaults be carried out; it counted for nothing. The confidence radiated by the vibrant little man with the jaunty upswept moustache was of no practical value. Putz had thrown in his reserve already and his artillery was standing abandoned in gas-stained gun-pits east of the Yser. His own moustache reflected the true state of affairs. It was remarkably long and drooped dismally in the manner of the ancient Gauls. Despite a second visit from Foch during the day, Putz's efforts to regain the lost line were of little consequence, though his troops clung tenaciously to the outskirts of Streenstraat. Some French soldiers, cut off the previous day, voluntarily joined in British attacks. The 2nd DCLI, who had left their rest billets west of the canal at 2.30 and marched via Ypres and the Menin Gate to support the Canadians, recorded one such case. As they went into action an unarmed coloured soldier, possibly a Tirailleur, asked to join them and, having been shown how to use a Lee-Enfield rifle, was killed in the first assault. In this attack the DCLI shot a dedicated German artillery observer, telephone in hand, at a strongpoint called Turco Farm.

German guns dominated the battlefield on St George's Day, 1915. Allied control and command began to slip as communications were cut. Battalions found themselves linked in ad hoc formations - ever a bad sign. Still in the belief that they were acting in conjunction with the French, the British moved in strength against the enemy dug in on the ominously named Mauser Ridge. Individuals stood out in the clear spring light and the well-drilled khaki skirmish lines advancing by short rushes were easy targets. Few got to within 200 yards of the enemy positions. The open fields, swept by machine gun and rifle fire, were littered with corpses. By nightfall little territory had changed hands. The real tragedy is expressed in the words of the Official History:

'No ground was gained that could not have been secured, probably without any casualties, by a simple advance after dark, to which the openness of the country lent itself.'

For the Germans this useless sacrifice was a bonus. While the front-line troops held the British at bay, others were digging in gas cylinders opposite the Canadians.

Whatever eventuality may arise in the British Army, someone is responsible somewhere in the system. The first reaction of the professional soldier to the gas attack was that, as its most lurid symptoms were physical, it was a matter for the medical branch. Its representatives were promptly confronted with evidence extracted from the battlefield. All the clues – brass buttons which had turned green, descriptions of the cloud and its smell – indicated that chlorine was probably the chemical agent used. Intelligence files were hastily sent for and the report of the French Tenth Army on 30 March studied. Prisoners taken by the Canadians near Kitchener's Wood (they were from August Jager's 234th Regiment) were closely questioned. 'Mouth protectors' were thoroughly examined. The following day the Director-General of Medical Services, Sir Arthur Sloggett, advised that buckets of sodium bicarbonate should be placed in the trenches. In the event of a gas attack men should dip their handkerchiefs or rags in the liquid and cover their noses and mouths until the cloud had passed.

In the likely eventuality that no bucket would be available, let alone sodium bicarbonate (though supplies were being rushed up to the trenches), a man might give himself some protection by urinating on a rag, thus providing neutralizing ammonia, or make a pad by filling a cloth or a piece of sandbag with moist earth. This he had to hold to his face. There was even a forlorn suggestion that a bottle with the base knocked out could be stuffed with earth. The owner could then suck in air via the neck, thereby filtering out the gas while being careful to breathe out only through his nose! Whether any hero tried the latter device is unrecorded.

While the staff tackled the job of getting the information round the fighting troops, steps were taken to organize masks similar to the captured specimens. The nearest drapers being unable to supply the quantities of gauze, flannel and elastic required, officers were sent post-haste to Paris to buy what they could. Every woman with a sewing machine in Hazebrouck and the small towns near Ypres was called on to help. The nuns in Poperinghe convent, using lint bandages, were among the first to start 'production'. Across the Channel the details of a telegram received from Sir John French (dated 23 April) were being studied. The message read:

'Germans used powerful asphyxiating gases very extensively in attack on French yesterday with serious effect. Apparently these gases are either chlorine or bromine; will send further details later but meanwhile strongly urge immediate steps to be taken to supply similar means of most effective kind for use by our troops. Also essential that our troops should be immediately provided with means of counteracting effects of enemy gases which would be suitable when on the move. As a temporary measure, am arranging for troops in trenches to be supplied with solution of bicarbonate of soda in which to soak handkerchiefs.'

The commander of the British Expeditionary Force left Kitchener and the rest of the authorities involved in no doubt as to his idea of what the priorities should be. Retaliation came first.

By dint of hard fighting and the liberal use of shells containing T-stoff, the Germans extended their bridgehead across the canal during the night. They consolidated their hold on Steenstraat and captured the neighbouring village of Lizerne, then stuck fast. The link between the Belgians and the French remained firm. In the War Diary of the German XXIIIrd Reserve Corps this check was attributed to the fact that 'the infantry had become enfeebled by trench warfare and had lost its daring and indifference to heavy losses'. The bulk of the men were inexperienced reinforcements, it was stated.

The smoking ruins of Lizerne were still being contested when a heavy bombardment began to the north. The Canadians had been standing-to, waiting for the dawn and shivering in the chill breeze. Signal rockets bursting over Pilckem village first attracted their attention and a bombardment began. At 4 am three red flares were fired from a captive observation balloon and the shelling increased. According to some reports Germans wearing helmets and apparatus of the type used by mine rescue teams climbed out of the trenches opposite and actually held the nozzles of the gas projectors in their hands.

Most troops saw only a greenish-yellow cloud growing taller as it floated swiftly towards them. In some places the trenches were only 100 yards apart. Men pressed damp handkerchiefs or rags to their faces as fumes swirled round them. Empty cotton bandoliers were soaked and used by some. The discharge, on a front of 1,000 yards, lasted for ten terrible minutes and then the cloud began to thin. By this time many whose natural instinct had been to remain crouching where they had previously been sheltering from the rain of high explosive, sprawled helpless in the bottom of the trenches. For those already badly wounded there was little chance of escape as the heavy gas found the lowest levels. The majority, however, were still fit enough to man the parapet as the Germans approached along a front much wider than that affected by the gas. Duke Albrecht's Fourth Army had drawn its assault units from corps which had been only lightly engaged up to that time and, coming forward en masse, they made easy targets at close range. At only one point were the Canadians forced back to a support line, otherwise the 8th Battalion (Winnipeg Rifles) and 15th (48th Highlanders of Canada), at the centre of the onslaught, held their positions. On their left, where there had been no gas, corpses in dark blue uniforms piled up in no-man's-land – German marines, brought up from the Nieuport sector.

The gas cloud was the prelude to another bloody and bewildering day. Whatever the consequences for the unfortunate enemy infantry following in its wake, it had achieved surprise and created widespread anxiety. Only garbled information could be obtained from the casualties streaming to the rear, some gassed, some wounded by bullets and shrapnel. The German heavy artillery opened fire again in preparation for a renewal of the assault and the British could offer little in response. A solitary 9.2-inch howitzer was brought into action during the day, supported by a battery of 60-pounders firing from west of the canal. These guns could hit hard but were too few to be decisive. By contrast there seemed to be plenty of troops available,

1. The true father of chemical warfare, Admiral the 10th Earl of Dundonald (1775–1860). He got the idea of gas warfare while operating in the Mediterranean during the Napoleonic Wars when he visited the Sicilian sulphur mines.

2. On 24 March, 1915, almost a month before the Germans used gas at Ypres *The Illustrated War News* published these pictures of a soldier wearing a 'safety muzzle'. The caption explained that the fumes given off by an exploding shell were 'hardly less fatal than the flying fragments'. This led both sides to suspect the other of using poison gas shells before they were actually introduced.

3. A group of officers of the 2nd Seaforth Highlanders enjoying the spring sunshine at Ypres in 1915 – all wearing 'cap comforters'. Second from the left is the Medical Officer, Lieutenant P. W. James. The first gas attacks began shortly after this picture was taken. At the beginning of May, after one gas cloud, James recorded few fatalities but the battalion was 'incapable of further action'.

4. William Howard Livens, (later DSO, MC) pictured here at the beginning of his service as a wartime officer. Inventor of the Livens projector, he co-operated with his father, Frederick Howard Livens, in the production of a flame-thrower and other weapons. F. H. Livens was Chief Engineer of Ruston and Hornsby Ltd (previously Ruston Proctor & Company) of Lincoln.

5 & 6. Two methods of delivering gas. Above a line of railway wagons loaded with cylinders – most likely containing a mixture of phosgene and chlorine. The train was driven near the front line under cover of darkness and the cylinders opened simultaneously by means of an electrical contact system. Below a line of Livens projectors are seen dug into an emplacement preparatory to receiving the drums of gas. The projectors were also fired electrically.

though not always of the right type, or at the right place at the right time.

Still keen to co-operate fully with Foch, Sir John French made his views known early on the morning of the 24th. The Chief of the General Staff, Sir William Robertson, who had started his career as a private soldier in the 16th Lancers in 1877 and had a reputation for candour, sent a message to Smith-Dorrien saying:

'Evidently not much reliance can be placed on the two French divisions on your left. We do not know where the division ordered from Arras[1] is at the present, but it ought to be in action by noon somewhere north of Poperinghe. We are inquiring.'

Sir John French, he added, was not fully aware of the Second Army's 'dispositions' or its situation, a handicap which did not stop the Field-Marshal from offering his advice that, 'Vigorous action E. of the Canal will be the best means of checking the enemy's advance from the line Lizerne–Boesinghe,' i.e. across the canal in the French sector.

Sir John placed the Cavalry Corps under Smith-Dorrien and suggested it should be concentrated behind Ypres, freeing the Northumbrians for use east of the city.

The Northumbrian Division (later renumbered the 50th) had arrived from England only a week previously. Its Territorials had never been in action. On the 23rd battalions had been rushed up to positions behind Ypres in requisitioned London buses. They drove along roads packed with refugees heading in the opposite direction (an experience Fifty Div was to repeat twenty-five years later). On the 24th, after the Canadians had been 'gassed', its units were ordered into the maelstrom piecemeal.

The 4th Green Howards passed four companies across a precarious pontoon bridge just before it was hit by one of many salvoes of shells. The vital machine gun section was held up on the west bank. The 5th Durham Light Infantry, marching through the dust and smoke of burning and collapsing buildings in Ypres, saw their first dead man – a Belgian civilian who lay in his nightshirt where he had been blown from his bed. The British had absolutely no way of matching the enemy's artillery superiority – they were even using two batteries of obsolete 5-inch howitzers which had been in action against the Dervishes in the Sudan seventeen years earlier – and as the danger to the southern edge of the Salient grew, Plumer and Smith-Dorrien decided it was time to go. The gradual arrival of the 4th Division from

[1] The 153rd Division.

GHQ reserve and the concentration of the Cavalry Corps gave them an opportunity to conduct a reasonable withdrawal. They were planning the operation together when a staff officer brought an order from Sir John: 'Every effort must be made to restore and hold the line about St Julien.'

Within the next forty-eight hours a series of hopeless mass attacks were made, directed by brigadiers or colonels substituting for brigadiers. Communications broke down everywhere and co-ordination at a higher level became impossible. The 5.9-inch howitzer dominated the battlefield.

Had the British been supported by adequate artillery and had the French lived up to Foch's promise, the outlook would still have been daunting. As it was the few guns the Royal Artillery possessed had to rely mainly on shrapnel shell, a projectile unsuitable for most of the fire tasks.

The powerful French reinforcements promised had yet to materialize. By the 25th, according to one account, 32,000 men had been brought up using a total of 1,480 lorries. British sources say that only the first brigade arrived that day.

In any case, on arrival the French naturally went first to the support of their compatriots locked in combat on the Yser; indeed, this area was giving Smith-Dorrien increasing cause for alarm as a break-through would allow the enemy to overrun British communications west of the canal.

One Corporal Berneteau, who went straight into action with the 418th Regiment at Steenstraat, wrote later:

'We were received by a frightful bombardment of gas shells[1] . . . . You can joke at bullets but to fall half-conscious into a trench with only three men to defend it . . . that's another matter, worse even than the rain of benzine and naphtha with which they tried to burn us out.'

A lieutenant in the 9th Zouaves de Marche, arriving at dawn, reported 'indescribable confusion, Territorials, Colonials, Canadians fleeing . . . lorries, headlights ablaze, making off at full speed.'

British anxiety eased a little when a brigade of the French 152nd Division was made available on the 26th to join in another attempt to clear the enemy from Mauser Ridge. The Indians of the Lahore Division, which had been resting after the battle of Neuve Chapelle, had also arrived and promptly deployed. By 2 pm the Indians were

[1] Probably bromacetone tear gas – 'B-stoff.

advancing on a two-brigade front with the French on the left of their line. For the Germans the situation looked menacing.

The enemy local commander let the attackers reach his wire. Then he ordered the release of gas from cylinders which had been dug in for use in a further assault. The cloud reared up in front of the French but the breeze swept it along the ranks of the Lahore Division. Even if they had been provided with masks the troops would have had no time to use them. Many fell back in disorder as the German fire intensified. Others tried to force their way across the entanglement. The attack broke down.

Of the two British battalions[1] involved, the Connaught Rangers lost fifteen officers and 351 men. In the six Indian battalions the 47th Sikhs alone had 348 casualties. No unit lost fewer than 200 of all ranks. They had fallen victim not so much to the gas as to the confusion and sometimes panic it caused. The new weapon was proving flexible. A practical means of protection needed to be found urgently.

[1] The brigades of the Lahore Division were composed of one British and three Indian battalions. Three battalions of British Territorials were also attached to the Division.

CHAPTER 6

Widow's Weeds

Even as the Indians were recoiling in horror from the gas cloud on Mauser Ridge, two soberly-clad civilians were making a grim tour of casualty clearing stations at Bailleul. One was Dr John Scott Haldane, a distinguished physiologist and brother of Lord Haldane, former Secretary of State for War. The quietly-spoken 55-year-old academic was the author of the Blue Books on *The Causes of Death in Colliery Explosions*, published in 1895, and of many other scientific papers. Accompanying him was Professor Herbert Brereton Baker, of the Imperial College of Science and Technology, sometime chemistry master at Dulwich College, London, and headmaster of Alleyn's. He was the author of such papers published in scientific journals as 'The Influence of Moisture on Chemical Action' (1894) and 'The Drying of Ammonia and Hydrogen Chloride' (1898).

The scientists inspected a laboratory improvised at Sir John French's headquarters at St Omer before going on.

Dr Haldane reported on what they saw at Bailleul: 'Men were lying struggling for breath and blue in the face. On examining (blood samples) with a spectroscope and by other means, I ascertained that the blueness was not due to the presence of any abnormal pigment. There was nothing to account for the blueness (cyanosis) and the struggle for breath but the one fact that they were suffering from acute bronchitis, such as is caused by the inhalation of an irritant gas.'

One of the casualties died soon after Haldane's arrival and a lieutenant in the Royal Army Medical Corps carried out a post-mortem examination. The results made him conclude that the man had died of 'acute bronchitis and slow asphyxiation caused by an irritant gas'.

The lieutenant also examined the body of a Canadian sergeant who had been brought in from the Salient. All the facts, wrote Haldane, pointed to the 'use by the German troops of chlorine or bromine for purposes of asphyxiation. There are also facts which point to the use in German shells of other irritant substances, though in some cases at least these agents are not of the same brutally barbarous nature as the gas used in the attack on the Canadians. The effects are not those of any of the ordinary products of the combustion of explosives.'

The publication of Dr Haldane's findings in the national Press brought an immediate public outcry which, as General von Einem had forecast, became a 'tremendous scandal' worldwide.

People were quick to point out that everyone should have realized that something was afoot when the enemy accused the British of using gas shells east of Ypres a few days before the chlorine attack. In fact the Germans had genuinely suspected the British of using gas shells even earlier. Professor Haber had been sent to the front after one complaint and identified the offending shell as the same one which had caused the allegations during the South African War – the fumes were caused by the picric acid in lyddite.[1]

On 24 March, a month before the first gas attack, *The Illustrated War News* published two photographs of a British sergeant in the Royal Artillery, wearing 'a respirator-protection against shell gases'. The caption explains: 'Hardly less fatal in effect than the flying fragments from bursting shells . . . are the fumes that are given off at the moment of explosion. The poisonous gases pervade the immediate locality, and themselves have often killed men outright.' A 'safety muzzle' illustrated closely resembles a modern paint-sprayer's mask with what appears to be a metal filter.

Undoubtedly some Germans remained convinced that the Allies had already used gas. Major[2] Octave Beliard, a medical officer serving with a battalion of the 66th Infantry Regiment, described an incident when a number of prisoners, including an officer, were bitterly abused because their country had employed poisoned gas contrary to all the laws of war.

'The officer showed genuine surprise. "Why reproach us when you started it?" he asked.'

To a persistent Frenchman the German replied bluntly: 'That's a

[1] 'The shells exploded with an appalling bang, emitting green and yellow fumes that gave one a burning sensation in throat and chest' – Deneys Reitz, *Commando*, Faber 1929.
[2] Major was the rank given to medical officers by the French as opposed to Commandant.

lie. I am your prisoner, so I can't ask satisfaction for your insults. Kill me if you like but don't abuse me.'

Beliard was convinced that the man was sincere and wondered whether the reaction was due to the spreading of rumours by the French about the terrifying powers of a new explosive invented by a Monsieur Turpin.[1]

In Britain the fact that the German official communiqué on the renewed fighting at Ypres made no mention of the chlorine cloud was taken by some to indicate their shame and their anxiety not to be seen gloating over this new display of 'frightfulness'.

The clamour for retaliation in kind grew. Why were the authorities waiting?

Gas to the Edwardians meant coal gas, generally regarded as a beneficial product of the industrial age; there were gas-lit streets, friendly lamplighters, gas-mantles which gave a reassuring 'pop' as they lit the interior of working-class homes. True no one lived by choice in the vicinity of a reeking gas works, with its fuming piles of coke, but people did so without coming to any harm. That gas could be lethal under certain circumstances was well enough known from occasional reports in newspapers of unfortunate young women who solved their personal problems permanently by 'putting their head in the gas oven'. It was difficult for the average citizen to understand that the gas used against their soldiers was completely different.

A debate developed over whether or not one should stoop to the depths of the Hun. When Sir John French asked Lord Kitchener if he was going to initiate steps to retaliate against the Germans, he received the reply:

'The use of asphyxiating gases is, as you know, contrary to the rules and usages of war. Before we fall to the level of the degraded Germans, I must submit the matter to the Government. These methods show to what depths of infamy our enemies will go in order to supplement their want of courage in facing our troops.'

The authorities did not rush to point out that Britain's solitary factory producing liquid chlorine manufactured only one ton a day. German output was so prolific that Falkenhayn had felt no compunction in releasing the equivalent of about six months' British production in a few minutes at Ypres.

Apart from knowing they lacked the means to make an immediate response in kind, there were sincere reservations among the members of Asquith's Liberal Cabinet to employ such an unconventional

[1] The so-called Turpinite.

weapon. Their hesitation was not feigned. International law was not something to be despised, any more than foreign public opinion. The legal implications of such a step were considered seriously. Deeper still than ingrained respect for treaties were the ethical considerations involved. Britain was then still a country where it mattered very much just how you 'played the game'.

In a handwritten note[1] to King George, referring to a Cabinet meeting held on 27 April, the Prime Minister reported 'with his humble duty to Your Majesty' that:

'Some discussion took place on the recent resort by the enemy to the use of asphyxiating gases. As the gases are apparently stored in and drawn from cylinders and not projectiles the employment of them is not perhaps an infraction of the liberal terms of the Hague Convention. Our soldiers are being provided with face and mouth pads of cotton steeped in bi-chlorate.' [written bicarbonate in the original, the carbonate being crossed out.]

An echo of the efforts of the Earls of Dundonald crept into the next paragraph:

'The Admiralty has been for some time experimenting with a view to the production of smoke in large quantities for a screen.

'A suggested scheme for destroying the enemies' crops by means of incendiary pellets dropped from balloons or aeroplanes did not meet with much favour.'

Even if the morality and legality of the question should be resolved so that gas was allowed into the country's armoury the practical problems were serious. Actual ammunition expenditure, HE and shrapnel, had wildly exceeded the peacetime calculations made for war. Millions of rounds were needed to replace those already expended and to furnish the wherewithal for future battles. To divert factories, workers, scientists and research facilities to the development of a new weapon of which little was known could be counter-productive. There were doubts about Britain ever being able to match the Germans in expertise and output.

The Cabinet hesitated but time was not on their side. Sir John French was pressing Kitchener and he was fixing his uncompromising gaze on the Government. It was up to the civilians to make up their minds. The Government consulted the leading scientific men of the day. They were not anxious to become involved. Leaders of the home chemical industry were also consulted. With a greater commercial incentive than the savants they expressed every confi-

[1] PRO CAB 37/127/40

dence in being able to deliver the goods. Asquith was left to resolve the dilemma.

By 5 May the artists employed by *The Illustrated War News* had found time to produce their impressions and across two pages was published a picture of 'The Germans' "Brutally Barbarous" poisoning of French soldiers near Ypres by suffocating gas-fumes.' The caption described the white puffs which marked the opening of the cylinders, the cloud 'like the yellow wind of Northern China'. After the gas had passed over the Allied trenches the Germans had swarmed out 'bayoneting, it is alleged, all Frenchmen they found not dead'.

Overleaf another two-page sketch, somewhat out of proportion, purported to show the battle for Lizerne—Zouaves charging the bridge followed by dwarf Belgian cyclists pedalling hard.

On the back page the magazine reproduced in gravure 'This interesting picture, showing how the clouds of asphyxiating gases released by the Germans near Langemarck rolled towards the French trenches', and announced it would be 'given as a colour-plate with the *Illustrated London News* (its sister paper) for May 8'.

The study of reeling 'Turcos', hands over face and eyes, was something of which the firm could be proud.

'The use of colour for war work affords one more example of the enterprise and initiative of that paper, which, it will be recalled, led the way in using colour-photography and in adopting special photogravure machinery for current illustrations.'

Other sections of the Press were also active. An appeal to the women of Britain by Lord Kitchener was widely publicized. Lord Northcliffe's *Daily Mail* was vociferous. Thousands of respirators loosely based on captured German models were rushed to France. For the most part they proved useless. The cotton wool or lint used as a pad for the mouth and nose was ineffective if dry, for the gas simply passed through it. If wetted it became more often than not a sodden pulp through which no air could pass. After large quantities had been distributed the medical authorities in France had to issue orders that the home-produced variety of respirator was not to be used. In its place squares of flannel and even cap comforters[1] were sent up the line to be treated on the spot with a chemical solution – where available. Work on more practical types of protection went on day and night as the tiny laboratory in St Omer fed information back to England and its staff worked on a prototype mask. In Britain production of an interim model was already under way.

---

[1] Woollen headwear issued to the troops.

They called it the 'veil respirator' because it was held in place by a length of black tulle of the type which Queen Victoria had made almost obligatory for widows. By the spring of 1915 this was being produced in bulk. The veil was folded so that it held a pad of cotton waste over the mouth and nose. The waste was soaked in a solution of sodium hyposulphite, washing soda crystals, water and glycerine, the last-named being included to ensure the pad remained moist. A waterproof satchel was designed to hold the mask so that it did not become saturated in muddy trenches or dry out in the wind and sun as troops marched. Pulled up over the eyes the mesh effect of the veil, originally intended to hide a woman's tears, gave some protection against the lachrymatory or 'weeping' gases.

Through an unfortunate misunderstanding initial production of the veil mask was held up. The first solution prepared for the dipping of the pads contained caustic instead of washing soda. The resultant mixture was so corrosive that the factory workers could not handle it. The mistake was quickly spotted but valuable time had been lost.

The order banning the *Daily Mail* mask was issued on 5 May. Distribution of the flannel pads and cap comforters had begun two or three days earlier at the rate of 5,000 per infantry division; the cavalry divisions, with fewer men, were allotted 3,000 each.

The confusion created by the original chlorine cloud had never been resolved, least of all by General Foch. In accordance with the lessons he had preached as a professor at the Ecole de Guerre before the war, he urged a series of headlong attacks to regain the lost ground.

It was a counsel which paid little heed to the numerous howitzers and well-sited machine guns of the enemy. By this stage of the war, Foch's exhortations would probably have resulted in only a modified response from French commanders. As early as September, 1914, Foch himself had been forced to acknowledge the efficacy of modern fire-power. General Eydoux, whose corps of Bretons had suffered severely making reckless bayonet charges, was able to inform his officers after the Marne that Foch was strongly recommending everyone to dig in ('*remuer la terre*') and disappear from the eyes of the enemy. A more cautious, even cynical, attitude developed and what might start at a high level as an order for a grandiose attack could finish up as a mere demonstration at the front. At Ypres in 1915, however, Sir John French was at first apt to take Foch at his word. The consequences were unfortunate.

The British Second Army consisted, at this time, of V Corps under Plumer and II Corps under Lieutenant-General Sir Charles

Fergusson. The latter was committed to the struggle for Hill 60 and there was a limit to the help he could send his neighbour. Such reserves as GHQ possessed were being drawn in piecemeal and worn down to little purpose. Smith-Dorrien, appreciating the realities of the situation, sat down in his report centre in Poperinghe on 27 April and prepared a long letter for dispatch to St Omer. As he wrote splinters from a 15-inch shell ripped into the walls of the house; the Germans would have used the gun earlier but the cement of its platform had been slow to set.

'I fear the Lahore Division have had very heavy casualties and so, they tell me, have the Northumbrians, and I am doubtful if it is worth losing any more men to regain this French ground unless the French do something really big.'

He could not ignore the threat to his rear which would develop if the Germans succeeded in expanding their thrust through Lizerne and beyond the canal.

Without a determined effort by the French 'the situation might become such as to make it impossible for us to hold any line east of Ypres'. In the absence of such action he suggested pulling back his troops to a less exposed line and he included the relevant map references for such a move in his letter.

Smith-Dorren insisted he was not being pessimistic but simply that he had to prepare for every eventuality. He showed his grasp of the broader situation by acknowledging that, as Haig was preparing the First Army for an offensive, there was not much point in borrowing troops from him.

Sir John French's reaction to the letter was ungenerous and unsympathetic. He had not forgotten or forgiven Smith-Dorrien for disobeying orders to retire and for fighting the battle of Le Cateau the previous August, especially as it was generally accepted that the action had saved not only II Corps (then Smith-Dorrien's command) but had gone a long way to preserving the rest of the BEF. This time there must be no misunderstanding.

First of all a message was sent to Second Army headquarters saying that Sir John did not consider the situation as unfavourable as Smith-Dorrien had made out.

This was followed by an uncoded signal directing Smith-Dorrien to hand over the command of all troops 'in the present operations about Ypres' to Plumer. It was timed 4.45 pm.

A letter was sent the same day to Plumer telling him to prepare a line ready for occupation 'if and when it becomes advisable to withdraw from the present salient'.

The following morning French put Smith-Dorrien's arguments for a withdrawal to Foch who was so alarmed that he put *his* thoughts in a letter which was delivered the same day. General Foch had 'the honour to observe' various things. They amounted to an almost hysterical demand that no British retirement should be ordered and that the attack towards Langemarck should be continued. He promised the arrival of a strong force of artillery the following day.

Foch's protests fell on deaf ears. Preparatory orders for a withdrawal to a less exposed line were issued by Plumer on the morning of 29 April. The troops, designated Plumer's Force, would take up the line suggested by Smith-Dorrien.

Plumer wrote to his wife: 'Things have not been made any better by Sir John French slighting Sir Horace and taking practically all my force away from him and leaving me independent of him. It is the last thing I wanted. It is not fair because Smith-Dorrien and I were in absolute agreement as to what should be done if I had remained under Smith-Dorrien.'

Plumer added that the losses had been very serious, with three brigadiers and a great many senior regimental officers killed.

'All the troops,' he declared, 'without exception have behaved splendidly,' and he made special mention of the Northumbrian Division which had faced a 'pretty severe test'. The 'test' included the loss of almost a whole brigade in a single attack.

Sir John French, having dealt with Smith-Dorrien, went to see Sir Douglas Haig at First Army Headquarters on the 30th and showed him a letter he had prepared for Foch. This was in the nature of an ultimatum. If General Putz did not succeed in advancing, British withdrawal to prepared positions, still within the Salient, would start that night.

Haig, whose first comment on being told of the introduction of gas was that the French should never have allowed themselves to be surprised, agreed that it was essential to pull back out of what he regarded as a 'death trap'.

Sir John then unburdened himself of his worries over Smith-Dorrien, a full general reduced to the command of a single corps, who still had not had the decency to resign. He was very complimentary to Sir Douglas who, he said, had never given him a moment's anxiety. After he had gone, Haig confided to his diary that Sir John was looking very well.

On churned-up, charred and blasted Hill 60 conversation was more basic. The 1st Dorsets were trying to improve their crumbling trenches unaware that less than 100 yards away the indefatigable

German pioneers were checking new batteries of gas cylinders.

May Day was one of decision. At 4 pm came the order to start withdrawing from the nose of the Salient. The first troops, remnants of the Lahore Division's battalions, were to move off at 8 pm. They did so to the familiar music of German guns pounding Hill 60.

Some time earlier the 1st DCLI, holding trenches near the Hill, noticed that the Germans had withdrawn from the front line and were firing from their supports. As they watched, a concentrated bombardment crashed down and cloud gas was released, taking the Dorsets by surprise. Until that moment they had only heard of gas and not experienced it. One company was actually doing gas drill at the time, unfortunately with dry protective pads.

The enemy then attacked the flanks of the Dorsets, advancing along the trenches behind a hail of grenades. As they did so their artillery laid down curtain fire on the approaches to '60'.

The range was short, the content of the cloud highly toxic. Soldiers reported that at one point they could see the gas pouring from the nozzles of the projector pipes only forty yards away. Instinctively some men took cover in the trenches. Others followed the example of a second-lieutenant who grasped the significance of the gas being heavier than air and jumped onto the parapet. Heavy rifle fire met the advancing Germans, who wavered. This momentary hesitation gave supporting troops time to charge up through the thinning yellow curtain. Bombers of the Devons and Bedfords, using home-made devices such as jam tins stuffed with gun cotton and nails, or captured 'potato mashers',[1] repulsed the threat from the flank.

The fighting was fierce. Private Edward Warner of the Bedfords won a VC by clearing a trench almost single-handed and then beating off all attempts to recapture it.

Hill 60 remained in British hands and the news went round the Salient that, for the first time, the Germans had failed to gain ground with a gas attack.

'The enemy was as much surprised at his failure as we were elated at our success in repelling it,' wrote an eye-witness, 'but many poor fellows died in terrible agony.'

All night bearers stumbled down the hillside with laden stretchers. The advanced dressing stations were crowded with gasping, retching soldiers. Of the Dorsets, ninety died in the trenches. Another forty-six died soon after reaching aid posts. Some lingered for days. The attack had cost them 300 men. Among the fatal gas casualties was Pte Warner.

[1] German bombs shaped like a common Victorian kitchen utensil.

'Clean killing is at least comprehensible,' wrote a Dorset officer afterwards, 'but this murder by slow agony absolutely knocks me. The whole civilized world ought to rise up and exterminate those swine across the hill.'

Alas, 'those swine across the hill' were incorrigible and at 5 pm the next day made a gas attack on a front of three miles. It fell on troops of the 4th Division[1] which had taken over the trenches facing Mauser Ridge with the French on their left. The 4th had been equipped with primitive gas masks and held its ground.

Only the 2nd Lancashire Fusiliers were slow in putting on their 'protectors', an order having been delayed, and they suffered accordingly. One company fell back from its trenches but, due to the iron will of a private soldier[2] who hauled his Vickers on to the parapet and kept it in action, reserves were able to restore the situation. To reach the Fusiliers, Territorials and dismounted regular cavalry had virtually to wade through a tide of gas which rolled forward waist-high. The 2nd Essex, though they donned their masks in time, also fell back but recovered the ground later.

Invaluable aid was given by French 75s which opened flanking fire aimed behind the gas cloud immediately it appeared, catching the assault troops as they deployed.

Despite the second successful defence of a 'gassed' line in two days the power of the new weapon had been once more dramatically displayed. In the Lancashire Fusiliers 450 officers and men were taken to hospital where many died, including the intrepid machine-gunner, Private Jack Lynn, awarded the Victoria Cross post-humously. The Essex gas casualties totalled 178. In both battalions many men were also killed and wounded by shot and shell.

The 2nd Seaforth Highlanders were holding trenches 600 to 800 yards from the German line that day. On being ordered to 'stand to' they watched what appeared to be a fog bank about thirty feet high roll down on them. A medical officer, Lieutenant P.W. James, attached to the battalion recorded that coughing and spluttering was heard the moment the 'smoke' reached them, though some troops had worn pads which had been dipped in water or a solution of bicarbonate of soda. Men tried to leave the trenches to escape the cloud and had to be 'led' back. James was struck by their exhaustion. There was no infantry assault and about three hours later the lieutenant himself had to lie down.

'All night in the trenches one heard groaning, not that of pain, but

[1] Brought up from GHQ Reserve.
[2] Without a mask.

just the low muttering that is often heard in disease.'

The Seaforths seem to have been badly informed about the new menace because the next morning most of them were found lying in the bottom of their trenches, where it lingered longest, as if sleeping off a poisonous drug.

'That night the battalion was reported incapable of further fighting.' Only four men died in hospital afterwards but the gas had removed temporarily a very fine battalion from the fighting line. Ironically, General von Hugel, whose troops made the abortive attack, had been wondering if the gas had been in sufficient concentration and whether his opponents were now fully equipped with efficient respirators.

The stealthy British withdrawal continued. By 4 May they had skilfully pulled back their more exposed forces to a line forming a broad curve averaging about three miles from Ypres. On their left, west of the canal, General Joppe's 152nd Division linked up with the British 4th Division at Turco Farm. The 28th and 27th Divisions occupied the centre of the arc and the 5th Division held Hill 60 on the right flank.

The following day the mound was lost after a morning gas attack in which the cloud drifted not over but along the trenches where many of the occupants were sleeping after a hectic night. So thick were the fumes that the cotton waste pads dried out quickly and it was impossible to keep them moist.

Bravely or rashly, depending on one's point of view, but certainly dutifully, the Rev. Owen Watkins enjoyed a 'delightful canter' over the fields to an advanced dressing station; he was attached to the 14th Field Ambulance of the 5th Division. His companion was an RAMC captain. Near the front 'to our horror we found men lying all along the road gasping out their lives, and with sinking hearts we recognized the deadly effects of the German gas. At 8.30 the death-cloud had swept down upon them, the men had not been able to face it. . . . These had run gasping until they fell, black in the face and dying – some had run three miles.'

Watkins found the dressing station filled to overflowing, with casualties streaming in: 'In 24 hours they had over 1,200 cases to deal with; more than 100 died in the dressing stations'. The stalwart Methodist said that for the first time in his life he felt real hate in his heart: 'Nothing seemed bad enough for the men who had done this thing.'

Hand-to-hand fighting went on spasmodically during the day among the humps and hollows which had once been trenches. In the early hours of the morning it was all over.

Smith-Dorrien, still responsible for Hill 60, felt the loss deeply. While the Germans were congratulating themselves on their success he sent a letter to British GHQ in which he gave Sir John French the opportunity he had been waiting for. It was 'for the good of the cause' – and because of the evident lack of trust in him – that he thought it would be better if he were to serve elsewhere.

According to legend, Sir William Robertson rang him from GHQ, paraphrasing Sir John's reply: ' 'Orace, you're for 'ome.' Plumer took over the command of the Second Army.

CHAPTER 7

Luck of the Irish

Fighting at Ypres died down after Hill 60 changed hands. Two small gas attacks were made along the Menin Road, but both failed. During one of them the cloud blew back over the enemy troops. Two battalions advancing in strength found themselves exposed to the view of an alert British machine gun detachment which took full advantage of their predicament.

For a time the struggle in Flanders diminished because ammunition priority had been switched from the Fourth Army to Prince Rupprecht's Sixth Army in Artois. There the French offensive launched on 9 May flattered only to deceive. Haig's attack on Aubers Ridge made no headway and had to be called off almost immediately.

In London the mounting casualties and the number of gas cases among them finally drove the Cabinet to make a decision. All scruples seem to have been overcome by May 18. On that day it was decided that the enemy should be repaid in his own despised coinage. Within a week the gas war began again. All the unexpended cylinders on the front of the German Fourth Army had been dug in at points around the Salient to await a favourable wind. It arrived on 24 May.

Four telltale red flares were seen, followed by two more at the first glimmer of dawn. Shells immediately crashed down and the enemy infantry opened rapid fire. Where no-man's-land was narrowest the hissing of cylinders could be heard through the pandemonium.

Makeshift alarms – suspended shell cases beaten like gongs or, in places, klaxon horns – sounded the alert. Sleeping men were roused and began fastening on their respirators. Not all had them at hand and frantic searching began. Those who clambered on to the firestep saw what appeared to be a long low cloudbank moving towards them, dipping and swaying. Aiming points such as trees, even houses, became blurs in the thickening mist and then disappeared. The oncoming cloud was estimated to have reached a height of forty feet.

Twenty-four hours earlier the 9th Lancers, of the 1st Cavalry Brigade, had taken over 900 yards of trench astride the Menin Road at Hooge, with Bellewaarde's artificial lake, part of the area's complicated drainage system, to their left front. They had been looking forward to a 'bright summer day with cloudless skies'. That was what had been forecast and all the signs were favourable. It was Whit Monday and Empire Day. In England the children were parading with Union flags.

Because there were only 350 Lancers, some 500 Green Howards and DLI of the 50th Division were placed under the command of the regiment.

They stood waiting for the assault which must come, hardly able to see one another. The wind was light and 'masks became so saturated (with gas) as to afford no protection'.

Some men simply ripped them off even though the gas 'drifted into our trenches and hung about for an hour and remained even after that in hollows and in trees'.

The line was pierced on the left of the Lancers and at 4.30 am the 2nd Buffs in reserve received a message from a cavalry officer saying his men were 'on their knees' but holding out. A company was sent to reinforce him. It moved along the Menin Road under black shrapnel bursts, past scores of wounded and gassed soldiers heading for Ypres.

'Eventually about 150 men . . . filed into the Hooge trenches, the occupants of which were suffering badly from gas – especially the officers. Besides the 9th Lancers there were . . . 18th Hussars, 4th Yorkshires, York and Lancasters and 5th DLI. Captain Grenfell VC, 9th Lancers[1] was in command.'

The Buffs formed a new firing line to enfilade the enemy pushing past the obstinate strongpoint.

Five miles away at Dickebusch troops in reserve felt the effects of the gas which was strong enough to make their eyes sore. Large numbers of tear gas shells were also reported during the day. In the firing line lingering wreaths of chlorine claimed victim after victim, especially in a tangle of trenches and trees known as Railway Wood, through which the Ypres–Roulers line had once run. The 3rd Royal Fusiliers reported later that, where it did no worse, it 'made men incapable of all effort; and yet the time had come for a superhuman effort'.

[1] Captain Francis Grenfell was killed that day. His brother, Riversdale, had been killed in 1914.

Somehow some soldiers found reserves of strength and the struggle continued.

North of Hooge the enemy broke into the line near the village of Wieltje and captured a shored-up, sandbagged ruin which had been known as Shell Trap Farm during First Ypres until some discerning staff officer changed its name officially to Mousetrap Farm. The 2nd Royal Dublin Fusiliers and the 2nd Royal Irish Regiment fought side by side there. Gas, shells and bullets caused heavy casualties but they resisted until about noon. Only a few survivors returned to tell the tale.

The Germans, exhausted by their efforts to overwhelm the Irish, were unable to exploit their success at Wieltje.

Some men gassed on this occasion might have been spared their ordeal if safety drill had been commonplace, but it was difficult to carry this out while the troops were trying to rebuild trenches – it had rained heavily earlier in May – and perform their normal duties. Where battalions had got to grips with the problem casualties were low. Opposite the 1st Royal Irish Fusiliers, whose gas discipline was good, all the enemy's attempts to advance were beaten back.

Though large supplies of veil respirators had been distributed, instruction on their use, even when given, had not always been understood. The masks had been designed so that they could be worn without the pad having to be dipped in a neutralizing solution. In the heat of the moment, or out of sheer ignorance, some men still soaked the protective cotton waste when the alarm was given, rendering it useless. Others still put their faith in the pure cotton wool pads sent out by well-meaning women in Britain.

Cases were reported of soldiers putting masks over their mouths and leaving their noses exposed to the poisoned air. Others are said to have applied cotton waste pads to their chests because that was where they felt pain.

Most of the rank and file were simple men: a glance at the Book of Remembrance in any military cemetery will reveal scores of cottage addresses. One of the most popular songs of the day got to the heart of the matter when it asked: 'Where are the boys of the village tonight?'

None of the exhausted troops was aware of it but on the 24th one of the most gruelling battles in history was drawing to a close after thirty-four days.

Almost as a reflex action the British delivered two counter-attacks. The first, 'at teatime', was made by a threadbare brigade[1] which had

---

[1] 84th Brigade – 2nd Northumberland Fusiliers, 1st Suffolk, 2nd Cheshire, 1st Welch, 1st Monmouthshire.

suffered severely at the beginning of May. It recaptured some lost ground and dug in. The second counter-attack, just before midnight, was betrayed by the all-revealing moonlight. Four battalions lost heavily to no purpose[1].

Earlier that evening Duke Albrecht issued fresh orders. Major operations on the front of the Fourth Army were to cease forthwith. The 1st DCLI recorded that on 27 May the battalion called in all cotton wool respirators and burned them, receiving veil gauze masks in their place. A 'proper system of gas drill was introduced and the sounding of gas alarms.'

Critics said afterwards that Falkenhayn disclosed his new weapon too soon and without sufficient thought. And, in retrospect, there may be good grounds for this argument. At the time, however, he acted before anyone knew what effect a chlorine gas cloud would have on a battlefield; and he had other objectives in view. These he achieved. On the day the British scored their second defensive success against a gas attack – Sunday, May 2 – the divisions secretly railed from the Western Front had joined in the great attack in the East. A gap of some twelve miles was torn in the front of the Russian Third Army. The Tsar's troops began to fall back to the line from which they had begun their offensive in 1914. The Battle of Gorlice– Tarnow was to have far-reaching consequences and for a moment Falkenhayn may have believed that Russia would be forced to come to terms, that the 'Easterners' were right. Soon, however, he reverted to his quest for decisive victory in the West.

At Ypres Duke Albrecht may have failed to eliminate what he preferred to call the 'bridgehead' rather than the 'salient', but he had, without necessarily appreciating it, inflicted irreparable harm on the British Army. The shock effect of the gas cloud seems to have numbed the mental processes of the Allied commanders.

At the time of Second Ypres the first eight regular infantry divisions of the British Expeditionary Force had already been through severe trials. Their battalions lost heavily in men and, in percentage terms, more so in officers.

When the 27th, 28th and 29th Divisions had been formed from units recalled from abroad they represented the last of the available highly-trained foot soldiers in the Empire. They could have formed an invaluable nucleus for the New Armies then being organized. Instead the 29th suffered heavily at Gallipoli and the 27th and 28th were squandered in fruitless mass attacks in Flanders, contrary to all

[1] 2nd Shropshire LI, 3rd and 4th KRRC, 4th Rifle Brigade.

their training; the Boer War had brought home to the humblest private the need for cover from view and fire.

Even the confusion resulting from the cramped conditions of the overcrowded Salient, even the failure of communications and the inability of the higher command to control the battle, does not explain the British obsession with numbers in both attack and defence.

Apologists pointed to the inequality of the artillery engaged; not having enough heavy guns, the British were obliged to hold their trenches with more men than would have been the case normally.

The numbers, however, led to more losses and greater weakness, not increased strength. The 3rd Royal Fusiliers had only one officer left out of seventeen on the night of May 24. More than 500 men had been gassed or killed by small-arms and shell fire. It earned the grisly reputation of being the battalion's worst day in the whole war – and perhaps saw the heaviest losses suffered in a day by any of the Regiment's many battalions which fought in the Great War. Unhappily the Fusiliers were not an isolated case.

More than 59,000 officers and men were killed, wounded or captured between 22 April and 31 May, British, Canadian and Indian. French casualties were also severe. The Germans, despite their attacking role, suffered 34,000 casualties.

The comment in 1926 of the British Official Historian, Brigadier-General Sir James Edmonds, a graduate of the Staff College, merits attention:

'These [the British] casualties were certainly heavier than the German, but in view of the infantry attacks and counter-attacks made in haste and without adequate support from guns, and of the enemy preponderance in artillery this is not extraordinary. That the line was held at all was due to the heroic sacrifice of the infantry, cavalry and engineers [Sir James was a Sapper], a very large proportion of whom were untrained soldiers, who could be relied on for defence, but, hardly, with their lack of military training, to win a battle.'

Few things are more 'extraordinary' than Sir James's comments – a dismal requiem for the many men who died without even reaching the enemy trenches on Mauser Ridge and for the corpses jamming the ditches at Railway Wood and Shell Trap Farm.

Sir John French was not so ambiguous in his praise of the Second Army. He punctiliously toured formations and units to thank them. Vilifying the enemy, he declared that they had resorted to a 'mean and dastardly practice, hitherto unheard of in civilized warfare, the use of asphyxiating gases'.

He did not add that ways of employing the object of his anger and loathing were being sought by the Allies as a matter of urgency. The British Army was to have its own genie, its own bottles. It was already looking for men to extract the corks.

CHAPTER 8

Stinks Masters All

Major Charles Foulkes was leading a company of Sappers to a rendezvous with the Guards Brigade near Festubert when a message arrived telling him to report to the B.E.F.'s Advanced Headquarters at Hazebrouck. He sent back word that he would have to carry out his mission first and plodded on. A second terse order left him no option and, mud-stained and shabby as he was, he climbed into the car sent to fetch him.

Why Sir William Robertson selected him to become the Army's first 'Gas Adviser' is not clear, as Foulkes, a professional soldier who had joined the Royal Engineers in 1894, knew nothing of the subject and had not witnessed the attacks made by the Germans in the previous weeks. The Chief of the General Staff may, however, have remembered some service rendered by him ten years earlier. Foulkes had shown an original turn of mind by spending part of his leave spying on the fortress of a foreign power, taking photographs of it through a telescopic lens and finally producing plans.

Sir William disregarded Foulkes's statement that he knew nothing about gas. He did not think it mattered.

'I want you to take charge of our gas reprisals here in France,' he said and ordered Foulkes to London to find out what was being planned there. He was to report back with proposals for offensive gas warfare as soon as possible. The date was 26 May – two days after the great gas attack at Bellewaarde and Hooge.

Foulkes, who had been promoted lieutenant-colonel, arrived in London on 27 May and went immediately to the Master General of Ordnance, General Sir Stanley Brenton von Donop, to present a letter of introduction from Robertson, which stated:

'The employment of gas may develop into a big thing, and all branches of the staff here feel that gas may become a fifth arm and that we need some officer at GHQ who will deal with the question as a whole.

'The C-in-C. has therefore appointed Major Foulkes, R.E., for this duty. He has no pretence to technical knowledge, as far as I know, and it is not considered that he need have very much. But he has had much experience at the front, and can explain generally what we need and how we can perhaps best use it.'

Foulkes was certainly a combat veteran, having seen action at Ypres in November, 1914, and been involved in later operations at La Bassée, Givenchy, Festubert and Aubers Ridge. His service before the war included duty in various unhealthy parts of West Africa as well as three years in South Africa during the Boer War. A commonsense, practical man, he came from a middle-class background, had been educated at Bedford Modern School and had played hockey for Scotland (1907–9). He did not think it at all strange that he should be given the task allotted to him.

General von Donop, who, despite his name,[1] was the son of a British admiral, was something of a scientist himself and had been Superintendent of Experiments at Shoeburyness before the war.[2] After reading Robertson's letter, he sent Foulkes off to consult with the special department which had been set up at the War Office to deal with gas warfare. Two days later Foulkes was back in France.

He told Sir William Robertson that there were plentiful supplies of chlorine at home but there was only one plant capable of converting it into liquid form. A hoped-for consignment of 1,500 cylinders would not be available before the end of June. There were production problems.

As for the possibility of making gas shells, experiments were in hand. Furthermore, at Mr Churchill's suggestion, tests were being carried out by naval airmen to see whether it would be practical to drop gas bombs.

Having described the scene in Britain, Foulkes then proceeded to make a number of suggestions which proved extremely shrewd. He advised that all talk of retaliation for the gas launched at Ypres should be stifled as far as possible so that when action was taken the enemy's surprise would be all the greater. He also requested that no gas attack should be attempted until enough cylinders had been accumulated for use on a large scale.

[1] General von Donop, born in 1860, stuck to his name despite the inevitable ill-feeling it caused. In 1917 he was sent to command the Humber Garrison.
[2] He foresaw the value of heavy artillery and sponsored development of the 9.2 in howitzer.

Other points included outline proposals for the creation of a gas service.

Foulkes was told to find and set up a suitable headquarters. Wasting no time, he selected Helfaut, a village on a quiet stretch of heathland about four miles south of the British General Headquarters at St Omer. Sir John French, probably prompted by his friend Mr Churchill, leaned towards the idea of gas bombing by planes but was careful to give his Gas Adviser an almost free hand. Foulkes concentrated on learning as much as he could about gas cylinders and on 4 June was back in England watching a trial chlorine discharge at the Castner Kellner works at Runcorn, Cheshire. On his return he urged that no time should be wasted in recruiting Royal Engineer companies to fight the gas war.

After the examination season of summer, 1915, college education authorities wrote to chemistry graduates and students to say that there might be special opportunities for qualified men in the Army. What these might be they did not specify, except to say that volunteers would be employed on scientific work overseas. Scores of innocents thereupon signed on 'for three years or the duration' and found themselves in khaki, still unaware of what they had let themselves in for.

About twenty experienced scientists had been hurried to France and sent to various corps in May to act as gas advisers, but the bulk of the rank and file had still to be found. While he awaited the arrival of these troops to form three 'Special Companies RE', Foulkes explored all possible means of using the new weapon. He listened to everyone and looked at anything anyone was prepared to show him. Encouragement and a valuable suggestion came from an unexpected source – Lieutenant-General Michael Rimington, commanding the completely misemployed Indian Cavalry Corps. Rimington, who had taken a degree at Oxford before joining the Inniskilling Dragoons, had been impressed by a demonstration of a new weapon, the 3-inch trench mortar. There had been a good deal of criticism of this primitive piece of equipment and it was regarded in high places as too dangerous to use. The General, however, felt that this was just the thing for Foulkes and might be employed to fire bombs filled with gas. A letter was immediately sent off to Mr William Stokes, the inventor of the mortar, asking him to design a larger version. Within a month he had produced a 4-inch model. Not long afterwards General Rimington disappeared from the Flanders scene to become Inspector of Cavalry in India. He was remembered more for his books *Our Cavalry* and *Hints on Stable Management* than for his appreciation of the value of the Stokes gun.

Foulkes's exploratory mission also took him to a run-down factory on the Channel coast, a place discovered by a French liaison officer, Captain Gerschell. The plant had produced chemicals for the dye industry before the war, but most of its workers had been mobilized. Nevertheless experiments were conducted on animals which indicated that another gas promised to be even more effective than chlorine. Foulkes set off for London again, taking a cylinder containing phosgene for further examination.

The first laboratory tests showed the chemical to be an indifferent poison. Foulkes was not prepared to accept the verdict. He insisted that the laboratory apparatus be checked. It was found to be faulty. Further experiments showed the gas to be highly toxic.

On his return to France Foulkes encountered another snag. Patriotic the factory owner might be, but his formula for producing the phosgene was a trade secret. He had to be suitably and legally indemnified before he would part with it. Eventually satisfactory agreements were drawn up and a number of French soldiers found themselves recalled from the trenches back to their old jobs at Coulogne, near Calais. The United Alkali Company opened a new factory at Lancaster and everyone involved was sworn to secrecy. Foulkes, who had great faith in the new gas, stressed its potential when he met Mr Lloyd George, the Munitions Minister, on a visit to France. The production of phosgene was clearly going to take some months, however, and in the meantime the Allies had to rely on chlorine.

In respect of factories to produce chlorine the French were even worse off than the British. Their politicians too had suffered qualms of conscience about stooping to such depths as their enemy and took even longer than the British Government to decide whether they should reply in kind. The shock of gas warfare on the French had been profound, despite the warnings that had been received. On 25 April Foch's Chief of Staff, Weygand, had issued an instruction which advocated the use of the same protective chemical as the Germans. As this was patently not available the next best thing, he suggested, was to rush through the gas cloud as quickly as possible towards the enemy and against the wind. Joffre had the mining districts scoured for breathing apparatus and requisitioned stocks of similar equipment from the Paris fire brigade, but the quantities involved were insignificant.

The faculties of chemistry at the Sorbonne and of pharmaceutical research at the College de France were called in to apply themselves urgently to the problem of protection, and a total of around 100 chemists were soon at work in specialist laboratories. Others concentrated on developing a practical gas shell. At Helfaut Foulkes devoted himself to making sure all was ready for the reception of his own cadres of 'BScs' and 'stinks masters'. They were going to be needed much sooner than any of them had expected.

On the morning of 7 July Foulkes saw Sir Douglas Haig.. The commander of the First Army had already exchanged pleasantries with the Crown Prince of Serbia, touring British troops in the company of Prince Arthur of Connaught, and was in a receptive mood. Sir Douglas agreed with Foulkes that 'the use of asphyxiating gas' should be delayed until it was available in sufficiently large quantities to make the best of the element of surprise. He suggested that an excellent place to use it would be Aubers Ridge, scene of the bloody repulse in May, and that it should be employed on a front of five miles. Exit Foulkes to carry on training.

The first drafts for the Special Companies began to arrive at Helfaut in mid-July, each man wearing the two stripes which had been given him to compensate for the sacrifice of his career and perhaps to reward him for his rashness in volunteering for the unknown. The men had been given no clue as to their duties when they carried out their basic 'square bashing' at Chatham. The first hint they received was as they left. An old NCO had sent one squad on its way with the words: 'Gas every one of those bastards back to Germany when you get to France.'

The enlightenment process was completed by a lieutenant-colonel, who, after the briefing, told the new arrivals that anyone who wished could return to England. Only half-a-dozen men from all the 1915 draft ever took advantage of this offer. The others settled down to learn the tricks of the trade and soon discovered that their academic qualifications were of little use. They were required first and foremost to be adept at heaving ugly iron cylinders weighing up to 130 lbs around Helfaut's common. The most primitive of them had simply to be picked up by two men and carried on the shoulder. A third man followed to relieve the carriers. The more sophisticated version in general use had handles welded to it. Through these two rope loops were threaded. A pole was thrust through the loops and the cylinder was borne off like a tiger fallen victim to a maharajah's gun. The third man still followed. Ultra-modern types had handles adapted to take the carrying pole without ropes, but the burden was still awkward and tiring. A man might acquire an affection for his rifle or even his field-gun, but no one ever learned to love a gas cylinder.

To make them even more unlikeable they could not even be

referred to by their proper names. In messages and in conversation some other name had to be used for secrecy's sake. 'Roger' was one official name, but they could be called 'Oojahs' without causing offence. More colourful names were discouraged in public.

Just how many Allied troops died from gas poisoning in the Second Battle of Ypres will never be known. The Germans occupied the French lines and disposed of the dead after the battle of 22 April. The Canadians and the British fell back from the positions held on the 24th and later withdrew from a large part of the Salient. During the battle officers and men marching 'up the line' often reported passing trenches filled with the bodies of men who looked as though they had been gassed, or passed apparent victims lying by the road. No one actually went round every corpse checking to see whether death had been caused by a bullet, shell splinter, blast or gas.

Up to and including the attack of 24 May a total of 7,000 British gas casualties were estimated to have reached field ambulances and casualty clearing stations. Of these about 350 are known to have died before the end of June (a month when there were no gas attacks). The Canadians lost 1,850 dead during this period but for the reasons stated the proportions of chlorine cloud victims cannot be known, only the fact that there were many of them.[1]

The realization of the potential of gas to inflict casualties provoked a British response which did not lose momentum throughout the war. Even before Foulkes was appointed to explore offensive techniques, 56-year-old Colonel William Horrocks, a hygiene expert and, among other things, an honorary surgeon to King George V, was appointed to head an 'anti-gas' committee, which consisted of military and civilian members. Laboratories were equipped at the RAMC College on the Thames at Millbank and the Royal Society formed another committee to investigate the effect on the human body, not only of chlorine gas but other toxins that might appear on the battlefield. Colonel Horrocks, whose son Brian[2] was taken prisoner while serving in the Middlesex Regiment in 1914, wasted no time in setting about the task of finding an adequate respirator.

The very first production models were rushed to France during May. Said to have been inspired by the report of a Canadian sergeant who saw a German pulling a 'bag' over his head while opening a

[1] An estimate of French casualties is given in the *British Handbook of Land Service Ammunition*, Part I, Chapter I (Historical) 1971: dead 5,000; gassed 15,000, prisoners 6,000.
[2] Later Lieut-General Sir Brian Horrocks, of Second World War fame.

cylinder, the respirator consisted of just that – a flannel bag which had been treated with the same fluid used to moisten the cotton waste pads.

Variously known as the 'smoke helmet' or 'hypo-helmet' (after the hyposulphite of soda in the chemical treatment), it was fitted with a rectangular mica window. In action the helmet was pulled over the head and the open end was tucked into the collar of the tunic, which buttoned up to the throat. The gas was neutralized as it passed through the impregnated material and the wearer was able to breathe.

A few of these 'gas bags' had been issued to machine-gunners at the time of the great gas attack of 24 May but the eyepieces cracked and became useless. In less than a fortnight celluloid had been substituted for the mica. By the first week in July all combat troops had been equipped with the new model and the veil mask was retained as a reserve.

A vast increase in the use of T-shell by the Germans also had to be countered; lachrymators or 'weeping gases' were to remain a nuisance throughout the war. They were able to penetrate the flannel gas bag to some extent and, in any case, were often used without a chlorine cloud accompaniment. At first celluloid goggles were issued so they could be tied on with tape independently of the mask, but they were not successful. It was decided to set goggle lenses in thick rings of sponge rubber.

From the end of April Vermorel sprayers became part of a unit's equipment – far from the cherry orchards of Kent in which they were originally destined to combat insects. The sprayers, filled with a weak mixture of the gas bag's protective solution, were used in attempts to neutralize pockets of fumes hanging about dugouts and trenches.

The scientists also looked ahead. They foresaw that the Germans would try to increase the potency of the gas cloud and calculated that the agent most likely to be encountered was phosgene which was not susceptible to the chemicals in the masks and smoke helmets designed to protect the troops against chlorine.

A new respirator was therefore designed of tougher cloth which could stand being soaked in a mixture of carbolic acid and caustic soda to react against chlorine *and* phosgene. A simple non-return valve was inserted so the wearer could breathe out without letting gas in. The tube for the valve was gripped in the teeth and the troops sometimes called it a 'tube helmet' or 'the booger with the teat'. The one-piece celluloid window had come in for much criticism and strong lenses set in metal frames were inserted in the new mask. Efforts were made to supply each soldier with an improved model so that he could carry the original gas bag as a spare.

The first rudimentary 'gas schools' were coming into operation by early summer and subalterns were despatched to investigate their mysteries. Nineteen-year-old Edmund Blunden in a Service battalion of the Royal Sussex Regiment stayed in a pleasant farmhouse while attending a course at Essars, then an untouched village on the Bethune–Neuve Chapelle road. Students went to lectures in a cluster of huts and sat in various gas chambers to obtain practical experience.

'It was all very leisurely, alarming and useful.'

Blunden was exempted from running while wearing his gas bag because he was slightly asthmatic.

The political need for an offensive in the West was not disputed. Lord Kitchener, on a visit to France in August, explained to Sir John French and to Haig that the Russians were facing collapse. Warsaw had fallen and the Germans were marching on Brest–Litovsk. The British must join the French in an offensive even though it might lead to heavy casualties. There could be no question of waiting until the New Armies, formed in response to Kitchener's call, were fully trained.

Sir John French quickly fell in with Joffre's proposal that the First Army should attack alongside d'Urbal's Tenth, making yet another thrust in Artois. It all fitted into the master plan. He rejected suggestions that it might be better to attack once more in the Festubert–Aubers Ridge area. Had not the stolid, solid, confident Joffre himself said that Haig would find the front selected 'particularly favourable'?

Joffre's primary aim was to free the occupied territory, a huge salient with the town of Noyon, eighty miles from Paris, at the deepest point. With General Edouard de Curières de Castelnau's Central Army Group he intended to strike in the Champagne country at the base of the salient. A total of thirty-seven divisions would be launched around Rheims.

The Northern Army Group under Foch would launch twenty-three divisions – seventeen French on a twelve-mile front and six British on a front half that width.

For success in Artois the French depended largely on heavy artillery – 420 big guns with plenty of ammunition.

Foch, carried away with hopes of victory, overruled a plan put forward by d'Urbal for an advance in three stages. The three steps proposed had to be combined into a giant leap. The Tenth Army had to 'achieve a strategic breakthrough capable of producing decisive results, and to push . . . rapidly towards Douai'. Douai lay way beyond Vimy Ridge, still littered with the unburied dead of previous unsuccessful assaults.

Argument with Foch was something that few people relished, least of all his subordinates. In 1914 d'Urbal had been a humble cavalry brigadier. Within a fortnight he had been promoted to the head of a division, quickly made the step to corps and within months had assumed leadership of an army. He owed much to Foch. The plan was changed as instructed. When it was seen by General Marie-Emil Fayolle, who had spent ten years as a professor of artillery at the Ecole de Guerre, he said only one word: '*Diable!*' His XXXIII Corps was scheduled to take Vimy Ridge and open the way for the rest of the Tenth Army.

Fayolle[1] is one of the most interesting of the First World War generals, thanks to his secret diaries which were not published until 1964. Recalled from a barely commenced retirement in 1914, he was given an infantry brigade and by 1918 was commanding a group of armies. From the beginning he recognized the scientific and economic nature of the conflict and made up for his ignorance by making frequent visits to the trenches. He was labelled the 'Duckboard General'. Though a devout Catholic, he raised no religious objections to the use of gas, seeing more clearly than some that if it is intended to kill or incapacitate, one shell is very much like another. He had personal experience of German tear gas and in July, 1915, when the enemy captured the hotly disputed cemetery of Souchez, in Artois, the General recorded that his batteries were so '*incommodées*' that they could not continue in action. Fayolle was strongly opposed to the wasteful attacks ordered by Foch in 1915. He had a reputation for looking after his troops and lost his temper with them only when he found evidence of their vandalism behind the lines, especially in abandoned churches. His diaries paint a grim picture of the battle in Artois.

On the Champagne front the French expected the Germans to conceal machine guns and reserves in the copses and woods and asked the Secretariat des Inventions for help in dealing with them. In August a number of staff officers gathered in the garden of a headquarters building to see a tree splashed with a liquid resembling mercury. It burned like a torch. There was much talk of it being dropped from the air so that the *boches* would be '*grillés comme les rats*'. Everyone was delighted with this forerunner of napalm. They called it 'revenge for the gas'.

Gas, however, was not a significant part of the programme. Again it was the artillery that would bear the burden of breaking the

[1] Made a Marshal of France in 1921, he died in 1928. His grandson was killed leading a RAF Hurricane squadron over Dieppe in August, 1942.

German line with high explosives. Castelnau's army group alone would be able to draw on stocks of 2,500,000 shells for the 75mm cannon with 600,000 shells for the heavy guns. Joffre had amassed a formidable battering train, even if some of the pieces were elderly. He had achieved this concentration by borrowing naval guns and stripping the fortresses in quiet sectors such as Verdun.

Sir Douglas Haig was not so fortunate as his ally in assembling either shells or guns. At the end of June, 1915, it was estimated that in the whole of the B.E.F. there were only seventy-one guns and howitzers of a calibre of six inches or more. This made gas an attractive proposition. Haig saw that, in some degree, it could compensate for his weakness in artillery. Its use also appealed to the authorities responsible for producing munitions; the cylinders did not require high grade steel or precise machining. Like their contents they were comparatively cheap. Used in large quantities gas might stun and demoralize the enemy as well as any bombardment.

Haig's orders were to secure the line Loos-Hulluch and the area extending to the La Bassée Canal on his left. On his right he was to take a prominent feature known as Hill 70 near Lens. Far from being 'favourable' ground, the whole area was ideal for a defensive battle, at least under normal circumstances. Hulluch and Loos were two large villages in the middle of what had been a thriving coal-mining area. It was dotted with deserted red-brick colliery houses and the pit-heads were marked by silent winding engines and overhead railways from which the dumper tubs still hung. Two rusting skeletal towers of iron girders dominated the neglected fields around Loos, surviving all attempts by the British gunners to demolish them. The troops called them Tower Bridge (see map p. 79).

Other natural features buttressed the front to be stormed. South of Loos was a huge slagheap known as the Double Crassier. In the centre there were quarries and a chalk pit. On the northern flank was another group of pit heaps – Fosse 8 and a veritable Table Mountain of spoil and shale known as The Dump. The Germans had used the timber and rails on the spot to turn mountains of industrial waste into bastions.

Prince Rupprecht's Sixth Army had applied itself diligently during 1915 and dug two deep trench systems between two and three miles apart. They were linked by strongpoints sited in the spoil heaps and the villages. Belts of barbed wire up to forty feet deep protected the approaches to both positions. Some of the wire was strung on low posts, forming a deadly spider's web hidden in rank grass and flourishing weeds.

To carry such formidable works under 'normal' circumstances, big guns and lots of them were called for. As the British did not have the required heavy metal, gas took on a still greater importance.

On 22 August Haig and his corps commanders had been impressed by the successful demonstration of a cloud attack. With chlorine Haig thought he could responsibly commit his troops to an otherwise dubious operation. It was possible to argue that the ground really was suited to its use. The heavy fumes would fill the quarries and chalk pits, sink into the workings and the deep trenches and seep into the machine gun nests built into the village cellars. Weather permitting, gas would be the key.

Two plans were made. If gas were used, two corps each of three divisions would attack in line. On the left I Corps under Hubert Gough, at 45 the youngest lieutenant-general in the British Army, would seize the labyrinth of trenches known as the Hohenzollern Redoubt, storm Fosse 8 and take the Dump. On the right, Lieutenant-General Sir Henry Rawlinson, 51-year-old ex-Commandant of the Staff College, would seize Loos and Hill 70 with IV Corps.

Gough was an Irish cavalryman (16th Lancers) with a reputation for dash. His grandfather, an uncle and his younger brother had all won VCs. The latter, Brigadier-General John Gough, had been Haig's chief staff officer when killed by a sniper earlier that year. The Goughs had been prominent in the Curragh Incident just before the war when it looked as though many officers were going to resign if ordered to act against the Ulster Protestants.

Rawlinson had joined the King's Royal Rifle Corps in 1884 and served as ADC to Lord Roberts for a time. He was considered to be a very wily soldier – 'Rawlie the Fox'. The operations to which Gough and he were committed on the chalky Artois plain were to call for all the dash and guile they could muster.

As the days passed, Haig, who, despite new deliveries, still had only 177 heavy guns for his attack, became more and more convinced that gas would be the deciding factor and was very concerned that cylinders seemed to be slow in arriving. On 17 September he sent an urgent message to Sir William Robertson at St Omer. Without gas he would have to launch an offensive on a restricted front, thereby exposing his troops to the full weight of the enemy artillery with the inevitable loss. In Haig's opinion the attack scheduled for the 25th ought not to be made without the aid of gas.

Robertson replied immediately that the fault lay in Britain. Just as promptly Haig sent off another message, despatched at 10 pm, urging

Robertson to send a special envoy to England to insist that the 'gas factory' should work round the clock and not the eight hours a day which he believed to be the current practice. Special arrangements should be made for the shipment of cylinders.

In fact there had been production hold-ups. By the third week of July the number in France was about 1,000 less than Foulkes thought adequate. There had also been difficulty in obtaining flexible copper and lead pipes to 'jet' the gas from the cylinders over the parapets.

Originally the offensive had been planned for 15 September and it was with relief that Foulkes heard of its postponement. It meant that he could have time to train a fourth Special Company which had been authorized on 9 September. The shortage of suitable pipes had presented a new problem. The troops would now have to make use of rigid iron substitutes, each a tiresome ten feet long. They were something else to carry. In action one pipe would lead from a cylinder propped upright in a trench in the front line and the other had to be screwed in at right-angles just before the discharge. Sandbags had to be used to keep the discharge pipe in position. Constant practice was required by the Special Companies, whose scientific Sappers already had enough to think about.

Apart from a revolver with which to defend himself, each operator carried spanners to operate the tap for turning on the gas and for opening the outlet valve. Not all the cylinders were alike. Underneath the domed safety cap protecting the tap and the valve he might find a rectangular connecting rod or a more convenient wheel handle. A blind nut covered the outlet valve and had to be removed before the jet pipe could be connected. With the right equipment the removal, opening and fixing were unlikely to tax the wit of educated men working in a training trench on a dry day.

To drop a spanner on a wet and windy night was a different matter, even in training. What might happen under battle conditions, no one could say. Only a few of the men of the Special Companies had seen action before, those who had already been in Service battalions when the call was made for qualified men for an unspecified task. No one, however, neither Foulkes nor the survivors of early battles, had actually 'let off' gas in anger.

CHAPTER 9

While You've a Lucifer

The first of the Special Companies completed their training at Helfaut at the end of August and on 3 September were harangued by a Brasshat about their importance in the coming battle. The next day they breakfasted at 5.30, had another encouraging address, this time from Foulkes, and set off in style for the war. Buses took them to the forward area where they went into comfortable billets and waited. The weather was fine and for a week the troops enjoyed themselves, helping to bring in the harvest, all the male peasants having left in 1914.

The men of No. 186 Company (the others were 187, 188 and 189) left this bucolic existence the day Haig sent the message asking Sir William Robertson to speed up delivery of the gas cylinders. Roused at 4 am, they were off by lorry an hour and a half later. Wearing full marching order, they rattled through Bethune to a railhead. The rest of the day was spent at the sidings lifting cylinders from wagons. All were full. For secrecy all were packed in wooden crates – many addressed personally to Foulkes. All were heartily cursed.

The exhausted company slept that night in a disused factory and returned to their task of unloading boxes of Oojahs the next day. From the railhead the cylinders were taken to distribution points by lorries or horse-drawn wagons. Infantry working parties took them to the firing line. The corporal-chemists supervised the placing of the cylinders in emplacements and in firing bays. For many of them it was their first experience of the front line.

The dry spell ended and wet and misty weather set in. Gough, keeping an anxious eye on the weather reports, was concerned about the added strain which the installation of the cylinders put on the infantry. Some of them had to be hauled for two miles along muddy trenches in rain and darkness. The meteorologists brought little comfort. They talked only of the possibility of a favourable wind for the attack.

By the 23rd more than 5,000 cylinders containing around 150 tons of chlorine – a similar weight to that used by the Germans on 22 April – were ready. That night the RE Special Companies left their billets and marched up the line carrying their spanners and 10-foot-long projector pipes. Some sections were issued with an extra jar of rum as an 'emergency ration'. They tramped to the front in pouring rain, their way lit by the flashes of guns already firing on enemy positions.

None of them had undergone more than six weeks' gas training. Many had done less. Foulkes had been obliged to go personally to London and tour the War Office to get the postings documentation completed by the relevant administrative branches. None had been informed of the urgency involved. At Chatham he had even discovered some officers posted to him were being held back so they could take their turn escorting drafts of Sappers for non-specialist duties. He was still short of leaders when the companies deployed for action and the last to be formed marched up the line under volunteer subalterns he had 'borrowed' from resting infantry units.

The 24th was spent checking the cylinders in position. The Oojahs were in groups of from three to twelve, with each corporal responsible for up to six. Every man wore a cloth armband in pink, white and green stripes to identify him to the trench garrisons, and save him from the attentions of the 'battle police' looking for men who failed to go over the top at zero hour.

Once again the weather had changed. During the morning the sun came out and the chalky soil began to dry. The bombardment continued but experienced observers were not impressed. The thought went through some minds that perhaps shells were being saved for a furious burst just before the assault.

The units which were to form the first waves were now crammed into the trenches with all their battle paraphernalia waiting to mount the scaling ladders. Along the rest of the British front word was awaited to launch dummy attacks and create diversions. The Special Company troops fixed the first of their pipes to the cylinders and checked the wind direction for the hundredth time. They were not the only ones.

Haig's position on 24 September was not an enviable one. He, Gough and Rawlinson met in the afternoon and were briefed by Major Gold, the Royal Flying Corps Officer responsible for 'met' reports. The wind was still uncertain. Sir John French and Sir

William Robertson arrived at First Army headquarters in Hinges Château in the evening, after seeing Foch, and reported that the French would attack at 11 am the next day. Haig promised to fix his zero hour by 10 that evening, 'if it were possible'.

He was astonished to learn that Sir John meant to leave Robertson in charge of B.E.F. headquarters in St Omer the next day and was going to Lillers where he would not be in direct telephone contact with Haig. This was particularly disturbing as Sir John had insisted on retaining the three divisions of the general reserve – XI Corps – under his control, the location of which had already been the subject of argument. Haig thought they were too far from the front, but had accepted assurances that they would be made available to him in time.

After his visitors had gone, Haig received more weather information with 'a slight bias towards the favourable'. At 9 pm he issued orders for the major attack, though making it plain that it was still subject to cancellation.

The 'Big Push' was to begin at 6.30 am after the gas discharge. When Haig had gone to bed the breeze dropped. At one time it was blowing gently *from* the German lines.

In another room in the château, Foulkes and a tiny staff spent the night at a trestle table on which a large-scale trench map had been spread. As hourly reports came in from the forty officers in the firing line small flags were pinned to the chart to indicate the wind direction in the sector concerned. From time to time General Butler, Haig's chief staff officer, looked in to obtain the latest news. It became clear that in places the wind would be adverse and might blow into our own trenches. This did not cause Foulkes undue concern as he had given orders that cylinders were under no circumstances to be opened unless conditions were favourable and only the officer on the spot could be the judge of that.

Just before midnight, on the extreme left of the assault front, the wind had been blowing steadily from the west. This was exactly what was wanted. Towards dawn, however, it veered to blow very gently from south to north. As the sky lightened it became clear that this would definitely carry gas over part of the British line.

Captain Percy-Smith, on attachment from an Indian Cavalry regiment to command 186 Special Company, was under no illusions. Acting according to Foulkes's orders, he made a determined effort to cancel the discharge in his sector.

Robert Graves, in his classic *Goodbye To All That*, writes of the RE captain in the front line phoning 2nd Division headquarters at 5.30 am with the message: 'Dead calm. Impossible discharge accessory.'

'Accessory' was the code name for gas.

The reply, according to Graves, was: 'Accessory to be discharged at all costs.'

Corporal Martin Fox, of 186 Company, sharing a bay with three cylinders and a philosophical sentry, concluded: 'Such a decision seemed suicidal, and our officers were compelled to obey against all common sense.'

At 5 am, when Haig had taken the morning air, it was almost flat calm. A non-smoker himself, he set his ADC, 39-year-old Major Alan Fletcher, of the 17th Lancers, 'smoking furiously' and noted in his diary: 'The smoke drifted in puffs towards the N.E.'

Haig ordered staff officers to be alerted in case a postponement was necessary. His diary entry, as edited, for the crucial moment contains a mystery. Having recorded his order to the staff to stand by to 'counter' the order to attack, he added:

'At one time, owing to the calm, I feared the gas might simply hang about *our* trenches. However, at 5.15 I said "carry on". I went to the top of our wooden look-out tower. The wind came gently from S.W. and by 5.40 had increased slightly. The leaves of the poplar trees gently rustled. This seemed satisfactory. But what a risk I must run of gas blowing back upon our own dense masses of troops.'

The passage contains nothing to indicate the grounds for his decision. Having had misgivings he suddenly said 'carry on'.

Colonel John Charteris, 38-year-old head of the First Army's intelligence branch, saw the puffs of Fletcher's cigarette smoke drift 'perceptibly' towards the enemy lines but die down after a few minutes. Haig then had a message sent to Gough asking if the attack could still be held up.

A sheaf of signals had been typed: 'Attack postponed; taps not to be turned on until further notice'. Runners and despatch riders were standing by and telephone lines had been manned. It was an excellent arrangement on paper but it could not be effected instantaneously. The troops of the Special Companies had been standing by their cylinders all night. After being told the attack was 'on', their officers had made their way along crowded trenches to synchronize watches and reveal the gas zero hour of 5.50 am.

Foulkes understood that 'it had been agreed that it would not be safe to depend on a message issued from Hinges and passed in turn through the Corps, Division and Brigade headquarters . . . in any less period than two hours.' Hence his instruction leaving it in the last resort to the officers on the spot to decide whether or not conditions were appropriate to turn on the gas.

According to Gough, Haig's message asking if the attack could be held up reached him at his battle headquarters half an hour before it was due to take place.

'I considered it too late to get the orders to the men in the front trenches.'

Charteris: 'I was with D.H. when the reply was brought in. He was very upset. Actually I think Gough was right. There would have been great confusion if any attempt had been made to postpone the attack.'

Charteris, a Sapper who had served under Haig in India and when he was commanding at Aldershot, was noted for his unswerving support of Sir Douglas. His comment underlines the doubts that plagued the First Army headquarters until the last minute.

The first signs of action occurred as diversionary operations began on other parts of the front. For example, in compliance with general orders the 8th Royal Fusiliers, in trenches near Houplines, in Flanders, had thrown bundles of damp straw over their parapets that night. These were to be lighted at 4.30 am. With fifteen minutes to go they received a message to delay the smoke cloud for an hour. This news did not reach the neighbouring division which dutifully sent up dense white clouds at the original time. There was silence until about 5 o'clock when 'voices from the German trenches inquired when the battalion were going to light their straw!'

On the Somme, where the British were taking over French trenches, every gun in the artillery of the 5th Division fired one round at 4.45 am. As for the infantry: 'All companies in the trenches showed their bayonets over the parapet and cheered. All men, except look-out men, then withdrew to their shelters, leaving bayonets showing, to avoid possible artillery fire. The enemy took no notice whatever of these antics and made no reply whatsoever'. The artillery had sounded 'very feeble indeed'.

The tactics devised by Foulkes took two important points into account: the nature of the German masks and the supply of cylinders available. The enemy riflemen were belived to be equipped with an improved gauze 'mouth protector'. This was a pad which had to be soaked in chemicals from a bottle which each man carried and was held in place by tapes tied behind the head. Officers and machine-gunners, however, were reported to have an apparatus which contained half an hour's supply of oxygen. To ensure that the deadly 'emma gees' were neutralized, it was therefore necessary to force enemy soldiers equipped with the sophisticated mask to wear it for at least thirty minutes. As there was not enough chlorine to discharge

continuously for half an hour a plan had been devised by which at
5.50 am:

GAS   would be run for 20 minutes then switched off;

SMOKE   would be discharged for 20 minutes;

GAS   would be switched on once more and run at full
              pressure until 6.38.

By then it was hoped the enemy machine-gunners would have used
up their oxygen supply and fallen victim to the fumes around them.
The possibility of their carrying spare masks of the gauze type does
not seem to have been considered. Whatever happened they would
still be the target of the First Army's artillery.

In front of Loos Corporal Fox, a soldier since August and in the
front line for his first battle, thought the preliminary bombardment
had started at 5.30 am when British shells began streaming overhead.
The ground shook repeatedly with the vibration of explosions.
German guns opened up on the British battery positions in reply.

'After a quarter of an hour of heavy firing . . . there came a lull for a
few minutes, but at precisely 5.50 am the bombardment roared again
to its maximum intensity. This moment was zero hour for the
discharge of our gas.'

Fox had already put on his gas bag, tucking it well under his collar
and buttoning his tunic. The friendly sentry, who was wearing his
tube helmet rolled up around his head so that it could be pulled down
if required, did not bother to lower it. With the ejector pipe in
position over the parapet, Fox applied his spanners and anxiously
watched the cylinder to see that all was well. When his section
sergeant rushed into the bay he was able to report that there were no
leaks. The sentry standing on the firestep called down that the gas was
moving forward 'nicely'. Fox jumped up to join him:

'I could see a green wave of chlorine pouring away directly towards
the enemy line; evidently the wind was all right for me.'

The gas delivered from the bays on either side was also going in the
right direction.

From the top of Haig's observation tower Foulkes saw 'the whole
countryside to the front, as far as the eye could see, being enveloped
in what appeared to be a vast prairie conflagration; for apart from the
fumes and dust caused by the artillery drum-fire and the clouds of gas
and the smoke from 11,000 candles, 25,000 phosphorous hand
grenades were spurting out dense white fumes and the thousand
bombs from the 29 four-inch Stokes mortars . . . were burning in
front of all the German strongpoints and were enveloping their
artillery observers and machine-gunners in an impenetrable cloud.'

Though direct observation was obscured, the German artillery was still able to bring down fire on its SOS lines – pre-selected targets for which the ranges had been calculated and charges prepared. As the multi-coloured bilious cloud soared and swirled over no-man's-land shrapnel shells from the .77mm field guns began to burst over the British front line, spraying the bays with iron balls. Earth erupted where the 5.9s fell in and on the trenches, burying men, sometimes piercing cylinders and snapping or twisting the clumsy iron projector pipes, so that the contents hissed in all directions. Despite the deluge of explosive a remarkable number of 'Oojahs' remained unscathed.

Fox's second cylinder began to leak slightly but not enough to worry the sentry who, with his gas helmet still rolled up, joined in the task of throwing smoke 'candles' over the parapet at the appointed time. A third cylinder was gushing well when, two minutes before the infantry zero hour, the sergeant returned and ordered Fox to turn it off; time was up. The NCO hurried off to the next position where he arrived just as it was hit by a shell.

Private Frank Richards, of the 2nd Royal Welch Fusiliers, was in an assembly trench in the same sector as Fox. To him the gas 'looked like small clouds rolling along close to the ground. The white clouds hadn't travelled far before they seemed to stop and melt away.'

Robert Graves recorded that in a certain section of trench the spanners did not fit the cylinder nuts.

'The gas men rushed about shouting for the loan of an adjustable spanner. They managed to discharge one or two cylinders, the gas went whistling out, formed a thick cloud a few yards off . . . and then gradually spread back into our trenches.'

Troops in the front line, the 1st Middlesex and 2nd Argyll and Sutherland Highlanders, abandoned the fume-filled assault positions which had been dug in no-man's-land and re-occupied what had been the old front line. When the discharge was over they advanced again but many were caught by enemy machine guns before they reached their own wire entanglements.

A survivor of the 1st Middlesex wrote later: 'It was just Hell with the lid off . . . .

'At 5.45 on Saturday morning we turned the gas on the devils . . . it was an awful sight . . . and at 6.30 we climbed over the parapet and charged them. I carried a field telephone; four of us started; I was the only one to reach the first German trench which was full of dead, about three or four deep, all gassed. But they had machine guns in their third line and they mowed us down.'

Gough, who had been up most of the night, began to receive

LOOS – 25 September 1915

Gas cylinders were deployed from
south of Givenchy to Double Crassier

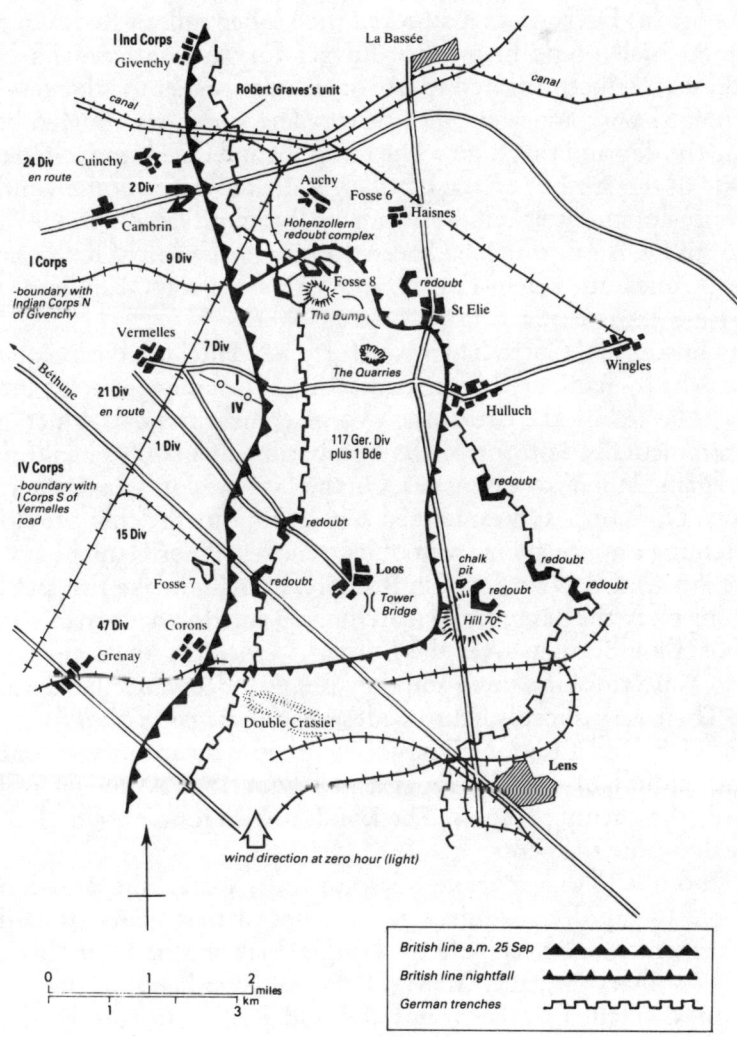

I Ind Corps
Givenchy
La Bassée
canal
Robert Graves's unit
canal
24 Div
en route
Cuinchy
2 Div
Auchy
Fosse 6
Haisnes
Cambrin
Hohenzollern
redoubt complex
I Corps
-boundary with
Indian Corps N
of Givenchy
9 Div
Fosse 8
redoubt
The Dump
St Elie
Vermelles
7 Div
The Quarries
Wingles
Béthune
21 Div
en route
IV
Hulluch
1 Div
117 Ger. Div
plus 1 Bde
IV Corps
-boundary with
I Corps S of
Vermelles
road
15 Div
redoubt
Fosse 7
redoubt
Loos
chalk
pit
redoubt
redoubt
47 Div
Corons
Tower
Bridge
redoubt
Hill 70
Grenay

Double Crassier
Lens

wind direction at zero hour (light)

0   1   2 miles
1   3 km

British line a.m. 25 Sep
British line nightfall
German trenches

conflicting reports: 'The gas was going across the enemy lines'; 'The gas was hanging about'; 'The wind was taking it up no-man's-land'; 'It was taking it over our own lines'; 'The discharge had to be stopped'.

His left division, the 2nd, was required to secure the flank of the 9th (Scottish) Division as it stormed the Hohenzollern Redoubt and Fosse 8. Such of its men who did get forward suffered like the Middlesex, which formed part of it, or ran into thickets of undamaged wire and were shot down. The survivors crawled back during the day and that night. The Redoubt and the Dump fell to one brigade of the 9th but on the left the gas drifted over another, and in the confusion the attackers were 'practically annihilated'. To the right of the 9th Division, which had been the first formation of Kitchener's New Armies to reach France, the 7th's regulars captured the Quarries.

Rawlinson's IV Corps had mixed fortunes. The 1st Division on the left was badly hampered by the gas, found the entanglements intact and was lashed by the fire of the two machine-gun posts which had been accidentally left out of the bombardment plan. A handful of men regained their own trenches. On the 1st Division's flank the 15th Scottish Division was mesmerized at zero hour by the chlorine cloud which hung ominously in front of its trenches. Piper Daniel Laidlaw of the 7th King's Own Scottish Borderers finally broke the spell by climbing on to the parapet and marching up and down no-man's-land playing 'Blue Bonnets over the Border'.[1] Once the Scots got going there was no stopping them and they plunged deep into the German lines. Their very success led to widespread disorganization.

The 47th (2nd London) Division's Territorials advanced steadily behind 'clouds of smoke, sluggish low-lying fog' as the gas rolled towards the enemy parapets. The London Irish found themselves in Loos alongside the Scots.

By about 9.30 that morning, despite heavy losses, the British had managed to capture considerable stretches of the enemy front-line trenches which had been held by a single division, the 117th, backed up by a solitary brigade. Many of the well-sandbagged, deep-dug redoubts had fallen. Some groups of dazed, excited and disorientated Tommies found themselves well inside the enemy position with only fugitives before them. The opportunites for exploitation were obvious to many of the officers on the spot. Hence the desperate cries for reinforcements and the need for the commitment of the reserves.

[1] He was awarded the Victoria Cross.

It was too much to expect the exhausted, depleted assault units to go on. The clamour went unheeded.

Apart from one brigade which was in immediate support of Gough's troops, the men of XI British Corps were seventeen miles behind the lines. As Haig had feared, this was too far. The infantry of the 21st and 24th Divisions, part of Kitchener's New Army, had been in France for about three weeks. They had never seen a battlefield. Carrying a full pack and rifle, largely unfed, they tramped towards the growing roar of conflict, struggling against a flow of wounded men and ammunition wagons returning for replenishment. On the 26th, after an appalling night of confusion, they were marshalled like the Confederate infantry at Gettysburg and led to an even worse fate. For them there was no preliminary bombardment, no gas, no smoke and precious little hope of survival.

If Lieutenant-Colonel Charles Foulkes was certain of anything it was that the performance of his troops and the battlefield value of gas would be the subject of close examination. As a Regular he was wise in the ways of the Army; well aware it would be foolish to rely on officers of other arms of the service to provide all the evidence on which judgment would be passed. Shortly after the first trenches had been captured that day specially selected individuals went into them and he joined them soon afterwards. While the fighting raged they examined the grey-clad corpses, ransacked their haversacks and made notes of the causes of death. It emerged afterwards that in the front line the German riflemen had been equipped with an improved version of the original gauze mask which had to be tied over the mouth and nose. Possibly because the British gas cloud had come as a complete surprise and some of the defenders had taken time to find their masks, many of them had been killed by the fumes. In the support trenches the garrison had been supplied with only the minimum protection – a chemically-treated pad which had to be held over the nose and mouth (though this came out later after prisoners had been interrogated). Unable to keep the pad over their faces and use their weapons at the same time, the troops had either been overcome or fled. At one stage of the battle the well-wired strong second line had been virtually abandoned but by the time the British 21st and 24th Divisions appeared on the 26th the German fire-steps were once again manned by determined troops.

Trump cards had been played but the game remained open. The French had gone into action after receiving an Order of the Day from Joffre, described in one account as 'being in the style of Bonaparte delivered by a gendarme'.

The infantry had been told: 'Soldiers of the Republic you are going to attack along the whole front . . . your elan will be irresistible. The first rush will carry you to the enemy batteries.'

In Champagne the forecast almost came true. The German first line was carried and 14,000 prisoners taken. Their second line held and, after reinforcements arrived, the irresistible elan merely produced a longer casualty list.

The offensive launched by d'Urbal's Tenth Army alongside Haig did not take place until nearly 1 pm on the 25th and failed dismally. The 'giant leap' demanded by Foch barely took the sorely-tried infantry over their own parapets. Fresh bodies piled up in the hotly disputed Souchez cemetery which was won, lost and won again; divisions fell back to their jumping-off points. Vimy was not captured. On 29 September Generaly Fayolle recorded dispassion-ately in his diary: *'Situation stationnaire'*

Discreetly Joffre began to transfer formations from the Loos front to the Champagne where there was still some hope of improvement. In Artois the French, as Falkenhayn said, had 'achieved no success worthy of mention'. On the other hand, he conceded that 'the English (*sic*) on the first day of their attack and by the employment of gas, succeeded in occupying our foremost positions over a breadth of 7½ miles'.

What was left of the supply of gas cylinders the British continued to use in local attacks. The Germans responded by lighting fires on their parapets, hoping to create a draught to carry the fumes upwards.

These secondary operations were mounted by the survivors of the Special Companies who had made their way back to their own bases at the end of the first day. Most had inhaled some gas. Many sought relief by sniffing at ammonia ampoules carried for emergencies. There was no reluctance to carry on.

In 186 Company five men had been killed and sixty affected by gas or wounded. The dead included the sergeant-major, saturated by a jet of chlorine released when, in his excitement, he put a bullet into a reluctant cylinder. In the four Special Companies the casualties totalled 14 per cent. A composite unit was formed and set out in lorries next morning to install salvaged cylinders in the notorious brickstack position at Cuinchy. They were dug in near the corpse of an Argyll and Sutherland Highlander whose entire body, uniform and equipment had been turned grass-green. He had been standing in a bay next to a cylinder smashed by shell fire.

The gas was released in perfect conditions on the evening of the 27th, carried by a westerly wind of four miles an hour, and was followed by a raiding party of the Scottish Rifles. The attackers reported that many casualties had been inflicted on the enemy but, due to a freak ground condition, the fumes had blown back in places. They had suffered casualties too.

Despite its limitations when released in small quantities, the British continued to use chlorine as fresh troops came up to relieve the spent formations and to try to recover the ground won back by the Germans.

The atmosphere at 10 Downing Street was also becoming unpleasant. A meeting of the Dardanelles Committee,[1] chaired by the Prime Minister, started well enough with the French coming under attack –a 'soft target', as they were not represented. Lord Kitchener, returned from a joint meeting at Calais, reported his allies as being 'very optimistic' about the offensives in the Champagne and near Arras.

'Absurdly so,' said Mr Balfour, First Lord of the Admiralty, who had also been at Calais. Then Churchill (at that time Chancellor of the Duchy of Lancaster) raised a disturbing issue: he had heard 'authentic accounts' of the failure of two divisions in the New Army and that the Loos casualty figure had reached 75,000.

Thunder echoed around Mount Olympus. Lord Kitchener said he had no information on these subjects.

This was an outrageous admission coming from the Minister for War on his return from the Western front, and Churchill grumbled that the War Council ought to get some account of 'those battles'.

Perhaps feeling slightly guilty, perhaps knowing more but being embarrassed by Kitchener's cavalier treatment of his Cabinet colleagues, Balfour tried to defuse the situation: it was unreasonable to expect an account while the battle was in progress.

Coolly Churchill retorted that *nothing* was going on. The staff were merely engaged in counting casualties; the Germans were shelling the British lines with a view to counter-attacking.

The rumours were 'most calamitous', rumbled Sir Edward Carson, the Attorney General.

This was too much for Sir Archibald Murray, who had taken over as Chief of the Imperial General Staff the previous month. He declared that there was another side to the story. The 9th and 15th Divisions had behaved with extraordinary gallantry, (so it wasn't they who had failed).

[1] PRO CAB 42/4/3

How much more did he know? Before the question could be asked, the Prime Minister added his contribution. The previous day the King had told him that 'the two divisions which were said to have misbehaved' had been given a very long march at night, at the end of which they had been ordered to attack a hill without having any breakfast.

Clearly the King had better sources than the War Minister. Even the Secretary of State for the Colonies, Mr Andrew Bonar Law, was able to add to the sorry tale. He had heard the divisions had gone without food and water for forty-eight hours.

The Chancellor of the Duchy of Lancaster, the Attorney General, the CIGS and the Colonial Secretary, even the King, knew more than the celebrated War Minister.

Kitchener unbent – slightly. He undertook to make enquiries.

At this point Mr Lloyd George (Munitions were in the know as well) said drily that he had heard that the reserves had been held too far back.

A cloud attack planned by the newly-formed Guards Division was forestalled by a massive German assault on 8 October. After this had been beaten off the Guards carried up and dug in 840 cylinders. These were discharged when the 46th (North Midlands) Division stormed over the Hohenzollern Redoubt on 13 October. A thick haze enveloped the enemy trenches and for a time it looked as though they had fallen. In the end the German bombers drove out the British, who still had no effective reply to them. The first consignment of the highly efficient Mills grenades, 9,000 in number, had arrived at the front but been issued to the Guards.

Corporal James Lennox Dawson, of 187 Special Company, was in charge of an emplacement which was damaged by shell fire during the battle for the Redoubt. Ordering the infantry out of the assembly trench, he managed to get three leaking cylinders hoisted over the parapet and, under heavy machine gun and rifle fire, rolled them away. From a safe distance he pumped rifle bullets into them to free the gas which drifted over the enemy instead of filling British trenches. Dawson lived to receive the Victoria Cross.

The 12th (Eastern) Division captured a strongpoint known as Gun Trench the same day and gained a foothold in the Quarries. The men went 'over the top' carrying greatcoats, groundsheets, a filled waterbottle, 250 rounds of ammunition, empty sandbags, gas helmet ready for use and goggles on the peaks of their caps in case tear gas was encountered. The divisional artillery had been liberally dosed with this on the 8th when the gunners had to wear masks for two hours – a serious handicap to their performance during the German counterblow.

By the time the battle of Loos was over the British had suffered more than 50,000 casualties. Of these 2,361 were believed to have been caused by their own chlorine cloud. Ten men were reported to have been killed when cylinders were burst by enemy shells and only fifty-five of the other cases were classed as severe. Many medical officers said they'd had so little experience of handling chlorine gas casualties that often they were uncertain whether or not a man was suffering from poisoning. They were more confident when dealing with tear gas cases of which 550 were recorded as having been treated during the battle. *The Medical History of the War* states: 'The majority of casualties resulting from British gas about the time of the battle of Loos were really more frightened than hurt.'

CHAPTER 10

Came Christmas

It came as an unpleasant surprise to the German front-line soldier to experience a lethal gas attack at Loos within six months of the first use of the weapon. The impression had been created that the Allies did not possess the means of retaliation. Immediately a cry went up for an improved mask to replace the cotton-waste type. For the sake of morale as well as physical protection another version was needed urgently and the scientists did not let the troops down. The new mask covered the face completely.

It was made of a rubberized fabric through which no air could pass. A metal plate was fitted to the lower part of the mask and onto this was screwed a drum containing neutralizing agents and layers of crushed brick or pumice stone. Air was breathed in and out through the drum, each soldier carrying a spare he could screw on if the original was damaged. The eye-pieces were held in metal rings.

By comparison with the British P-helmet the vision was good and there was no uncomfortable tube to grip with the teeth. Nor did the wearer suffer from blistering of the forehead and neck as did the British troops from time to time – the chemicals from the flannel of the helmet were apt to inflame the skin of the wearer in hot weather.

If the German mask had a weakness it was its dependence on the fit of the fabric to the face. This, held in place by elastic bands, had to be airtight. Captured German masks were studied closely in the expanding laboratory at St Omer. The idea of a metal container or box to hold chemicals to filter the gas was already under consideration. In the meantime the protective power of the cloth helmet had to be maintained. In this respect the British and French were in luck.

After the cloud attack at Ypres the Germans had transported thousands of newly made small cylinders to the Eastern Front and at the end of May these were released at Bolimow where the original T-shells had been fired. The result was a grisly victory with thousands of unprotected Russians reported dead. The chlorine content of the containers had been reduced to make way for five per cent phosgene. A similar mixture had been suggested for use in Flanders in April but had been considered to be 'too provocative'.

Out of this disaster came some good, however, as Russian scientists discovered that the chemical hexamine was an excellent absorbent for phosgene. They passed on the information to their allies in October, 1915 and trials began immediately. From the end of January, 1916, all cloth for helmets was treated with a new solution containing hexamine.

Since the opening of the first gas offensive on 22 April, the British had produced a series of masks, beginning with the protective pad and the veil respirator, followed by the smoke helmet with its unsatisfactory eye pieces. Next to be introduced was the P (phenate) or tube helmet to counter phosgene (should it appear) and then the PH (phenate-hexamine) helmet containing the stronger absorbent identified by the Russians.

Production of a PGH helmet for specialist troops such as artillerymen and machine-gunners was begun early in 1916. Goggles set in rubber sponge mountings in the mask and, held in place by elastic bands, gave greater protection against weeping gases.

'Re-dipping' centres for masks which had become ineffective through use were opened in Abbeville and Calais. There the cloth was chemically treated again and, if torn, repaired before re-issue.

The achievements of the scientists in the new branch of warfare had been considerable in a matter of months but there was to be no let-up. Other scientists saw to that.

Sunday, 19 December, 1915 was a day full of interest to the British Army. At Gallipoli the last troops were successfully withdrawn from the beaches at Suvla Bay and Anzac Cove.

It was a campaign in which gas was not used despite the urgings of Mr Churchill. Some of his Cabinet colleagues felt the Turks would respond by massacring British prisoners.

However, as late as 20 October Churchill was concerned that 'large gas installations' had arrived at Constantinople and wanted new respirators to be rushed to the Dardanelles to replace those of the earlier pattern already issued.[1]

'I trust that the unreasonable prejudice against the use by us of gas

[1] PRO CAB 42/4/4

upon the Turks will now cease. The massacres by the Turks of Armenians and the fact that practically no British prisoners have been taken on the Peninsula . . . should surely move all false sentiment . . . indulged in as it is only at the expense of our own men.'

Churchill added: 'Large installations of British gas should be sent out without delay. The winter season is frequently marked by south-westerly gales, which would afford a perfect opportunity for the employment of gas.'

Like Haig at Loos, Churchill sought an instant solution to a deadlock, for there is little doubt that had the ammunition reached the area it would have been used. In his reference to the expected gales he seems to have been grasping at straws: strong winds dissipate cloud gas. The dosage is inversely proportional to the wind speed; e.g. ten times as great in a two-knot wind as one of twenty knots.

No matter. For a time he may have had hopes. The conscientious Asquith penned another note[1] to the King after a Cabinet meeting on the 22nd in which he said: 'Mr Lloyd George (Minister of Munitions) reported the preparations he was making for sending Gas to both France and the Dardanelles'.

It was a cargo that was never delivered. On 19 December, as the dream faded along with many military reputations, and with Churchill's own influence, there were signs of a new dawn in France. Sir Douglas Haig took over the British Expeditionary Force that day from Sir John French, who returned to London to become Commander-in-Chief Home Forces. French was paying the price for mishandling the reserves at Loos and, what in some eyes was even worse, for trying to lay the responsibility on someone else. The outraged Haig had not hesitated to use his personal friendship with the King to secure justice. He had seen it as his duty.

It was certainly true that the Field-Marshal had kept the 21st and 24th Divisions too far back and held on to them so long that they arrived exhausted and too late to be of real use. That was blatant incompetence for which he was demoted.

But it was also true that Haig, who, only a few weeks earlier, had expressed doubts about the use of the same raw troops as reserves, had recklessly sent two divisions to a bloody fate against unbroken defences. Here too was incompetence – but he was promoted.

19 December was also a landmark in the careers of many front-line soldiers in the British 6th (Regular) and 49th (West Riding) Divisions. Before the first glimmerings of dawn over the ruins of

---

[1] PRO CAB 37/131/34

Wieltje, where the Irish battalions had died in May, the Germans unleashed a large and powerful gas cloud. It was the first of its kind they had used against the British for seven months. At Vlamertinghe, five miles away, prudent soldiers put on their masks.

The high concentration of gas delivered swiftly in darkness caught many troops unprepared. Fifty men died in or near the trenches and slightly more than 1,000 sufferers endured a trying wait until nightfall when they could be evacuated to the casualty clearing station at Poperinghe. Their condition disturbed the RAMC doctors. An unusually high proportion of the gas victims were found dead when the Red Cross train which took them from Poperinghe to the base hospital was unloaded. The gas had clearly had a delayed action. For the British, though it was not immediately recognized, the phosgene era had begun.

Used by the Bayer Company and the Badische Anilin und Soda Fabrik in the production of violet dyes, phosgene was more poisonous than chlorine. 'A cloud of phosgene containing one eighth by weight of the concentration of a chlorine cloud will have the same lethal properties.'[1]

One of its most important qualities as a war gas was that it could be breathed for some time without causing obvious distress. Hours might elapse before a soldier succumbed, his lungs filling slowly with fluid.

It seems to have been accepted in 1915 that its appearance was only a matter of time and, after experimenting with it in the East, the Germans used an increased dose against the French in the Champagne in October. Considerable casualties were inflicted though no important ground was seized.

The troops[2] who had carried out the Champagne operation also delivered the attack at Wieltje when it was estimated later that the poison cloud had been 75 per cent chlorine, the rest being phosgene.

The German report on the incident concluded: 'In spite of the relatively favourable conditions, the gas had not had the expected effect . . . a breakthrough of the enemy position solely on the ground of the gas discharge would not be possible.'

Though the British were on the alert for a gas attack it is clear that the P-helmet was not entirely reliable. It was just as well that the phosgene content of the cloud had not been higher and that the PH helmet was on its way.

[1] Fries and West, *Chemical Warfare*, McGraw Hill, New York, 1921.
[2] Pionier Regiment 36.

Eventually a warning went out to the troops that phosgene smelled like 'green corn' or 'musty hay', descriptions which can have meant little to the thousands of city dwellers in the ranks and may have confused countrymen.

Another new gas, reported on 19 December, was contained in what was designated 'K' shell. Though considered poisonous, it did little harm on this occasion, though those who experienced it reported suffering a 'choking sensation and a feeling of tightness in the chest'.

The victims of the Wieltje attack were buried in the graveyards which flourished at Ypres and their comrades were left wondering 'What next?' In 1915 there was no truce of the sort that had marked parts of the front at Christmas, 1914.

Only gradually was the delayed action of phosgene understood. Early in February, 1916, the RAMC gave instructions that confirmed gas cases were to be kept at casualty clearing stations until doctors were confident patients were in a condition to travel. Some doctors insisted that even suspected phosgene victims should be carried and not allowed to walk to dressing stations.

Gas discipline became ever more important, since, once a soldier had adjusted his helmet, he could expect to be safe from all but the densest of clouds; at least he would have done all that was possible for his own protection.

By this time, despite the cries of horror with which its appearance had been received, gas had become almost respectable. The Prince of Wales, who was serving in France, attended a demonstration put on by a Special Brigade unit and turned on a chlorine cylinder. The spanner he used was regarded as a valuable souvenir.

All the belligerents began to develop their particular preferences in chemical warfare. The British, for want of a suitable projectile, favoured cloud attacks. The French and Germans applied themselves to designing and producing shells. The ability of the artillery to bombard distant positions with gas avoided the wind problem, though it greatly reduced the quantity that could be delivered unless thousands of rounds were fired.

The gas shell was seen by many French and German commanders as a valuable ingredient in a plan of attack, but its evolvement was slower than they would have liked. The soldiers expected their requirements to be met instantly but the production route was a difficult one. The chemicals were likely to be corrosive and filled rounds difficult to store. The ballistic properties of liquid agents were very different from those of high explosive. Some gunners felt it essential to be able to mark the fall of shot – not easy when the bursting charge was small. Smoke could be included but the generating material cut down still further the space left for gas. Furthermore, smoke was useless as a guide at night, the best time for a surprise bombardment. The efficiency of a shell was low, the chemical content being as little as 7 per cent. The massive rates of fire required to build up a concentration of gas carried penalties. Britain was short of steel and explosive throughout the war; she had to meet high demands from the Royal Navy which laid down extraordinary scales of reserve ammunition for its battleships and, indeed, all its ships.

As none of his superiors seemed to have any deep thoughts on the use of the 'new' weapon it was left to Foulkes to promote its merits as a means of inflicting casualties.

As the year turned the Special Companies applied themselves conscientiously to their duties. Lorries took the gas Sappers as near as possible to the front line where they were to operate. Thigh-booted, they waded along flooded trenches cursed by the infantry helping to carry the heavy cylinders. If enemy flares lit the way from time to time they made the night seem all the darker when they spluttered out.

It was no fun to sit on a muddy firestep waiting for orders. Always it was a question of waiting for the right wind. Amid a score of makeshift indicators the one most favoured, when it was light enough to see, was a hessian strand taken from a dry sandbag and tied to a piece of wire.

If the wind were in the right direction at the appointed time the gas would be released. The first thing the equally cold and wet German sentry was likely to notice was a pale cloud looming from the darkness, 'whiting out' his own wire as he hastily adjusted his respirator and sounded the alarm.

In the British trenches those responsible for the cloud took cover, knowing that German shells would arrive quickly in reply.

Worse than anything was the receipt of a message to postpone an attack because of a change in the wind direction. Cylinders had to be made safe and covered with sandbags and pipes disconnected and stored in a suitable dugout. The detachment in charge of the cylinders then had to make its way back through the trenches and find their lorries, which had often been moved back because of shell fire. The next night the same rigmarole had to be repeated.

Three times in December Corporal Fox made his weary way up the line through communication trenches filled in places with mud the consistency of pea soup. The attack was called off at 2 am the first night, at 10 pm the second, at 3.30 am on the third.

'December 21st was the blackest night of all, but this time the wind was in our favour. We were able to discharge 700 cylinders of chlorine at the zero hour of 8pm [he had been in the trenches since 2 pm]. The enemy retaliation with whizz bangs and mortars did much damage . . . .In the next bay to mine Corporal Hoare, a cheerful London lad, was killed immediately. So ended our final operation for the year.'

Hoare was buried the next day in a section of Cambrin churchyard reserved for British soldiers. While a chaplain conducted the service a battery of 18-pounders fired steadily from fields nearby. There was no coffin. Hoare was buried in his groundsheet. Never again would he join in the 186 Special Company chorus:

> Corporals all, sitting on the fire step,
> Corporals all, with their spanners in their hands,
> Corporals all, lying on their bellies,
> Gassing back the Germans to the Fatherland.

Early in 1916 the original Special Companies were expanded to become the Special Brigade. The old numbers disappeared and sixteen companies, each with a working strength of about 200, were listed alphabetically – thus A to D formed the 1st Battalion. There was no I company. Four more special companies, perversely numbered 1 to 4, were trained to handle other chemical weapons, such as smoke mortars, and a fifth company, designated Z, was to be equipped with flamethrowers.

The unique 'corporals all' establishment vanished and privates were posted in as 'pioneers'.

A Directorate of Gas Services was created in France with a brigadier-general as its first head. Henry Fleetwood Thuillier,[1] then 49, came from an Indian Army background and had joined the Royal Engineers in 1887. Eight years later he took part in the Chitral Relief Expedition on the North-West Frontier.

As the Great War gained momentum and regimental officers found early graves or accelerated promotion, the demand for professionals increased. Thuillier was given command of the 2nd Infantry Brigade and at Loos saw his command cut to pieces on undamaged wire. The slow-moving and unpredictable gas cloud had also caused difficulties and Thuillier knew a great deal about the new medium from bitter experience.

---

[1] Pronounced 'Tillyer'.

Thuillier had two assistant directors. Foulkes took charge of offensive operations and the other headed the defensive branch. Though originally this had been a post for a medical man it was decided to make the Gas Service part of the Royal Engineers and it was filled by Lieutenant-Colonel Harold Hartley, a 39-year-old-Fellow of Balliol College, Oxford. Hartley had seen service in the Leicestershire Regiment before becoming a Sapper and acting as chemical adviser to the Third Army. The Central Laboratory came directly under Thuillier.

The reorganization provided a gas school for each of the four British armies on the Western Front; there were five when the Reserve Army[1] was formed late in May, 1916.

Senior officers attended a two-day course; junior officers and NCOs went to corps schools and divisional schools were abolished. Each formation had its gas adviser and the organization went down to the level of sergeant or corporal at company level. The NCO was responsible for inspecting and replacing helmets or respirators, checking the gas-proofing of dugouts and for maintaining stocks of Vermorel sprayers and a much-discussed propeller-like fan, turned by hand, supplied to blow gas out of trenches after an attack. The fan was the brain-child of Mrs Hertha Ayrton, the widow of William Ayrton, a distinguished electrical engineer. Mrs Ayrton was herself a scientist[2] and had a redoubtable personality (her husband is recorded in the *Dictionary of National Biography* as a 'supporter of women's rights'!). The War Office found it easier to accept her product than turn it down. Ayrton fans were highly regarded at the front as firewood though even today it is possible to find serious scientific support for them.[3]

The gas NCO also had one other important duty: he was responsible for regularly noting the direction of the wind in his sector.

In Britain the War Office bought an area of downland at Porton on the edge of Salisbury Plain where field trials were carried out under the supervision of Lieutenant-Colonel Arthur Crossley, a distinguished Mancunian chemist who had studied at Wurzburg and Berlin Universities among others.

The system certainly aimed at being comprehensive. One weak point, however, was the break in the link between the Sappers and the

---

[1] Later designated Fifth.
[2] Awarded Royal Society medal, 1906.
[3] A member of the Porton establishment defended them in conversation with the author.

RAMC, though a junior medical officer remained on Thuillier's staff. The appearance on the battlefield of a new enemy gas was always treated with the greatest secrecy to prevent the Germans accurately assessing the effect of any unpleasant chemical they employed. According to the *Official History*:

'The casualties came for treatment into the hands of medical officers[1] who only slowly obtained information regarding the nature of the gases used, and this information was even less widely disseminated in England than it was in France.'

From the cool wording it is fair to assume that the doctors found the Sappers obstructive on occasions. It was not until 1918 that a Chemical Warfare Medical Committee was set up.[2] For much of their information the RAMC had relied on the stark evidence of post-mortem examinations and work done at Porton on animals in support of clinical evidence.

At the 'sharp end' the Special Brigade still worked in companies spread along the front. The Fourth Army, destined to bear the brunt of the forthcoming summer offensive, had the lion's share – seven 'gas companies' and three of the four equipped with mortars (48 four-inch Stokes guns, though none of these fired gas bombs).

There were changes in equipment. The projector pipes were halved to make them more manageable, though they had to be screwed together. An amazingly inventive officer, Lieutenant William Howard Livens, who had been with 186 Company from the beginning, designed rubber hoses for linking the cylinders to the parapet pipes. It was not to be his only contribution to the war effort.

The gas itself was 'improved'. Plain chlorine cylinders which bore a red star were supplemented by others with a blue motif, indicating that the contents included 20 per cent sulphur chloride.

The Germans continued to add phosgene to their cylinders and though in 1916 they made only five cloud attacks against the British,[3] all inflicted severe casualties. In the first on 27 April smoke and gas were released at 5 am across the wasteland of the old Loos battlefield around Hulluch. After it had dispersed, many of the British front-line troops laid aside their masks and began to prepare breakfast. About an hour and a half later the enemy unleashed a poison cloud. The unwary were caught.

---

[1] Comment by interested party (scientist) in 1980s: 'Then as now their skills were greater than their staff work.'
[2] Nevertheless, pamphlets compiled by physicians and physiologists were distributed in June, 1915, and July, 1916, with supplementary notes later.
[3] Two attacks on the French.

Despite the pains taken to educate the troops in gas warfare there was still a great deal of ignorance about it, as was underlined by the fate of a company of the 9th Black Watch. After the first attack their commander, being under the impression that the chemicals in the helmet fabric were rendered useless once they had been exposed to gas for a time, ordered the men to unmask. When the second cloud arrived this misunderstanding cost eighteen lives, including his own, and landed most of the men in hospital.

It was small consolation that enemy raiders were driven off, but the British took some satisfaction in machine-gunning groups of Bavarians who scrambled wildly out of their trenches when a counter-bombardment shattered undischarged chlorine cylinders.

Two days later, on a front of about two miles, the enemy delivered another lethal cloud attack in the sector immediately alongside the scene of the previous one. In a trench marked on British maps as The Kink, men of the Royal Inniskilling Fusiliers manned a parapet only fifty yards from the enemy line. The attack was in support of a raid and when the uproar had died down the thirty man-garrison of The Kink was still there, helmets correctly fastened – but all dead. Either the gas had been too much for their PH helmets or they had been slow in putting them on.

There was to be mourning in many Irish homes after the Hulluch attacks; the 7th and 8th Royal Inniskilling Fusiliers, the 7th Royal Irish Fusiliers and the 8th Royal Dublin Fusiliers counted 338 deaths, with many more men seriously affected.

The 16th (Irish) Division suffered a total of 900 gas casualties.

The first reaction of senior officers was to blame the high figure on bad gas discipline but it was an indisputable fact that most of the victims, like the men in The Kink, had their gas helmets properly adjusted. The sheer density of the cloud and its large phosgene content delivered at close range was later suspected to be the real cause of the incident.

That the Germans had a healthy respect for their own product had been made clear when part of the cloud suddenly blew back from the British trenches and bore down on its creators. Once again the Bavarians took to their heels, preferring to run through a British barrage then risk a whiff of the deadly fumes.

The day after the last Hulluch attack the enemy struck near Wulverghem opposite Messines. The front was manned by the 24th Division, brought up to strength after its ordeal at Loos. Having come from the desolation of the Ypres Salient, where they had spent six months, the troops found the comparatively undamaged countryside, almost undisturbed since 1914, a pleasant change.

On 25 April two German deserters brought the first news of an impending gas attack. The cylinders were in position, they stated, and a favourable wind was awaited. A warning was immediately circulated. On the evening of the 29th two more deserters announced that gas would be released that night and followed by a large-scale raid.

The British promptly manned their trenches and prepared to receive the attack. They were not kept waiting. Just after 12.30 am heavy machine gun and rifle fire ripped along a two-mile front and a white mist rose above the enemy line. The hissing of cylinders was clearly heard where the trenches were close. Barrages crashed down behind the attacked front. The discharge lasted for up to forty minutes in places after which, as the cloud drifted away on a ten-mile an hour wind, the enemy raiders appeared.

They were driven off with heavy loss but the 1st North Stafford-shire Regiment reported 112 gas casualties, while the 8th Queen's numbered 122, nearly a quarter of the battalion strength. It was deduced that the men had kept their helmets in their satchels until the moment of attack and the slightest hesitation at such short range – the lines were about 100 yards apart – was likely to result in fumes being inhaled. The 2nd Leinsters, whose trenches were up to 300 yards from the enemy's, and who had time to don their helmets, had suffered very lightly. So had the 10th Royal Welch Fusiliers of the neighbouring 3rd Division, whose low casualty return was attributed to their having worn their helmets rolled up around their heads ready to pull down.

A total of more than 500 gas cases were reported and a considerable number of men were also wounded by the hostile bombardment. All had to be carried down the pavé road from Wulverghem to a sandbagged farm about a mile from the village where the 73rd Field Ambulance had set up an advanced dressing station. There they negotiated the 'air lock' system which protected the dimly-lit entrance. First a thick curtain soaked in 'hypo' had to be pulled back and the stretcher carried in. The curtain was replaced carefully before a second could be drawn. One or the other had to be kept permanently closed to prevent the entry of gas. Though the dressing station had been directly in the path of the cloud it had remained secure and the staff worked on without masks.

Daylight revealed a sorry landscape. For three-quarters of a mile behind the line grass and bushes had turned an unpleasant yellow. Cows and calves lay dead in the scorched fields. Suffering cattle lowed repeatedly. The bodies of hundreds of rats were scattered in and around the trenches.

The gas had been detected as far away as Bailleul, six miles behind the lines. At Neuve Eglise, a hamlet near the trenches, the remaining inhabitants had heard the alarm and stuffed wet cloths round doors and windows. Some wore masks which had been provided. Several suffered slight effects but fortunately the village was on high ground.

The final military death roll was eighty-nine; but for the warning given by the German deserters it would have been much higher.

The Germans attempted a similar gas attack in the same area in mid-June. There was no infantry raid but one gas cloud was followed by another. The total casualties were somewhat higher than in April and the North Staffordshires were again badly hit, suffering nearly a third of the ninety-five fatal gassings.

In their final cloud attack of the year the enemy returned to the Salient. On 8 August he caught a worn division from the Somme in the process of relieving its battalions at Wieltje. The trenches were crowded and many of the men were drafts straight from England.[1] Of 800 gas casualties more than four in every ten died. Despite this tragedy one thing that was proven during the severe cloud gas attacks of 1916 was the effectiveness of a new type of British gas mask known as the Large Box Respirator (also Tarbox and Tower Respirator).

Chemical granules of a type produced and tested at Oxford University were packed in a metal container carried in a satchel. A rubber tube led from the box to a mask which covered the mouth and nose. Air entered by a valve in the bottom of the satchel, passed through the chemicals and was taken in through a metal mouthpiece. To ensure the wearer did not breathe through his nose (fumes might have penetrated the face mask) a nose clip was worn clothes-peg fashion.

Goggles, with sponge rubber around the eye pieces to keep out tear gas, were worn separately.

When wearing the large box respirator for long periods, the unnatural method of breathing in and out through the mouthpiece made it most uncomfortable but the apparatus proved to be highly efficient. Each of the four British armies was supplied with 7,500 of the new-style masks for use by specialist troops. First on the list were the 'gas companies', next machine-gunners, signallers and artillery-men. Issues began in February, 1916.

[1] According to A.F. Graveley, *Army Quarterly and Defence Journal*, October, 1980, some companies had sent their respirators on ahead of them in wagons.

CHAPTER 11

Crisis at Verdun

The year which saw the introduction of effective lethal gas shells was also the year of Verdun. It was a year in which the Germans rationalized their chemical war effort by co-ordinating the activities of many industrial companies under the umbrella organization of IG Farben – (*Interessen Gemeinschafte fur Farbenindustrie*).

After using a lead container to insert gas into a conventional shell, they had progressed to the stage where the liquid agent could be introduced directly into the projectile. The French had perfected a system in which they lined the inside of their gas shells with toughened glass. Thousands were to be fired as the great battle which began on the banks of the Meuse on 21 February developed into an artillery duel of stupendous proportions.[1]

Verdun, on the ancient invasion route into France, was protected by a ring of forts. The citadel itself dated back to the time of Henry II and its innards, hewn out of solid rock, were proof against the heaviest shell. The other forts were developed, built or improved by General Séré de Riviere after the 1870 war. They were generally similar in shape – a blunt arrowhead pointing towards the invader – and dominated ridges on both sides of the Meuse. Their reinforced concrete roofs were covered by many feet of earth and to some degree they resembled a cluster of tortoises crouched on the hills. They had been equipped with modern guns in retractable turrets but many of the heavier weapons had been removed by Joffre for his offensives the previous autumn.

The shattering of the Belgian forts at Antwerp, Liège and Namur had led military opinion to the view that in the event of a serious

---

[1] The Germans used 6,000 cylinders in a diversionary cloud attack south of the Somme on 21 February.

onslaught de Riviere's creations would also crumble under the fire of the massive Skoda howitzers. The fact that, in any case, they still offered a great deal of protection for, say, reserves waiting to go forward, were custom-built communications centres and magnificent observation posts was overlooked. Due to neglect and stupidity Fort Douaumont, one of the most formidable of the species, fell without a struggle on 25 February. Thereafter every exposed hill, splintered copse and pile of rubble was contested furiously.

As the Germans battered their way forward, the French, in desperation, asked their ally to agree to their use of a gas shell which it had been hoped to keep secret until large stocks were available. The new projectile contained phosgene – though the British and French Governments had not authorized the use of the gas until January, 1916, some weeks after it had been identified in the German cloud at Wieltje. Temporary relief was gained by the introduction of the shell into the protective bombardments, but the premature disclosure of the possession of phosgene gave the enemy time in which to take counter-measures. The fighting on the Meuse merely intensified.

With both sides suffering terrible losses, the Germans clawed nearer their goal. At the beginning of June another fort, Vaux, fell to them after a bitter struggle, ending only when its water supply failed. Fort Souville, the key to the whole system of the defence of the Right or East Bank of the Meuse, was threatened. From its shell-furrowed glacis and blackened walls French observers could see much of the convulsed battlefield. Only two and a half miles behind them lay Verdun.

The attack on the city had been von Falkenhayn's brainchild. The French, he reasoned, would never yield it without making the utmost efforts. He hoped to grind them into the dust. A mass of heavy artillery was assembled to blast a path for the reinforced Fifth Army under the nominal command of Crown Prince Wilhelm. What Falkenhayn had not counted on was the hypnotic effect the battle would have on his own side, where emotion and pride were also to stifle caution, reason and common sense. The French set up their own infantry pulverising plant. Guns of all shapes and sizes trundled up the narrow road to Verdun, the Voie Sacré. So dominant was the artillery and so confused was the fighting that sometimes it seemed that the opposing gunners had gone into business together. Foot soldiers on both sides complained frequently of being slaughtered by their 'own' 75s of 5.9s.

Disillusion reached the highest levels. The Crown Prince became

completely disenchanted with the whole affair and wished to call a
halt. General von Deimling, whose XV Corps had been transferred
from Ypres and had taken Fort Vaux, considered that in the end 'the
Hell of Verdun had an effect on even the best soldiers'. Nevertheless
Falkenhayn was prepared to sanction another attempt to register a
victory. General Schmitt von Knobelsdorff, the Crown Prince's
Chief of Staff, began enthusiastically to plan the operation. To help
him he was offered large stocks of a new gas shell. With these he
hoped to silence the aggravating batteries barring the road to Verdun.

The new shell was an improved version of the 'K' round reported
to have been used against the British at the time of the cloud attack on
19 December. The K-2 Stoff, also called C-Stoff, shells were filled
with another powerful lung irritant generally referred to as
diphosgene (chemical name trichlormethyl-chloroformate). The
agent was about as toxic as phosgene but had a higher boiling point
and was relatively inert physiologically. The civilian munitions
factories were not enamoured of the 'stoff' and finally 'filling stations'
were set up behind the front. As the woods burst into leaf on the
Woevre Plain, soldiers in their shirt sleeves stencilled green crosses on
the shells awaiting their poisonous contents. It was one way of
passing the pleasant early summer days.

The attack began at 6 am on 23 June after two days of the
customary violent bombardment. Large quantities of Green Cross
ammunition were fired the previous evening and during the night;
then, for the final 'preparation' the batteries reverted to conventional
high explosive.

It was a little while before the French realized they were being
gassed. The Green Cross rounds had only a small bursting charge and
could have passed for duds had there not been so many of them. By
the time many of the troops had donned their masks – and the French
M2 was not regarded highly by either the Germans or the British – it
was too late. One whiff was enough to affect a man. A soldier might
carry on at his post for a while, but, as noticed with the victims of
phosgene-chlorine clouds, he would eventually collapse.

The Germans had tried gas shells earlier during the battle, but not
in such quantities. For once, as the fire storm lifted to targets in the
rear of the objectives, the assault troops were not lashed by the rapid
salvoes of the defenders' 75mm batteries. To some eyewitnesses it
seemed as if the opposing artillery had been annihilated. Elements of
the crack Alpine Corps, I and III Bavarian Corps and the German XV
Corps scrambled hopefully forward. Grim evidence of the results of
previous advances and repulses littered the countryside, but they

went on. There was no shortage of courage in the German army. The ankle-high debris of the village bearing the mocking name of Fleury was captured. The shattered concrete of a mini-fort, the Ouvrage de Thiaumont, which had already changed hands many times, fell yet again.

CRISIS AT VERDUN – 11 July 1916

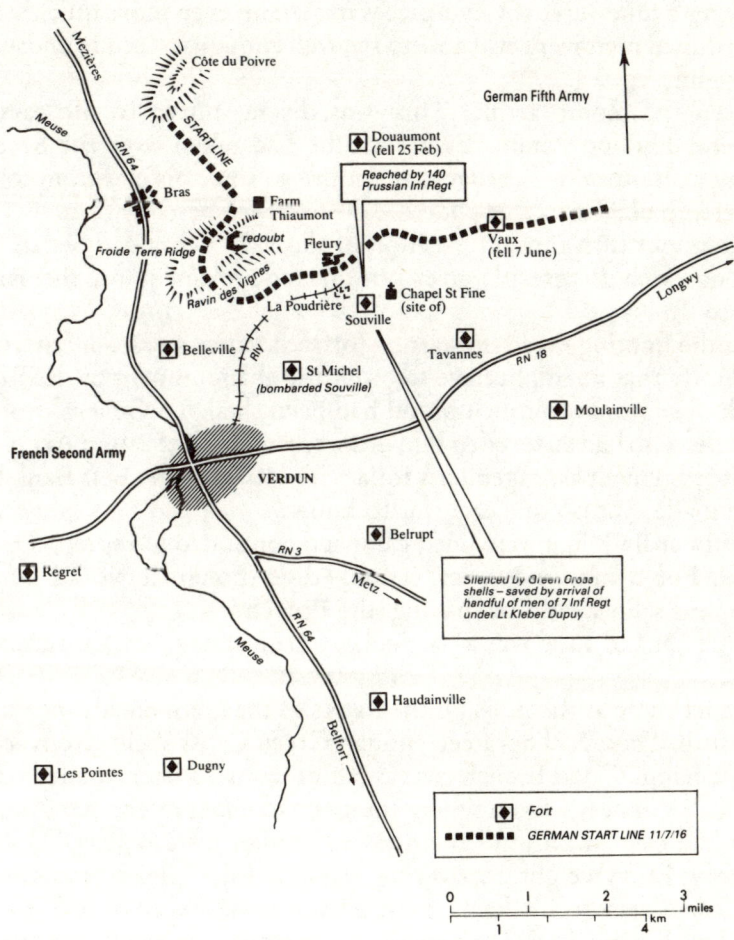

Then the familiar thudding of a single 75 was heard. And another. Larger shells began to scream down. The French batteries were firing again from the ridges where the heavy gas fumes had drained off into shell holes and ravines.

Some of the original gunners were still in action. The French M2 mask, not unlike the British PH helmet in appearance, was made of layers of 'cheese cloth' – thirty-two in the 1916 model – and, thanks to the information passed on by the Russians, the chemicals with which it had been treated included 'Hexamine'. It offered reasonable protection against Green Cross gas as long as it was put on in time.

The M2, unlike the British helmet, did not cover the whole head. It fitted like a horse's nose bag and was more comfortable to wear. Lacking a tube valve the eye-pieces misted up even more quickly but determined men were still able to see well enough to feed rounds into their guns.

Even spasmodic artillery fire was distant music to the ears of General Phillipe Pétain. Ever since he had taken over the Second Army at Verdun in February, and more so since his elevation to the leadership of Army Group Centre, he had been beset by fears that the battle might turn into a repetition of the 1870 débâcle at Sedan. He had no wish to preside over another encirclement on the River Meuse.

As the fighting raged he warned Joffre at Supreme Headquarters at Chantilly that he might have to order the abandonment of the Right Bank over which so much blood had been shed. To General Robert Nivelle, who had succeeded him in command of the Second Army, he confided that all arrangements for a withdrawal to the Left Bank had been made, but no one else was to know.

Outwardly Pétain remained calm and continued to repeat: '*On les aura*'. For a time, however, it looked as though it would be the Germans who would be 'having' the French.

'The 23rd of June was a particularly critical day,' Pétain admitted later.

Relief came as the guns on the flanks of the German advance took their toll. There had not been enough Green Cross shells to cover the whole front. (Total French gas casualties reported later totalled 1,600 – not all gunners). Even where the gas had taken effect, handfuls of men had carried on until the dead and dying were replaced. Like a wobbly heavyweight recovering from a solar plexus punch the artillery began to hit back. Steadily the noise began to rise to the previous lunatic level. The Germans crept to within less than a mile of Souville but the line held.

Falkenhayn approved a last attempt to shatter the bolt position and von Knobelsdorff again resorted to Green Cross shells, fresh supplies having been produced. German high explosive cut all French links with Souville on 11 July. No food, water or ammunition could reach

7. The 12th Earl of Dundonald. In 1915, then a Lieutenant-General, he raised the possibility of using sulphur clouds against the Germans. Sir Douglas Haig pooh-poohed the idea just before the Germans showed it to be practical.

8 & 9. Drawn on the spot, these sketches by Captain John Procter of the Gloucestershire Regiment (now in the regimental museum in Gloucester) show men of the Royal Inniskilling Fusiliers lying where they had fallen on the Somme in July, 1916. He made the drawing in August of the same year. The Irishmen had fallen victim to bullets or shells. About the same time he drew the picture (left) of gas victims which is equally grim. Though the facts are not stated it may be assumed that the gassed group are dead.

10 & 11. Two pictures of Charles Foulkes, profound believer in the effectiveness of British offensive operations with either cloud gas, projectors or shells. The picture above shows him as a Brigadier-General escorting King George V during a visit to France during the war, the one below, relaxing with the Royal Engineers billiards team when he was Chief Royal Engineer at Aldershot in the late '20s.

12. Early gas cylinders in a practice trench at Helfaut, training centre for RE Special Companies, 1915–18. Note the essential spanner and the flimsy projector pipes. Sandbags are jammed around the bases of the cylinders.

13. Later they were often dug into shelters as in the picture in which a sergeant is attending to two of his charges.

14. Australian troops wearing small box respirators, Garter Point, September, 1917.

the trenches on either side of the fort as the Green Cross projectiles thudded onto it and around it.

A French sergeant watching the gas barrage through binoculars saw 'the country disappear' little by little, 'the valley become filled with an ashy coloured smoke . . . things turn sombre in this poison fluid. The smell of the gas occasionally reached us despite the distance.'

By the time the assault began at 5 am the Green Cross curtain extended from Souville to Verdun. Thick black smoke arose as flame-throwers drove out the defenders of the shapeless compost heap that had once been an ammunition store – La Poudrière. The Bavarian Royal Guard stumbled past howling Frenchmen who rolled frantically on the ground trying to smother the flames on their burning clothes. The commander of the 225th Brigade, Colonel Coquelin de Lisle, emerged from his command post firing a soldier's rifle and was shot down. His men hung on and the Bavarian Guard went to ground near the Ravin des Vignes. A Prussian unit dug in beside the torn-up railway track. There were to be no excursions along the Chemin de Fer Meusien that summer.

The 3rd Company of the 7th French Infantry Regiment had set out early in the morning to reinforce a post north of Souville. The soldiers blundered through a heaving landscape strewn with bodies.

Forced to seek shelter, the survivors of the first leg of the journey scrambled into the debris-choked entrance of Souville. There were sixty-five of them, led by Lieutenant Klébert Dupuy, a teacher by profession and a pacifist by inclination. The refugees found the gloomy corridors jammed with groaning or unconscious Territorials. Cement dust rose in clouds and the lights flickered wildly as heavy shells hammered into the glacis. Deafening metallic clangs echoed through the dank tunnels as Dupuy scribbled a message for his colonel:

'Souville, 11 July, 6 am. Captain Soucarre gassed. Has handed over command of company with order to reach Carrières. Having passed through numerous barrages and poison gas clouds we have with difficulty reached Souville. Here, everything is in chaos. The commandant of the fort is gassed, the garrison is out of action. Unless otherwise ordered I will stay in the fort and assure its defence.'

A bold soul set off to the rear with this note. Dupuy posted his three machine guns and his bombers at vantage points and began to organize the collection of the wounded and disabled for evacuation when it became possible. During the morning a captain managed to get through and approved the dispositions. He announced that there was little hope of reinforcement; the 7th's cooks, pioneers and clerks were now in the line. In any case no body of troops of any size was going to be able to climb the splinter-swept slopes behind Souville. The captain disappeared into the hurricane to rejoin the colonel.

After a harrowing night Dupuy peered from the entrance of the fort. It was about 3.30 with the light improving. A dishevelled figure stumbled in – a medical officer. He had volunteered to bring word from a neighbouring unit after two previous messengers had been killed. The Germans were gathering east of Souville.

Dupuy posted riflemen and two machine guns in shell holes on the glacis. At 6 am a second-lieutenant returned from a hazardous reconnaissance to report that the enemy was advancing.

The Prussians, the 140th Infantry Regiment, came on in waves which made easy targets, but pressed ever nearer. Wounded Frenchmen loaded spare rifles for their comrades to maintain the rate of fire. The machine guns rattled incessantly. Dupuy and another officer hurled grenades at figures scrambling up the shell hillocks on their flanks. Groups of Germans finally succeeded in reaching the superstructure but all were eventually killed or driven to the shelter of the ditches.

At 9 am the exhausted defenders were able to pause for breath. At that moment more shells began to pound Souville – French shells. Observers at neighbouring Fort Saint Michel had assumed the worst. German guns joined in and it took a superhuman effort by Dupuy to get the men on the glacis under control. When the 25th Chasseurs counter-attacked and mopped up round Souville at midday they found the garrison of the fort consisted of Dupuy and fifteen haggard soldiers.

Falkenhayn and Colonel Tappen arrived at the Fifth Army's headquarters at Stenay after news of the repulse at Souville had been received. Reluctantly he instructed Knobelsdorff:

'As the objectives set for today have not been gained, despite the use of Green Cross shells and all other means, the Crown Prince's group of armies will maintain a strict defensive.'

Though Falkenhayn did not know it, Green Cross had brought victory within his grasp. Had the attack of 23 June been delayed until more shells had been accumulated, had the gas bombardment been extended and thickened, the result might have been different.

On 11 July the French gunners knew what to expect; their gas discipline had been improved, the helmets checked to ensure they were of the latest pattern. They did not expose their battery positions until the enemy struck.

Nevertheless the bombardment did knock out the garrison at Souville, the innocuous thump of the Green Cross shells being lost in the drumfire. There were air vents, observation slits, even the main entrance through which the diphosgene could drift. The problem of making a building as large as Souville 'gas-tight' was something the engineers were already studying. Their findings were to bear fruit later.

On 11 July it was luck that saved Verdun, luck and the decision of a humble lieutenant. The French High Command was shaken by the narrow escape. The truth about the desperate situation at Souville was long suppressed and came out only gradually *after* the war. The official communiqué at the time reported in three lines that the Germans, having 'suffered heavy losses, gained a small amount of ground in the vicinity of the chapel of Saint-Fine.' The chapel did not even exist; it had been pulled down before the war.

CHAPTER 12

A Beautiful Patina

In the run-up to the dismal sequence of massacres which became the Battle of the Somme, British gas operations were prejudiced by varying views developed after Loos.

Before 25 September, 1915, the chlorine cylinders were expected to provide a magic key to unlock the enemy defences. Afterwards, when it had sunk in that barbed wire could not be cut by a weapon with the substance of a wraith, critics abounded, rumours spread. Among the troops the belief persisted that the chlorine had done more harm to the attackers than the defenders. Some Tommies also believed contrarily and simultaneously that the British product was not as strong as their opponent's. As one old footslogger put it as he struggled up the line with one of the hated cylinders full of chlorine: 'The Jerries will simply inhale it and think they're having a champagne supper.'

Misconceptions were equally common among commanders at brigade and divisional level. One or two flatly refused to employ gas in their sectors, considering it to be more trouble than it was worth, drawing fire and adding to the dangers already present. Foulkes, as head of the offensive section of the brigade, found that part of his job was to convince his elders and betters that his units were effective. Obtaining evidence of the results of gas discharges was easier said than done, however, The weapon became in the eyes of many, if not old hat, commonplace.

The appointment of a comparatively junior brigadier-general as head of the service in France indicates the weight placed on the value of gas by the High Command, though Sir Douglas Haig was by no means dismissive of it and constantly badgered the War Office to invent and supply his gunners with 'lethal shell'. In fact the first

British-made projectiles did not contain a toxic filling but tear gas. A trial consignment of 10,000 of them reached France in the spring of 1916. During the four-month-long Somme battle 'practically the only gas shell fired on the British front was fired by French batteries lent for that purpose'. So says the Official Historian. There were, of course, quite a number fired by the enemy.

Lack of enthusiasm and understanding among commanders gave gas operations a low priority during the weeks before the assault began on 1 July. Just as the artillery fired mainly in support of the corps or division to which it had been allotted, so the Special Companies were fitted into the plan of their parent formations. Principally they were employed to create diversions. Spread along the front, their efforts were fragmented and the effect diluted.

Opposite the Thiepval spur, which, with its village, had been turned into a fortress, the 36th (Ulster) Division made its first acquaintance with the Special Brigade in late June when cylinders were dug into the edge of the wood they occupied.

The 'abominable stuff . . . brought no good fortune'. A German bombardment burst several cylinders and infantry and Sappers suffered severely. The gas was sent over during the night and followed two hours afterwards by raiders from the 13th Royal Irish Rifles who brought back a dozen or so captives.

'The prisoners denied all knowledge of our gas, nor did their respirators smell of it. It was occasionally the experience of the Division that the British gas services rated too highly the effects of their devices.'

More cylinders were dug into no-man's-land opposite Thiepval on the night of 30 June. Half an hour before zero hour the next day they were opened, German gas alarms were heard, but, when the infantry attacked, the enemy machine guns opened up on the Ulstermen 'as if there had been no bombardment'.

By this time the British were using 'White Star' cylinders, containing equal proportions of phosgene and chlorine. Thousands had been carried up to the front line during June. They were given a new code-name; 'Oojahs' became 'Rats' and were about as popular.

'A hostile gas attack is perhaps the only thing which a British soldier dislikes more than one from his own side. No one with experience of our gas services can fail to recognize the pluck, perseverance and self-sacrifice . . . or their skill at fighting the enemy at his own hellish game. But it must be confessed that, quite apart from moral principles, the "gas monger" was not generally popular.

'Even if spared the delights of carrying cylinders up narrow

communication trenches . . . the infantry often spent days, sometimes weeks, with these undesirable companions, praying that a
hostile bombardment might not burst them.'

When, after days of perversity, the wind turned favourable and the
gas was discharged, . . .'one result which could be reckoned on was
the enemy's retaliatory bombardment.'[1]

In a sentence: 'No soldier has ever laughed at that true invention of
the devil himself . . . which creeps silently and without warning over
its victims and having dealt the most horrible death, creeps on.'

The author of *All Quiet on the Western Front* shared this
sentiment.[2]

'All four of us lie there in heavy, watchful suspense and breathe as
lightly as possible. These first minutes with the mask decide betwen
life and death. . . . Is it airtight?

'The gas . . . creeps over the ground and sinks into all hollows.
Like a big soft jellyfish it floats into our shell hole and lolls there
obscenely . . . it is better to crawl out on the top than to stay where
the gas collects most. But we don't get as far as that; a second
bombardment begins.'

Lieutenant Ernst Junger, serving with the 73rd Hanoverian
Fusiliers, found himself in the centre of one of the diversionary cloud
attacks in June. At midnight at Monchy le Preux, on the Arras front,
alarm bells rang and a stream of distress flares went up.

'A whitish wall of gas, fitfully illuminated by the light of the
rockets, was moving over Monchy. As a strong smell of chlorine was
noticeable in our cellar we lit fires of straw at the entrances. The acrid
smoke nearly drove us out of our refuge, and we were forced to clear
the air by waving coats and groundsheets.'

The next morning he noticed that nearly all green vegetation had
withered. Snails and moles lay dead in the trenches and the noses and
eyes of horses were streaming with water. Shell splinters were
covered with a 'beautiful green patina'. The few civilians remaining in
the area demanded gas masks and were evacuated to villages in the
rear.

The British Special Companies were never idle during 1916. A new
system of attaching three or four cylinders to one outlet pipe had been
developed and the members of the original units began to wish they
had taken degrees in plumbing instead of chemistry.

At Hulluch 2,500 cylinders of phosgene were released in three

---

[1] *History of the 23rd Division*
[2] Erich Maria Remarque (Kramer) was deprived of his German nationality by the
Nazis because of his writing and took refuge in Switzerland.

waves on the night of 5 October. Huge clouds enveloped the German lines betwen 8 and 10.30. The 'gas mongers' were able to walk above the parapet freely as they retrieved their projector pipes. The raiders who followed up the discharge three hours later were not so lucky. A machine gun on one flank of the gassed sector caught them in no-man's-land as they returned and a long line of bodies lay just outside the British wire. Nearer the German trenches wounded twitched and cried out.

Both sides stared with disbelief as a stretcher bearer of the 2nd Devons walked upright and alone between the lines and, after talking to two German officers, obtained permission for a comrade to come out and help him to carry away the injured. In the wake of a gas attack this was courage indeed.

The gas legend was spreading beyond the Western Front, however. Some days after the Hulluch incident, Sir William Robertson received a signal from General Smuts, leading the frustrating pursuit of the enemy in East Africa.

'General Smuts to CIGS. OA 697 Secret.

'Within the next few months it is probable that the enemy may be concentrated into area where speedy end to the campaign might be made by use of gas. I would therefore urge advisability of sending out gas with technical personnel at early date for use when occasion arises.'

Sir William sent the request to General von Donop to consider. His reply was as follows:[1]

'Hitherto the War Committee have not considered the use of gas against any enemy force who has not employed it. If, however, the circumstances are considered to justify the use of gas then the following answer is suggested –

' "War Office to General Smuts . . .

' "Use of gas shell is not possible as there is no design of gas shell for artillery you have. Use of gas in cylinders not considered advisable in sharply accidented country nor in very dense scrub nor long grass, and of doubtful value in your local conditions owing to necessity of choosing exactly favourable weather and difficulty of replacing used cylinders. Also climate unsuitable for use of anti-gas appliances essential for our troops.

' "Cylinder attacks not considered effective at greater range than 200 yards. Considerable difficulty in securing trained personnel." '

Due to the higher temperatures, the increased pressure on the large cylinders, such as those used in France, was another factor which had

---

[1] PRO CAB 42/21/14

to be considered from the safety point of view. Smaller cylinders weighing 50 lbs each were possible substitutes but 3,000 would be required for a single attack on a front of 1,400 yards.

Smuts was told the smaller cylinders could be sent out 'in about two months' but 'considering above, do you still wish for gas?'

On careful reading Sir Stanley's suggested cable is a masterpiece of diplomacy, a perfect example of how to deal with an awkward question which no one wishes to handle. It was much easier to resort to the commonplace, the banal and the brutal when the Western Front was concerned. The chronicler of the War Committee meeting at 10 Downing Street on 17 October, 1916, summarized Sir William Robertson's opening remarks on the situation in France: 'There was nothing fresh. The casualties for the past week on the Somme were 11,500.'

The search for more devastating ways of delivering gas was pursued by the British throughout the Battle of the Somme and into the New Year. The aim was to unload as much as possible on the enemy in the shortest possible time.

The 4-inch Stokes mortars developed at Foulkes's request in 1915 were still not provided with gas bombs, though plenty of other ammunition was available for them. The Germans had adapted their much feared minethrower, the 17 cm minenwerfer, to lob a canister containing, at first, 27 lbs of tear gas – bromacetone. Later they substituted phosgene for B-Stoff but enemy interest in this field waned after the death of its foremost expert, a Major Lothes, at Verdun.

The amazing Lieutenant Livens continued to apply himself to the problem. On the reorganization of the gas service he had been transferred from 186 to Z Company. After much experimental work in England he reappeared on the eve of the Somme with a collection of ponderous flame-throwing devices. He did not consider, however, that walking towards the enemy with an unreliable hosepipe spouting fire was the best way to smoke out the foe. He improvised a crude mortar to throw an equally primitive container filled with fuel which ignited on hitting the ground. If inaccurate, it was nevertheless spectacular and could be guaranteed at least to frighten anyone near the impact area. Livens suggested using his invention for gas warfare and was recalled from Z Company to work in a laboratory set up near the headquarters of the Reserve Army at Toutencourt.

Completely absorbed in his work, he looked up one day to find himself under close scrutiny from the Army Commander, General

Gough, and his chief staff officer, Major-General Neil Malcolm. The two Old Etonians seemed concerned. Was it really necessary, Gough wished to know, to fill the laboratory and the surrounding area with so much gas? Was it not dangerous to Livens and everyone else?

Livens was astounded. Of course not!

Why was he so sure?

'Oh, I put some over that football field [next to the lab] while they were playing and they didn't mind a bit!

The Brasshats left.

The projector which bore Livens's name closely resembled a gas cylinder with the top cut off and was eight inches in diameter.

The tube was dug into the ground at an angle and fired a fat projectile containing 30 lbs of liquid phosgene about 1,500 yards. The propellant was a charge of gun cotton detonated electrically. A stout base plate prevented the 'gun' digging itself into the ground. With such primitive weapons accuracy was approximate and they were fired in batteries simultaneously. Staggered firings were apt to wreck the wiring connections.

Setting up a projector attack was easier than preparing cylinders, but it did mean that the Special Companies had to work above ground after dark digging the trenches and then burying the tubes so that only the muzzles showed. After the charges had been inserted and the bombs loaded, the firing officer removed the safety pins from the projectiles. He then returned to cover and, at the appointed time, firmly pressed the plunger of the firing dynamo. Wise men made sure the key of the dynamo box never left their possession.

Gough's army was the first to use the Livens projector. On the night of 28 October the inventor sent a shower of bombs[1] whirring into German lines near Beaumont Hamel. A gas cloud containing an estimated 2,300 lbs of pure phosgene enveloped the enemy trenches. After intelligence reports that many enemy soldiers had been gassed before they could put on their masks production of the projector was stepped up but its further use was forbidden until large numbers could be accumulated.

On their part the enemy were concerned to increase the lethal quantities of their Green Cross shell. This they did by adding another chemical – chloropicrin, a severe lung irritant with strong tear-producing qualities. First reports of the appearance of the new strain of Green Cross came from the Italian front where it was said to have

---

[1] Filled weight 60 lbs, giving an efficiency ratio of 50 per cent, compared with five to seven per cent in a shell.

caused vomiting and induced men to remove their masks, thus making them vulnerable. The Italians were equipped with a version of the French M2 mask. It followed that the British PH helmet incorporating the same principles would also be useless against chloropicrin, as proved to be the case. The PH helmet, however, was no longer in the first line of defence.

Chloropicrin had first been prepared by a Scottish chemist, John Stenhouse, in 1848, during peaceful research. He was also the inventor of charcoal air filters and respirators. It was fitting, therefore, that by the time the chemical appeared in shells in France the British were protected against it.

Anticipating events, the scientists had produced a scaled-down version of the Large Box Respirator. A container filled with chemicals filtered air which passed up the 'elephant's trunk' tube to a mouth valve. The valve was inserted into a mask with built-in goggles which covered the face. The nose clip was retained, giving the wearer a chance of survival even if the material of the face piece was damaged.

Issue of the new model began in August, 1916, and was completed early in 1917. Every soldier was supplied with one small box respirator and kept his PH helmet as a reserve. The 'SBR' was to remain in service for the rest of the war.[1]

The search for adequate protection proved to be easier than the production of an effective chemical shell, though not for want of trying. Porton's chalky acres quickly took on the appearance of a battlefield after the War Office acquired it in January, 1916. Projectiles of all descriptions descended on Gas Wood and the trench systems, some circular, which scarred the downland. Scientists and soldiers crouched in dugouts, with or without masks according to the nature of the task, to sample the fumes. Frequently they emerged retching and coughing, with eyes streaming. The dangers were real, as shown by the description of a trial carried out in May, 1917.

The 4.5 inch howitzer battery assigned to Porton fired 150 shells containing chloropicrin in twenty minutes. After a further twenty minutes an officer and six observers entered. Though the gas caused 'slight lachrymation' the concentration was not thought to warrant the wearing of respirators. At that time, said a later report, it had not been realized how small amounts of PS[2] when breathed over a period could prove to be very dangerous to health. Experiments of this

---

[1] In all, Britain produced a total of 50 million masks of seven different types for an army of around two million men – a remarkable output in three and a half years. See Prentiss, p.535.

[2] Chloropicrin-filled shells first investigated though apparently not produced by Lever Brothers at Port Sunlight.

nature meant that most of the staff at Porton were gassed in some degree during their service. In some cases scientists showed devotion amounting either to cold-blooded courage or recklessness.

The distinguished chemist Joseph Barcroft established a permanent place in the history of the establishment when he and a dog entered a chamber to test the toxicity of hydrocyanic acid,[1] present in a minute quantity.

Barcroft walked about to stimulate his breathing 'in order that the experiment might be as fair as possible'. The dog, which no doubt walked with him, died after one minute 35 seconds and Barcroft left the chamber. He commented:

'As regards the result upon myself, the only real effect was a momentary giddiness when I turned my head quickly; this lasted *for about a year*, (author's italics) and then vanished.'

For some time afterwards Barcroft found it difficult to concentrate for any length of time, but reported drily: 'It is hard to say to what extent this was due to the experiment.'

The evaluation of such trials took time. It was necessary to know why six goats which had been tethered in the trench system and bombarded with PS shells on 12 March were still hale and hearty 72 hours later. Rabbits and rats had died in large numbers. Why on another occasion did another group of goats (animals which feature largely in trial reports) appear to have survived unscathed after a gas attack only to succumb a week later? To the military mind the painstaking nature of research came as a disappointment if not a shock. The German trenches were never going to be stormed by waves of white-coated professors shouting 'Eureka!', that was clear.

Even the brighter Brass Hats were apt to take umbrage. Major-General Noel Birch, artillery adviser at GHQ in France, complained of the 'ghastly failure' of specially designed 4.5 inch incendiary shells (arriving from England at the rate of 5,000 a week). He complained to the head of Porton, Lieutenant-Colonel Arthur Crossley,[2] then visiting France, that they had in some instances started fires but these had gone out almost immediately.

Brigadier-General Thuillier, as head of the Gas Service with the BEF, had already been the target of the General's indignation and left it to his subordinate to deal with the technical problems involved. Patiently Crossley explained that it was essential for gunner officers to study the techniques of chemical warfare (under which heading the

[1] Prussic acid (*l'acide prussique*) derived from Prussian blue dye.
[2] PRO WO 142/209

incendiaries came). He cited the French and their 'thoroughness' in this respect. His 'long conversation' bore some fruit: 'General Birch said he would take the matter up at once and gave me an introduction to an artillery officer he had just detailed to Larkhill.'[1]

This encounter gives some indication of the gaps which existed between the soldiers and scientists, not due to ill-will but a lack of understanding and the absence of co-ordination in high places. Porton had no long-standing traditions, mess customs, hallowed buildings, revered old boys to fall back on. It had to go into business from day one, erect its own huts and laboratories, recruit its own experts and produce results at once. At the same time the demands grew.

By the end of 1917 British chemical shell production had expanded to the extent that lethal ammunition was available for the 4.5 inch howitzer, the 4.7 inch gun, the 6 inch gun and the 60-pounder.

It was a sterling achievement as far as Porton was concerned as the establishment had to conduct not only trials of the chemicals but the fuses of the missiles – fuses were a major headache throughout the greater part of the war – while assessing bursting charges and carrying out leakage tests. To see just how gas-tight the 60 pounder shells were, a number were solemnly dropped six feet on to concrete, first on their base, then on their sides. Boxed 60 pounder rounds were allowed to fall fifteen feet. The tests were successful.

It was only by the end of 1917 that a variety of British-made gas shells became available and during the previous eighteen months great interest was taken in the French 'Vincennite' or 'VN' shells which took their name from the proving ground at Vincennes. The major ingredient was prussic acid, a poison familiar to readers of Victorian and Edwardian detective novels: 'Note the smell of bitter almonds, Watson'. Suggestions that it might be used to murder German soldiers were rejected as barbarous for a time but the opposition was eventually drowned in the tide of casualty lists from the Champagne and Artois. Its sponsors gained considerable encouragement during the Somme fighting. (The French attacked on the right of the British.)

'Near the Bois des Riez, south of Combles, is a sunken road (five metres deep). It was twice unsuccessfully attacked by the French. On 13 September (1916) it was heavily shelled by the the French who used both 75 and 155 mm shell filled with VN and after the

[1] Larkhill, Salisbury Plain, a few miles from Porton and now home of the Royal School of Artillery, was also in the embryo stage.

bombardment . . . was easily carried by storm. No less than 500 Germans were found asphyxiated in the defile and all were wearing gas masks.'[1]

The VN mixture was tested in 60-pounder shells fired at Porton in January, 1917. Splinters were found 600 yards from the point of impact, so it may be assumed the gas contents must have been spread very thinly indeed.

By suppressing all temptations to use their newly developed weapons prematurely the British scored an early success in the spring of 1917. Large dumps of gas shell had been accumulated, some filled with a mixture similar to Vincennite and code-named JBR; another was a mixture of phosgene and arsenic trichloride – CBR.[2] The German mask gave excellent protection against the contents of these shells but they proved effective all the same.

The bombardment which preceded the Battle of Arras was one of the most carefully orchestrated of the war. It began on 4 April but it was not until twelve hours before zero hour on Easter Monday (9 April) that the enemy batteries and roads in the rear were deluged with gas shells. The German gunners were not killed but became exhausted with the strain of having to wear masks continuously. Draft animals were also badly affected by this gas which one report said succeeded in 'killing off horses like flies'. An official enemy assessment reads: 'Horses were greatly affected by the gas; in many cases the failure of the ammunition supply must be attributed to this. From the same cause it seems the timely withdrawal of the batteries could not be effected. Artillery activity seems to have been paralysed.'

The Livens Projector also made its reappearance; with a roar like a stricken shell dump, a total of 3,827 drums of phosgene were blasted into the German lines. Fifty tons of gas gushed from the ruptured containers. In the Blangy area alone it was later learned that 460 men had been killed.

The gas and artillery preparation paid dividends. The Canadian Corps captured Vimy Ridge and the British overran the enemy's front-line system in front of Arras. For a time it looked as though the sought-after breakthrough had been achieved. Then the old problem of the delayed deployment of reserves reasserted itself. Droves of cavalry waited in freezing slush, adding to the congestion behind the front. The battle degenerated into a dour struggle for points of vantage – a hill, a village or a factory.

[1] PRO WO 142/209
[2] For British gas shell code initials see appendix.

The Special Companies continued to bombard the enemy with the Livens Projector: 570 drums were fired into a position known as 'Electric Station' near Lens on 31 May. A captured stretcher bearer of the 88th (Nassau) Regiment said his battalion lost forty dead and sixty disabled. The 10th Reserve Regiment was reported to have had 400 casualties, of which 130 died.

A German general commenting on the 'projector method' described it as a very useful idea cleverly applied. From a technical and tactical point of view it represented 'the most important success of the gas war, and this importance hardly diminished towards the end of the war'. From a strategic point of view, however, he concluded that projectors did not approach the importance of artillery using gas shell.

The British also added a psychological element to their gas operations. Enemy units which were known to have been badly hit by a gas attack were tracked along the front through normal intelligence reports of changes in deployment. They became special targets for Foulkes and his men.

In a period of six months in 1917 the 1st Bavarian Reserve Regiment was 'gassed' fifteen times, the 1st Guard Reserve Regiment twelve times and the 10th Bavarian ten times. Between spring, 1916, and summer, 1917, the 9th Bavarian and the 161st Regiment each suffered fourteen gas attacks. These multiple attacks may have provoked the enemy into explaining to his own troops why gas attacks had been necessary in the first place. French intelligence reported that a Bavarian under-officer captured in May, 1917, was found to be carrying explanatory notes:

'While six metres of overhead cover gives protection against ordinary shells, gas shells cover a wide radius from their point of impact. Thanks to its density gas infiltrates the strongest shelters and affects the occupants. Finally a kilogramme of explosives costs 2.40 marks while a kilogramme of chlorine costs 18 pfennigs.'

By May, 1917, however, the French troops themselves were demanding explanations. The offensive which began on the Aisne on 16 April ended in disaster. Nivelle, who had replaced Joffre as Commander-in-Chief at the end of 1916, stubbornly clung to a plan which had been wrecked by the enemy's strategic withdrawal to what the Allies called the Hindenburg line. Falkenhayn, too, had gone, even before Joffre, dismissed for failure at Verdun and sent to command in Rumania. The Hindenburg-Ludendorff team from the East replaced him. By their withdrawal they flattened out a vulnerable salient and provided themselves with greater reserves. It was a brilliant move.

Three French armies concentrated for the main attack, intent on bursting open the front by brute force to let the cavalry pour through to Laon. Before them stood the fortified heights of the Chemin des Dames ridge, which took its name from the road along its crest. It had once been used by the daughters of Louis XV to reach the Château de la Bove. The slopes were a labyrinth of ravines and old quarries (*creutes*) from which stone for many towns and cities, including Paris, had been dug. Some of the excavations dated back to Roman times and before 1914 the French peasants had grown mushrooms or stored vegetables in them. The Germans turned them into shell-proof barracks and ammunition dumps.

Though the French Fifth and Sixth Armies fired more than five million shells from 5 to 16 April the enemy guns seemed to multiply, not decrease. Some gains were made but the assault foundered bloodily in cold wet weather.

Medical arrangements were inadequate to cope with the unexpectedly high number of casualties and led to their being spread among hospitals far to the rear. The troops, promised a walk-over, felt betrayed. Straight from the horrors of the battlefield, the occupants of a hospital train which steamed into the Gare du Nord late on the 16th were outraged by photographs in the evening papers. One showed a relaxed Poilu, rifle slung, smoking his pipe as he crossed a trench full of German dead. The men who knew the truth created an uproar. Rumours spread around Paris. The unrest grew. Mutinies occurred.

Captain Louis Spears, British liaison officer,had investigated *creutes* at St Gobain a few weeks earlier and thought gas alone would be effective against those occupied by the enemy. The French 'VN' shells were simply not good enough.

Lethal concentrations of Vincennite[1] were seldom achieved by the French though they stuck to it until the end. The Germans ignored prussic acid as an agent and the British, despite the slaughter of the German gun-teams at Arras, also dropped the idea – or at least they tried to. Representations were made by B.E.F. headquarters to restrict production but the accumulated supplies were still being fired off late in 1918.

The French 'Collongite' – a phosgene filling supplied by the Coulogne factory near Calais – was much more effective but its

---

[1] Now in the Red Army's arsenal for use with the multi-barrelled rocket-launcher which can achieve dense concentrations. Useful as it is non-persistent.

potency was reduced by the insertion in the shell of a smoke-producing chemical which took up part of the limited space available.

To achieve the best results gas shelling had to be concentrated, the fumes, when liberated, potent and, a prime factor, delivered by surprise. The last element was lacking all along the Chemin des Dames front where the results of the ten-day bombardment were unsatisfactory. Neither Vincennite nor Collongite made much impression on the *creutes* and the German respirator once again provided complete protection to the wearer. That caves, quarries and dugouts were good targets for gas ammunition was to be proved later on the Chemin des Dames but on this occasion the infantry were reduced to clearing them with haversacks full of grenades and incendiary bombs, if they could get within range.

Little mercy was shown by either side, yet Spears, standing among the reserves waiting to go forward, witnessed a remarkable example of humanity. The order was given: 'Gas masks on.' A wounded German sitting among his captors did not seem to understand. Some men half-removed their masks to warn him.

Spears: 'With tears streaming down his cheeks . . . he pointed to the empty smashed satchel around his neck. A huge French soldier, looking ferocious under a week's growth of beard, came up and, taking off his own mask, roughly clamped it on the German's face, then walked off, his handkerchief, an enormous dirty affair . . . printed in red checks, over his mouth.'

In the distance the pitiless battle for the *creutes* continued unabated.

The sense of failure spread swiftly. Nivelle, the name that had been on everyone's lips when Douaumont was retaken the previous October, had become an ominous word. After that coup, with his ruthless henchman, General Charles Emmanuel Mangin, he had boasted: 'We have the secret.' But the enemy had learned the secret in advance, been ready to meet it. Nivelle, artillery brigadier in 1914, Commander-in-Chief 1916, disappeared into the shadows in the early summer of 1917. A post was found in North Africa from where he watched events unfold on the Western Front.

Meanwhile the artillery of both sides continued to pound the opposing positions on the Aisne–Champagne front. The Germans introduced a more powerful version of the Green Cross shell while their own infantry were harassed constantly by the less toxic but debilitating French ammunition. The account of Corporal Ludwig Renn, who had been wounded on the Somme and arrived on the Aisne in April, makes it clear that gas had become a routine problem for the German in the firing line. Renn would have found it incredible to learn that in 1917 there were soldiers bound for the front quite unprepared to face chlorine and phosgene.

CHAPTER 13

American Patrol

The Yanks were coming all right but they weren't bringing an awful lot with them. Of men there were plenty. Equipment was a different matter. When the troopships set sail for 'Over There' in May, 1917, the American Expeditionary Force effectively had no artillery and did not possess a single gas mask. Not one of its soldiers had been given any gas training. Everyone had to begin at the beginning.

The Department of Mines took over the job of organizing a research programme the day after war was declared. Dr G.A. Burrell, the Bureau's chief chemist, set up a laboratory at the American University in Washington and quickly became a colonel.

In June the Ordnance Department started to look for a place to build a plant for producing poison gas shells. In November it settled on a pleasant rural site at Gunpowder Neck, Maryland.

Discussions began on the structure of a 'Gas Service' for the A.E.F.

With tremendous enthusiasm the Research Department examined all available types of protective equipment and decided that, in answer to a call for 20,000 gas masks, they would copy Britain's Small box respirator. Only they would improve on it.

They made the box for the chemicals larger and changed the style of the mouth piece. They altered the nature of some of the absorbent chemicals.

Just as the Germans had called on their industrial giants to fulfil military needs in 1916, the Americans turned to Big Business. The American Can Company plant on Long Island was the scene of the assembly operation; the Goodrich and Goodyear Rubber Companies at Akron, Ohio, produced face-pieces; the Day Chemical Co. in Pennyslvania provided the charcoal; Simmons Hardware in St Louis manufactured the satchels and the General

Chemical Company provided other essential items.

The first 20,000 masks reached Britain in July and were found to be useless. They provided no protection against chloropicrin.

Undismayed by the cablegram that brought the bad news, the researchers went back to the drawing-board. The US Army wanted 1,100,000 masks to be delivered within a year. A Mr Bradley Dewey was commissioned as a major in the Sanitary Corps and given the job of supervising production. The Hero Manufacturing Company at Philadelphia was brought in to help with the crash programme. Factories mushroomed.

The United States Army in France was also starting from scratch under the demanding eye of its commander, General John Joseph Pershing, a spry 57-year-old.

'Black Jack' Pershing had been commissioned into the 6th Cavalry in 1886 and had campaigned against the Apaches in Arizona and the Sioux in Dakota. He had also been an observer in the Russo-Japanese War and just before coming to Europe had hunted the rebel Pancho Villa on the Mexican border. Pershing knew nothing of gas warfare but had a strong personality and an open mind. Lieutenant-Colonel Amos A. Fries, of the Corps of Engineers, arrived in Paris on 14 August, 1917, tasked with organizing the army's transport. On the 19th he was asked to take over the Gas Service, then being raised. Given a night to think things over, he said yes. He was promptly handed some notes and told to prepare a paper for submission to the General. Fries got to work.

Two days later Pershing's discerning eye picked out one or two doubtful paragraphs and he asked some pertinent questions, such as why special gas troops would have to operate 4-inch Stokes mortars instead of ordinary gunners. 'Beat it to British Gas Headquarters and see how they do it,' said Pershing. With a couple of medical experts Fries set off forthwith.

At St Omer the Americans were shown statistics relating to gas casualties for the 12-month period covering almost all of the Somme battle and the attacks at Arras in April and at Messines in June. Despite the liberal use of Green Cross by the enemy the total number of men treated at casualty clearing stations was only 8,806, of whom 532 had died. Other deaths had occurred in the trenches but indications were that the numbers were small. It was concluded that cloud gas attacks were much more dangerous than gas shell bombardments.

A report on the Messines battle, in which a series of huge mines were exploded under the German lines on 7 June, contained some interesting facts. The British guns had fired mainly gas shell for thirty minutes at zero hour. A three-minute burst of lethal shell (CBR) was followed by another burst of shells containing tear gas and chloro-picrin (PS) and then bursts of purely lachrymatory shell (SK – so marked because it was the product of a team at the Imperial College of Science at South Kensington). Results were stated to have been very satisfactory.

As usual, this was a game at which two could play and the 3rd Australian Division was caught by a barrage containing phosgene and 'weeping gas' as it moved through Ploegsteert Wood to take up its assault position. The fumes hung thickly in the still air and caused 500 casualties.

Fries and his companions should have been able to draw some comforting conclusions from the casualty statistics supplied by the British. They indicated that over a long period the Germans had over-estimated the disabling properties of their gas shells. And up to the second week of July, 1917, that was reasonably true. Since then, however, much had changed. Eight thousand casualties in the period of a year had been followed by more than that in a single month.

Rawlie the Fox had been caught napping. Towards the end of June troops of his Fourth Army began to move to the Belgian coast near Nieuport. They were to relieve a French formation in preparation for an attack to be made in conjunction with a landing on the coast. The 1st Division had undergone special training, including the use of floating piers, forerunners of the Mulberry Harbours used in Normandy in 1944. It was due to do more training at Dunkirk later in July but for a period shared the custody of the Nieuport trenches with the 32nd Division, with which it constituted XV Corps, commanded by 52-year-old Lieutenant-General Sir Philip Du Cane.

The take-over had not been smooth. There had been differences over the artillery relief and in the end the French, who regarded the position as highly vulnerable, pulled out before the British gunners began to arrive in strength.

The position was a weak one on the east bank of the Yser, where a bridgehead about 800 yards deep was to act as a springboard for the forthcoming offensive. The French had never intended to defend the area, but to pull back across the river if attacked. Du Cane decided it had to be held at all costs in view of the operations impending. There was, however, little to hold. The forward trenches were simple sandbag breastworks and there were no deep dugouts. Australian miners, used to working in sandy conditions, were brought in to remedy this, but what was really needed was the missing artillery, most of which was taking part in feint attacks further south. The British holding the front line found themselves manning feeble barricades with a river up to 200 yards wide behind them and none of the usual artillery support. Only 181 of the Army's 583 guns had arrived. Worse, a stream ran into the Yser at one point, cutting off the two battalions holding the flank of the bridgehead next to the sea. The Germans found the situation most interesting and on 6 July, the day General Rawlinson opened his headquarters at Malo les Bains, they began to bombard the XV Corps area. On the 10th the enemy dipped deeply into 300,000 shells which had been made available, smashed the bridges behind the two most exposed battalions, blew down the breastworks and at 8 pm sent in stormtroops of the 1st Marine Division who reached the river twenty minutes later.

Of the 1st Northamptonshire Regiment only one officer and eight men escaped; of the 2nd KRRC a total of fifty-five came back; of fifty Australians four returned. All swam the Yser after hiding in the tunnels under construction.

While Du Cane protested to Rawlinson about orders to make a counter-attack as soon as possible (and won his argument), British specialists were studying reports of the bombardment which had been liberally laced with gas. It says a great deal for the organization that it was able to identify within a matter of hours the Green Cross and lachrymators that had been used. What was more interesting was the description of a new type of shell which 'burst with a loud report like H.E. but caused sneezing, slight irritation of the nose and eyes and tightness of the chest'. Immediately the search for an unexploded shell began, but none was found. By the following day a new phenomenon demanded urgent attention.

CHAPTER 14

Yellow Peril

Promoted Major-General, Thuillier had been delighted to receive command of the renowned 15th (Scottish) Division after a year spent as Director of Gas Services. When, in June, 1917, he handed over to Foulkes, who became a Brigadier-General, it looked as though developments in the chemical warfare department had reached a plateau.

Thuillier entered enthusiastically into preparations for the forthcoming Flanders offensive. There had been little attempt to conceal British intentions and on the night of 12 July the ruins of Ypres were subjected to a furious bombardment in which H.E., shrapnel and phosgene shells landed in mixed salvoes. The 15th Division was on the receiving end. In the midst of this noisome concoction someone detected a suspicious new smell.

It was variously described as 'resembling mustard, rubber, vulcanite, dead horses, diseased vegetables, petrol, garlic and lamp oil'. 'Horseradish' came to the mind of someone else.

Soldiers, used to the idea of gasses which seared the bronchial tubes and choked victims, were at first unconcerned about the new torment which stung their noses and made them sneeze. Some enemy lachrymators were mild enough to disregard and on this occasion many men did not even bother to put on their respirators. It was only later, as eyes became sore and inflamed, as skin blistered and men vomited, that victims began to make their way to the rear. With swollen eyes closed, the afflicted formed little files, holding each other's shoulders and following in the steps of lightly wounded guides whose sight had not been affected.

At the casualty clearing stations few showed symptoms of chest trouble though many were hoarse and coughed harshly. A few hours later serious symptoms developed. On the second and third days after being gassed men began to die. Falkenhayn's green genie released at Ypres more than two years earlier had returned in a more menacing guise.

Mustard gas may have been first identified in an impure form by Frederick Guthrie, sometime Professor at the Normal School of Science, South Kensington. When young he had studied under Bunsen at Heidelberg. A poet as well as a scientist, he can hardly have imagined that thirty years after his death his research would become the subject of an intense study in the middle of a world war.

Another of Bunsen's pupils (it would seem that Bunsen has a great deal to answer for) was Victor Meyer, a Berliner who eventually succeeded his old mentor at Heidelberg. The Royal Society thought so highly of his research in a number of peaceful fields that he was awarded the Davy Medal a few years before his death in 1897.

Using his purely academic method of producing the gas as a basis for their work, another generation of German scientists managed to build a large plant at the Badische Soda works in Mannheim which was making 300 tons of mustard oil a month when the first rounds were fired in anger.

Two 'blinds' (unexploded shells) were found at Ypres when daylight returned on 13 July. Both were marked with a yellow cross. One was sent immediately to London and the other examined at the Central Laboratory at St Omer.

Credit for finding the first shells is given to Major G.W. Monier-Williams, commanding a company in the Special Brigade, whose other claim to fame was that he was an authority on figure skating!

Credit for identifying the contents of the yellow cross projectiles is not so clear-cut.

The indefatigable Foulkes, Lieutenant-Colonel Hartley, the chemist, and Captain Claude Douglas, of the RAMC, a physiologist, were soon on the spot. According to Foulkes, though the new agent had not been identified by analysis, 'its compostion was . . . surmised'. A cautionary signal was sent out to each of the five British Army Commanders on the 14th and on the 16th a circular letter spelled out symptoms and effects and the cause of the casualties.

According to the *Official History* it took a 'few days' to identify the gas.

Another account is more interesting. It states that it was three weeks before the Army knew for certain that it was dealing with BB-dichlor-ethyl-sulphide, though its suitability as a shell filling had been suggested by an officer of the Anti-Gas Department in London some eighteen months previously, a Lieutentant Dudley. The Department, set up initially by Colonel William Horrocks, had been taken over by Professor E.H. Starling, by then a major in the Medical Corps, at the end of 1915. The Trench Warfare Committee, the high-level body responsible for such things, had been informed but nothing had been done. French and German scientists had looked at the potential of mustard gas[1] about the same time. At first Berlin did not react, but later had second thoughts.

Few things underline more clearly the damage inherent in carrying secrecy to the stage where it becomes counter-productive. While the Staff in one quarter was trying to identify the new threat a telegram to another quarter in London could have produced the right answer immediately. The Anti-Gas Department had it. Later Major Starling openly condemned the flaws in the system, was promoted to lieutenant-colonel and sent to Salonika as chemical adviser to the expeditionary force there. Realising he was wasting his time and refusing to be flattered by his newly-conferred rank, he reverted to civilian status and went to Italy where he performed vital work.

Batteries of 77mm and 105mm Krupp cannon continued to hurl Yellow Cross shells into the Salient. The French, British and Americans between them could hardly have filled a tin hat with mustard gas.

For Ludendorff the introduction of mustard gas to the battlefield was impeccably timed. The British had left no one in any doubt of their plans. Vast dumps of shells, stacks of stretchers, new camps, hospitals, railways, aerodromes – and gossip – filled the rear areas. Surprise, essential to the initial success at Arras and Messines, had been abandoned at Ypres.

Lieutenant Blunden: 'From Poperinghe forward the place was like a circus ground on the eve of a benefit.'

Captain Hubert Essame, of the 2nd Northamptonshire Regiment, whose unit was ordered into the Salient for a period of 'familiarization' before the big day:

'Signs of preparation for the attack were everywhere . . . east of the city the Germans held all the high ground and had perfect observation from both front and flanks. Movement in daylight, except by individuals, was impossible. Even a single man would attract a salvo. The low-lying fields were littered with the debris of two and a half years' fighting – destroyed wagons, blasted trees and heaps of rubble. The bodies of men and horses stuck up out of the mud.'

[1] Fries and West

The Northants, having 'familiarized' themselves, went into reserve in the massive ramparts but the 'shellfire was even worse here than in the forward rear'. At night parties emerged to carry ammunition up plank roads beyond the Menin and Lille Gates. The stink of decomposing horses and mules was overpowering and on each trip the infantry suffered casualties from shrapnel and 5.9s.

Sir Douglas Haig's reasons for attacking at Ypres have been the subject of much discussion. From his diary, however, it is clear that he wished to drive up the Belgian coast in order to eliminate U-boat bases there. (Admiral Jellicoe, the First Lord, had warned in Cabinet in June that if merchant losses continued at the current rate the war could not be continued.) Haig also thought it necessary to prevent the Germans concentrating against the French, still shaken by events on the Aisne.

In addition, he believed that any easing of Allied pressure in the West would revive German hopes and give them time to restock with arms and ammunition. In a detailed appendix to a memorandum outlining his views to the War Cabinet he stated that German manpower reserves were extremely low.

Robertson, as CIGS, had figures which contradicted Haig's assessment, but persuaded Sir Douglas not to submit the appendix, a most reprehensible act on the part of the Government's chief military adviser. Nevertheless Haig could not help blurting out at a meeting of the War Cabinet that he thought Germany was within six months of exhaustion, but only if intense fighting continued. He caused the Cabinet to think again. Lloyd George wanted 'no more Sommes'. There was talk of standing on the defensive until the Americans realized their potential and of sending big guns to help the Italians. All came to nothing, but not until 21 July did Haig receive official approval of his plan. He complained bitterly to Robertson of the absurd behaviour of the Cabinet in delaying their consent when an artillery battle had been raging for a fortnight. The original 'Z' day had been the 25th.

As late as the 29th Haig was writing to Lord Derby, the War Minister, of the 'desperate fight' to master the German guns.

The batteries of General Sixt von Armin's Fourth Army, especially those on the Gheluvelt plateau south-east of Ypres, bellowed a resolute defiance. British intelligence put the number of enemy guns at 1,500. Gough's Fifth Army had deployed 800 more than this – and was to be supported by Plumer's Second Army in subsidiary operations on the right and the French First Army under General

Anthoine on the left. Despite confident statements by GHQ's artillery adviser, General Sir Noel Birch, that the British were getting the 'upper hand', the enemy fire increased noticeably. After the Second Battle of Ypres nature had made some attempt to repair the ravages of the howitzers. Splintered woods had made secondary growth and peasants had even returned cautiously to some fields. As July passed, however, new large shell holes multiplied in the pasture land on the approaches to the city. Every night Yellow Cross shells flopped among their noisier brethren to belch out their corrosive contents.

Casualties on 12 July were put at 2,134, mostly in the 15th Division. Ninety of them eventually died and more than three-quarters of the total had to be evacuated to the rear.

Within three days of the first Yellow Cross 'blind' being recovered Foulkes had sent a complete description of the new shell, and suggestions for protection against it, to the five British Army Commanders. But the medical authorities still had to work out the correct method of handling casualties. Immediately after the 15th Division's ordeal the RAMC had been talking about the new 'mustard oil *lachrymator*' and suggesting that most men would return to duty within a fortnight. Second thoughts occurred as medical evidence accumulated.

On the nights of 20 and 28 July Armentières and Nieuport were doused with Yellow Cross. Nearly 6,000 soldiers had to be sent to hospitals outside the battle area: with an offensive imminent, casualty clearing stations could not be allowed to fill up with gas patients. An additional 675 civilians became victims at Armentières. The death toll, especially among the older citizens, was high and soon approached ninety.

British gas operations also increased as Z-day drew nearer. Four thousand Livens projectors were discharged by Special Companies on the nights of the 13th and 20th, smothering selected targets up to 1,500 yards behind the enemy forward line. This, however, had been only lightly manned for days. On the front of the Guards Division near Boesinghe the Germans had pulled back deliberately. The Fourth Army's Chief of Staff, Colonel von Lossberg, had a high reputation for directing defensive operations.

Large-scale aerial battles involving scores of fighters took place over Ypres as the tempo increased. A gradual assertion of Allied flying supremacy could not, however, block the view of the German observers in the concrete pillboxes on the high ground.

From 28 July the British concentrated against the enemy batteries using a large variety of gas shell, the contents including phosgene, chloropicrin and another lung irritant, stannic chloride. From midnight on the 30th the artillery had fired gas shells at all known opposing gun positions. Sir Douglas Haig recorded in his diary that the Fifth Army used 80,000.[1] At 3.50 am on the 31st elements of fourteen British and two French divisions advanced. The 'creeping barrage', a curtain of thunder and flame, flayed the ground before them.

It was unfortunate for the British that mustard gas decomposed very slowly in water. Rain set in on the afternoon of 31 July and continued for four days and nights. The drainage system collapsed completely under the weight of shell and the duck ponds fashioned by the howitzers filled rapidly. A swamp began to form. In most places the Fifth Army had taken only the first of four objectives set for Z-day and the depth of the conquered ground dwindled sharply as the line neared the Gheluvelt plateau. Most of the tanks which attacked along the front in small groups had stuck in the mud or been knocked out (seventy-seven out of 117 became non-runners on Z-day). The German gunners applied themselves zealously to making life as difficult as possible for the occupants of the sodden salient.

One 'blind' fired from Gheluvelt was found to be more interesting than most. It was marked with a blue cross. A probe into the innards revealed a glass bottle in a powerful charge of high explosive. Inside was a white compound derived from arsenic-diphenyl chlorarsine, which in its pure form is a solid. Subjected to the heat of the explosion the compound turned into an irritant 'smoke' composed of small particles,[2] some of them liquid, like cigarette smoke, and some solid.

Its effect on soldiers was to cause, in mild cases, sneezing, with additional complications such as burning sensations in throat and lungs, aching gums and a general feeling of misery, according to the amount inhaled. Occasionally some men seemed to lose their reason when gassed with Blue Cross. Though toxic, in practice fatalities were almost unknown. It took, however, up to twenty-four hours for victims to recover from a feeling of lassitude, a condition not best suited to inspire the defence of a trench. It was deduced that Blue Cross had been the unknown quantity used in the attack on the Nieuport bridgehead.

The Germans now had a full range of gas shell to apply as tactical

---

[1] See Appendix C for typical counter battery 'shoot'.
[2] Fortunately for the British not small enough to be fully effective. Vapourised correctly, the chemical was devastating.

conditions demanded. Broadly speaking, the ammunition stock could be divided into four types – those which could kill and those with a high nuisance value (toxic and lachrymators); and those which dispersed quickly and those which lingered (non-persistent and persistent).

During the Third Battle of Ypres the Germans could fire any mixture of these projectiles to hinder and harass their opponents. A colour guide made it easy for the gunners to load what was required.

A battery commander supporting Group Wytschaete, facing the British astride the Menin Road, might be expected to be familiar with the following range of markings:

Code	Effect	Technical name
White B or BM Black or Green T	Tear inducing	Lachrymator
Blue Cross	Sneezing/Irritant/ Depressant	Sternutator
White C White D Green Cross Green Cross 1	Choking/Suffocating	Acute lung irritant
Yellow cross	Blistering	Vesicant

The persistency of mustard gas was exploited to the full at Ypres. If it did not splash or affect someone the moment it landed it still lurked there, a menace for days. While the Germans could not actually flood the Salient with the liquid – their ammunition supply was limited – they did the next best thing. Shell after shell descended without the firers having to worry very much where they fell as long as it was behind the British line.

Stories of the powers of Yellow Cross spread quickly. Private Frank Richards, then serving at Arras:

'The worst yarn of all was that, even if a man did not inhale it, it would penetrate his clothes and burn certain parts of his body and leave him in the same state as a man in the last stages of venereal disease. The majority of the men believed this yarn and several lectures were given to reassure them that it was all bunkum.'

Later evidence showed that not all the yarns were as exaggerated as had been made out. Richards again:

'Our new box respirators were proof against it. I have seen cases where it burned through the gas mask and a few days later the men were temporarily blind, but in each case they did not inhale it. It would burn through the clothes and nasty blisters would break out. . . . If an area had been shelled with these shells, it was never safe to use a shell-hole as a latrine. . . . The gas would hang around . . . for a day or two.'

Kilted regiments were particularly vulnerable and new methods of cleaning stained clothing had to be devised. A man whose tunic was splashed by mustard gas or who leaned against the edge of a contaminated trench might walk away unaware that he was inhaling evaporating fumes. As the whole area smelled like an overflowing midden the slight odour could pass unnoticed. Even a small dose could inflict severe damage to throat and lungs.

Fortunately, as Richards says, the small box respirator gave adequate protection and the decision to retain the mouth valve and nose clip, uncomfortable though they were, proved correct. The British maskers had also scored another victory over the German gassers. After experiencing problems with stannic chloride from our own gas shells, the need for a filter to counter tiny particles of solids was recognized. One was added to the small box respirator's chemical container and incorporated in later models. Protection against Blue Cross had been anticipated.

Once the enemy had examined captured British respirators he revised his tactics. Instructions were given to fire Blue Cross shells at the beginning of a bombardment (the first salvoes being generally recognized as the most effective), so that sneezing would prevent men adjusting their masks. Green Cross shells could then be fired to spread their poisonous contents among troops who had been caught off guard. Mustard gas shells were normally 'concealed' in a barrage of noisier projectiles. All these and other niceties awaited the burdened figures in soiled khaki making their way nightly past the smashed Cloth Hall in Ypres, or slithering over duckboard tracks on their way to occupy some captured pillbox with a foot of water covering the floor. They could look forward to little else. All hopes of a quick breakthrough had vanished.

Sir Hubert Gough: 'When it came to the advance of the infantry . . . across the waterlogged shell holes movement was so slow and so fatiguing that only the shortest advances could be contemplated. In consequence I . . . advised that the attack should now be abandoned.'

That was early in August. Haig, who had earlier spoken of stopping the offensive if it was held up, insisted that it should go on.

Gas casualties continued to rise. They reached 14,000 in the three weeks after the introduction of Yellow Cross. By contemporary standards the death roll was low – about 500 – but the trend was serious; for the week ending 11 August there were 1,573 casualties;

during that of the 18th the figure rose to 1,890; on the 25th the reckoning for seven days was 1,263, and there was no relief in sight.

Haig was kept fully informed of the situation and on 10 August wrote indignantly to the War Office to complain that the Germans had forestalled the Allies by using 'a chemical substance which had proved to be of great military value'.

He requested that energetic action be taken to remedy the matter.

The letter brought the War Minister, Lord Derby, and Mr Churchill, Munitions Minister, to France. As a result the first inter-Allied gas conference was held in Paris on 16 September. (The previous week's figures for British Yellow Cross casualties had exceeded the 2,000 mark).

The delegates included Americans, Belgians, British, Italians and French. The latter, who had been immediately informed of the new development, were already busy with research into what they called 'Yperite'. A certain Commandant Peyron had spent fourteen minutes in a gas chamber at Hesdin on 23 July, wearing the French M2 mask, but with head and forearms (one of which was covered with vaseline) bare. He endured what was thought to be a low concentration of vapourised mustard gas.[1] Though he emerged cheerfully from his ordeal the vesicant took effect within four hours. Peyron did not recover for almost three months and suffered considerable pain including severe blistering of the genitalia. It is comforting to record that the M2 mask protected his lungs and eyes and that after an initial spell of sickness his digestion, appetite and organs were unimpaired.

The great problem for the Allies was to find a means of producing mustard gas for use against the Germans. By dint of great effort they had managed to expand their home industries to provide supplies of chlorine, phosgene and other agents, but the newcomer was a much more complicated challenge. The Meyer formula was known but was thought to be too academic to be adapted to mass production techniques.

Some of the finest brains in Britain worked on the problem, among them Professor William Pope, 47-year-old Professor of Chemistry at Cambridge, and his former research assistant, Charles Gibson, a Manchester Grammar School pupil who had distinguished himself at Oxford. Dr Arthur Green, 57, Head of Applied Chemistry at Leeds, was another. Dr Green was an expert on dyestuffs. The savants applied themselves to the study of Guthrie's original experiments.

At the Ministry of Munitions Churchill set up a special department

[1] Obtained from enemy 'blinds'.

and in October Major-General Thuillier left the 15th Division to become, reluctantly, Controller of Chemical Warfare.

The French, who already had a Directeur du Materiel Chemique de Guerre, called in leading scientists to find a method of producing mustard gas, as did the Americans. All said the same. There was no short cut. The troops would have to learn to live with the enemy's Yellow Cross.

'The effect of the explosion of such a shell was that its contents were spread partly as vapour and partly as a fine spray which was distributed more or less evenly over a radius of some twenty yards. When the spray fell to the ground it remained for a long time in the contaminated area, only slowly being hydrolyzed (destroyed by water) or evaporating.

'In fact on dry soil which was not exposed to direct sunlight, the contamination might persist for many days and continue to form a source of danger to troops advancing over that area.'

Woods and deep trenches were likely to remain dangerous for long periods.

At Ypres in 1917 the woods disappeared, leaving only blackened stumps to mark their passing. Deep trenches were rarely encountered because of the swampy conditions. The painfully-slow expansion of the salient, in which gains were measured in hundreds of yards over many weeks, meant that the slough was doused again and again with Yellow Cross.

An unexpected situation arose in which Gough, the dashing cavalryman, urged Haig to call off the offensive, while Plumer, the veteran foot soldier, continued to carry out Sir Douglas's orders to the letter. More and more the responsibility for the battle passed to the British Second Army. Haig was convinced that he was wearing out the enemy and Ludendorff in his *Memoirs* talks of the 'heavy strain' on the troops in the West.

'In spite of all the concrete protection [pill boxes of all shapes and sizes studded the ground under attack] they seemed more or less powerless under the enormous weight of the enemy's artillery.'

The wearing-out process worked both ways, however, and as division after division was drawn to Flanders, the British infantry took tremendous punishment. Mustard gas and Blue Cross constantly eroded the efficiency and sapped the strength of the attackers. The need for good 'gas discipline' was stronger than ever. Canadian gunners supporting an attack on Hill 70 at Loos on 16 August tried to ignore Yellow Cross when they first came across it. Because their rate of fire dropped when the eye-pieces of their respirators misted up, they took them off. They remained in action during the night, but infantry, marching back at dawn, reported seeing long rows of gunners writhing in agony from the effects of Yellow Cross.

Heavy concentrations of Blue Cross and Green Cross were also used increasingly in offensive operations.

On 1 September near Riga a two-and-a-half-hour gas bombardment, helped by a heavy mist, heralded a German assault on the Dvina. Their artillery silenced, the Russian infantry panicked and fled.

At Caporetto on 24 October the Austrians and Germans treated the Italians, still desperately short of heavy guns, to a similar gas deluge[1], inflicting heavy casualties and opening up a corridor through which the assault divisions crashed. The Italian mask was not up to the job.

On both sides gas had now became a critical factor. The French made good use of it at Verdun on 20 August when they launched an attack which, in five days' fighting, recaptured valuable observation points lost in earlier battles. Ludendorff correctly deduced that the French army was giving notice that it was 'once more capable of the offensive.'

---

[1] The Germans also made a projector attack, firing the drums from obsolete 180cm mortars.

CHAPTER 15

Just a Line to Say . . .

Huddled in quarry workings near the farm of Les Bovettes on the Chemin des Dames, Private Ludwig Pauquet wrote to his family saying that he hoped to get leave soon. It was impossible at that moment, however, as the French were blasting the area with shells of every calibre and had been for some days. The front line was only a row of craters, the second was half-filled-in and he and his comrades of the 20th Infantry Regiment were occupying a number of large caves. One of these had been partly blown in and forty men had been crushed to death under falling stone. Everyone wanted the enemy to attack so the shelling would cease. The 20th was a Berlin regiment (3rd Brandenburg) and its men were confident of giving their opponents a bloody nose. Private Pauquet had no intention of being taken prisoner just a short time before he was due to leave. What he could do with, however, was some rest. Unfortunately 'those who try to sleep are soon roused by the sentry's shout of "Gas alert". It is the same every night. You put on your mask and make a fire in the cave so the poison doesn't enter too far.'

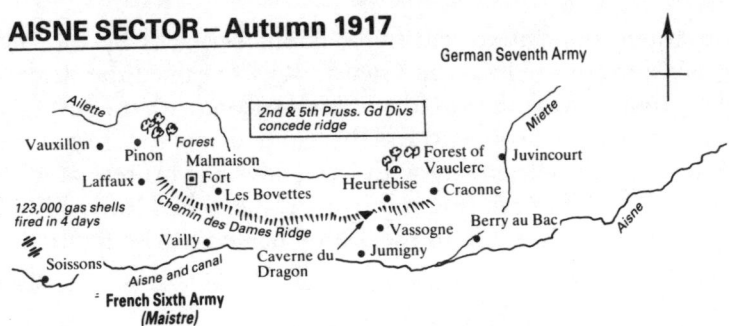

AISNE SECTOR – Autumn 1917

As for being gassed: 'Your eyes stream, you cough, your chest seems about to burst and you can't get your breath. Only one ration party has been able to get through the shelling and the gas. Even the lieutenant dare not leave the cave.'

The regimental postman also found his rounds too hazardous to make a regular collection. Pauquet put the letter in his pocket to give to him when the tempest abated.

The storm continued pitilessly. General Paul André Marie Maistre, whose Sixth Army was to carry out the attack, heartily approved of the preparation. An infantryman himself (he had joined the 60th Regiment in 1879), Maistre wrote on 9 September:

'The Chemin des Dames has just as bad a reputation in the country as with the troops. Another failure in this region would be disastrous. We must be certain of success and the first essential is to have a crushing superiority in artillery.'

Pétain had sent him 1,600 heavy guns including 105 super-heavies with calibres up to 17 inches, plus 120,000 tons of ammunition.

In an effort to forestall the attack the Germans concentrated 250 batteries and increased the allocation of gas shell, mainly Yellow Cross. From seventy-seven casualties on 13 October the toll rose steadily until on the 21st alone there were 1,000 victims in the Sixth Army. The French stepped up their fire just before the attack. They had one gun for every six yards of front.

Like Pauquet and his comrades in the 20th Prussian Infantry Regiment, the 20th Chasseurs à Pied were also finding sleep impossible. Many of them passed their time carrying gas shells for the gunners. In four days 123,000 poison and tear-gas shells were fired into the ravines and quarries.

J-Day[1] was fixed for 23 October, zero hour for 5.45 a.m. An intercepted radio message made it clear that the German Seventh Army was expecting the assault to begin at 5.30 when it intended to bombard likely assembly positions. Maistre changed the zero hour to 5.15.

Despite tough opposition and fierce counter-attacks by the 2nd and 5th Divisions of the Prussian Guard, Maistre gained the success he sought. His men took the old fort of Malmaison, with the strongly held cluster of quarries around it, and then surged over the crest of the Chemin des Dames. The enemy withdrew, covering his retreat with bursts of gas shell. The 65th Infantry lost 260 men, the 136th had 150 casualties and there were 120 in the 48th Chasseurs. The Ravin des

[1] From the French *Jour*, equivalent to modern D-Day and British Z Day of the Great War.

Grelines was flooded with gas. By the beginning of November the Germans had pulled back, leaving the blood-soaked Californie Plateau and other places of evil memory in the hands of their opponents.

The comparatively cheap success of the French at Verdun and the Chemin des Dames was due to the setting of limited objectives within the resources available. At Verdun 60,000 gunners supported 50,000 infantry; on the notorious ridge the heavy mortars – 'crapouillots' – tore the barbed wire to shreds and high explosive and gas penned the Prussian Guard in its bunkers and the deep creutes. Machine guns were concentrated in batteries; one of eighty mitrailleuses fired 120,000 cartridges round the clock for four days and for a finale on J-Day lashed its objective with 800,000 bullets. German ration parties found it impossible to reach the forward troops. Pauquet and his comrades went hungry and thirsty.

By the time the assault was delivered some Germans were waiting, haversacks packed, ready to go into captivity. Others died at their machine guns. The artillery continued to exact its toll.

Gabriel Chevallier,[1] serving as a runner with the 163rd Infantry Regiment, set off into the night with fifteen other agents de liaison, on being relieved. Though they had waited for a lull in the shelling it intensified while they were making their way past a notorious hot spot, La Ferme mal batie.

After surviving a fierce bombardment they thought themselves almost safe when:

'Zzziou-flac . . .Zzziou-flac . . .Zzziou-zzziou-flac-flac . . . Gas shells arrive and the 150s seem to return as well. We set off again. The road drops slightly. The lower end is covered in a menacing mist which smells unpleasant. Masks on!'

The march became difficult, the eye pieces obscured by sweat and a warm thin air difficult to breathe. The pace began to slow.

'Vououououou . . . the explosions begin again all round us. We tear off our masks and run for it, breathing in the poisonous fog.'

Fortunately the dip in which the gas lay was soon crossed and the shell fire diminished. The party lost one dead and one was slightly wounded. Crouching behind an earth bank they heard the explosions die away and laughed despite themselves.

The German withdrawal from the Chemin des Dames was in itself a lesson in tactics. Unlike Hitler's commanders, the Kaiser's generals could and did exercise considerable responsibility. If a position became too hot to hold they could pull back without having to

[1] Author of Clochmerle and many other books.

explain, as did their successors, a breach of a 'Führer Order'.

Ludendorff, who said that 'one division succumbed ... to an exceptionally heavy gas bombardment' added: 'In itself it was of no consequence whether we stood north or south of the Ailette [a stream running at the foot of the ridge] but having fought all summer for possession of the Chemin des Dames it was very difficult to order it to be given up. To hold on, however, would only have involved continuous wastage.'

With their experience of the German strategic retirement in the spring when the countryside had been infested with booby traps, the French followed up cautiously and examined the abandoned *creutes* with great care.

In one deep dry cave mines were found at the bottom of two flights of wooden stairs. Sappers dismantled them and a company of the 236th Regiment moved in. On 4 November something exploded and the *creute* filled with gas. It was so thick that ordinary masks were useless and rescuers had to call in artillerymen with sophisticated Tissot apparatus to help. One by one they brought out eighteen bodies and a live corporal who, without a word, ran straight to the aid post where he collapsed and died. The first mines had been decoys. Gas bombs with time fuses had been hidden in the roof of the cave. They cost the lives of thirty-eight young men. The Chemin des Dames might be French once more but it was still living up to its sinister reputation and would continue to do so. It had, however, done with – and done for – Ludwig Pauquet. His letter was collected by a French soldier searching corpses for Intelligence material.

While war correspondents wrote colourful accounts of the battle between the Blue Devils (the Chasseurs Alpins had played a leading part on the Chemin des Dames) and the Grey Wolves, the British, Canadians and Australians were floundering through the marshy approaches to the Houthulst Forest and Passchendaele's sodden brickdust. The landscape had begun to change soon after the battle began but men who had been pulled out to refit in August could not believe their eyes when they returned in late autumn.

Nearly all traces of buildings other than pillboxes had vanished. Wrecked tanks, shattered transport and dead men, mules and horses protruded from the mud which was gradually swallowing them. The flourishing woods of 1914 had been completely erased as if a maniac had run over the ground with a gigantic lawnmower, having set the blades at their lowest pitch. Both sides now manned lines of shell holes. Trenches had disappeared. The barbed wire covering the original enemy lines had for the most part been reduced to shreds, but determined German working parties were still stringing thick new entanglements which could produce nasty shocks.

The British main line of resistance now lay 800 yards or so behind the outposts. The enemy sheltered in concrete bunkers and tried to guess when the assault would begin.

General Essame: 'The morning artillery barrage had become a matter of habit for both armies, and this . . . had the advantage that we could make a good guess where the German counter-barrage would fall and could fix our assembly positions accordingly. When, however, we intended a serious attack the addition of a machine gun barrage relieved the enemy of any uncertainty of our intentions.'

The German defenders had to determine the appropriate moment to leave cover. It was a matter of life or death whether or not they could scramble into an adjacent crater and set up their machine guns before their opponents were on them.

To subdue the stubborn Fourth Army the British had to haul their 18-pounders and 4.5 inch howitzers to within range of the block-houses. This meant crossing a flooded stream which ran through the middle of the battlefield, the 'valley' of the Steenbeek. From mid-October until the offensive was finally halted in the second week of November, this dismal vale received nightly attention from German gunners well instructed in the latest tactics.

'Sneezing gas . . . which made it difficult to keep on the respirators was followed by mustard gas . . . which blistered the body and damaged the throat and eyes. Although only a few deaths were caused, some thousands of men of the infantry in support and reserve positions, of the artillery and of the working parties were disabled during this period.

'Large areas . . . including battery positions and bivouacs, became saturated with mustard oil and could not be reoccupied for some time.'

As early as 23 July 'in consequence of a steady rain of gas shells, gas masks at the batteries had to be worn for six hours' in the 29th Division. 'Mustard gas could hang about dugouts for days.'

Thanks to prodigious efforts, ammunition columns using pack mules kept the British field guns in action, but at a heavy price.

The artillery of the 63rd (Royal Naval) Division supported some of the final attacks at Passchendaele after their own infantry battalions had been withdrawn.

'Only by keeping one third of the gunners at Brigade Headquarters and another third at the wagon lines had sufficient officers and men been kept alive to carry on. The casualties of the two artillery brigades in this period were heavier proportionately than those of the infantry in the most disastrous battle of the war.'

Some idea of the damage done by enemy counter-battery work may be gauged from the losses of the 74th Brigade, Royal Artillery, which supported the Guards Division. During 'Third Ypres' forty-nine guns were put out of action of which thirty-three were 'write-offs'.

By a miracle of perseverance Passchendaele's squalid acres fell to the Canadian Corps on 10 November. Freezing rain scoured the earth. So did German shells. The struggle for gun supremacy, begun in mid-July, had never been settled. Haig called a halt.

The British *Official History* gives the total casualties for the Third Battle of Ypres as 244,897. That was from 31 July to 12 November when the battle was deemed to have closed. Total known gas casualties, not counting choking or blistered men who simply disappeared under the slime or into the depths of a waterlogged shell hole, were nearly 40,000 (counting from the first Yellow Cross bombardment on 12 July).

Ten days after Passchendaele had fallen Haig attacked again further south. On 20 November the Third Army, with 476 tanks under command, swept over the Hindenburg Line covering the approaches to Cambrai, taking 6,000 prisoners and scores of field guns and howitzers. To the disappointment of the Army's Commander, General the Hon Sir Julian Byng[1], the four mounted divisions concentrated behind the lines were unable to exploit the initial success. By evening the cavalry brigades were coming back to water their horses. Their opportunity had vanished.

At this point Sir Douglas Haig could have broken off the battle, an option he had kept open because of a shortage of troops and pressures in Italy. He chose, however, to fight on with the aim of securing Bourlon Wood, a dominating rounded hill still wearing its russet autumn finery. The cavalry remained in the area in hopes.

The battle degenerated into a familiar pattern, with the British doing their best to cram themselves into an excellent artillery target. Tank action on a grand scale was no longer possible. Apart from the wear and tear on tracks and engines the crews were exhausted.

A handful of machines restored to combat condition were knocked out in the tangled rides or simply disappeared. A number even penetrated Bourlon village but not many came back. The wood soaked up men and material like a great sponge. The 40th Division, the last of the Kitchener volunteer formations to reach France (it

[1] Sir Julian, seventh son of the Earl of Strafford, had joined the 10th Hussars in 1883.

arrived in the spring of 1916), was strong in numbers and highly experienced in trench warfare. Its battalions, which had been spared the Passchendaele ordeal, fought furiously, lost heavily and were withdrawn. Another attempt was ordered.

The 62nd Division of West Riding Territorials had been involved in a disastrous attempt on the Hindenburg Line at Bullecourt, south of Arras, in the spring but its morale was high after its part in the successful assault on 20 November. Reorganized, it went into the attack again at Bourlon but despite all efforts was stopped by a surfeit of machine guns. A final attempt to seize and consolidate village and wood was scheduled for the 27th despite opposition from some of those required to do the seizing.

On the 26th Major-General Sir Geoffrey Feilding, of the Guards Division, whose troops were committed to clearing Bourlon's lower slopes and the village of Fontaine on the Cambrai road, requested a meeting with the Corps Commander to explain his objections. Sir Charles Woollcombe, responsible for the operation, found himself in an unenviable position. Haig now had little confidence in him and had urged Byng to take a personal grip on the battle. Woollcombe was not made any happier when both his superiors joined the meeting. Sir Douglas departed after making it clear that he could see nothing wrong in one last thrust before winter but left the assembled generals to argue among themselves. Feilding produced his common-sense views in writing – but Byng had the last word. The attack was made the next day and failed as forecast. Sixty-one-year-old Woollcombe, who had joined the Army in 1876 and spent many years in India, was left in little doubt about who was to blame. Feilding, ten years younger, was on firmer ground. The Guards Division was consistently well led throughout the war and his opinion counted even though it might be critical, if not tart.

The Guards Commander took the view that the whole Cambrai operation was a limited one without strategic objectives.

'Had the British Commander-in-Chief, therefore, decided to break off the engagement after the first day's fighting and drawn back his line along the main Flesquières ridge (short of Bourlon), it would have been a perfectly justifiable tactical move which most practical soldiers with experience in the war could have commended – which no one in his senses could have described as a "pottering game of grignotage".'

The 'pottering' phrase is from a defence of Haig's generalship by a former member of his staff. 'Grignotage' comes from the French 'grignoter', to nibble or gnaw.

As far as the British were concerned gas did not play a major part in the opening phase at Cambrai, though some heavy projector attacks were made on the flanks: 1,320 Livens drums were fired into Honnecourt Wood and a total of 1,800 in the Bullecourt sector. Blazing oil drums and smokescreens were also 'projected' in diversionary operations.

On the German side there was some gas shelling of Bourlon Wood to start with but the fighting inside it was so violent and confused that they were able to step it up only gradually. This they did.

When the 47th Division took over the wood's defences on 28 November elements of seven British battalions were found there with more than forty machine guns. Gas shell was arriving in such profusion that the General, Sir George Gorringe, decided to thin out the number of troops on the ground simply to avoid casualties. A former Royal Engineer who had served on Kitchener's staff at Omdurman and in South Africa, Sir George had been severely wounded earlier in the war. His reduction of the garrison at Bourlon was a shrewd move. Though he did not know it, the gas was being fired in preparation for a German riposte.

The German counter-attack on 30 November took Byng completely by surprise, though one of his Corps Commanders, Lieutenant-General Sir Thomas Snow, an ex-infantryman and Zulu War veteran, did his best to alert Third Army headquarters. A barrage intensified slowly, leaving doubts about its purpose until the stormtroops advanced at 7 am. Field guns firing on Bourlon had been allocated 16,000 gas shells.

Casualties caused by a Green Cross-Blue Cross barrage mounted. The 141st Brigade was reduced to a composite battalion: in one of its units, the 1st/19th London Regiment, only seventy men were unaffected. The brigade machine gun company was put out of action. During the night two battalions of the 59th Division, the 2nd/6th North Staffordshire and the 2nd/6th South Staffordshire, had so many men gassed that they had to be relieved, along with the brigade mortar company. The Bourlon front held, nevertheless, though to the south the enemy scored a success almost equal to that of the British on 20 November, taking large numbers of guns and prisoners. As late as 3 December Lieutenant-General Otto von Moser, whose group of storm divisions was opposite Bourlon, ordered the wood to be shelled and gassed throughout the night. By this time, however, both sides were exhausted. The British successfully withdrew from the bastion which had cost them so dearly and took up a line with the village of Flesquières forming the 'nose' of a pronounced salient. It seemed to matter little as the snows came. Caesar, it seemed, really was going into winter quarters.

In the windswept huts on Porton Down typewriters rattled far into the night as clerks prepared Lieutentant-Colonel Crossley's precise reports: by the end of the war they were to reach a total of 1,189. How he found time to write them, join in field trials and visit France is worth a study in itself. There were few places that mattered across the Channel that he had not visited, few men of scientific significance he did not know.

Crossley saw Professor Urbain experimenting with phosgene in his laboratory in the Sorbonne, Professor Bernard up to something else in the Institut Pasteur and Professor Moureu working on tear agents at the École de Pharmacie. He appeared on the factory floor of the Triquet works where shells were lined with glass, made himself at home on the ranges at Vincennes and inspected chlorine cylinder filling at a site built 'for the duration' at Pont de Clais, near Grenoble.

The French said they weren't kept in the picture with regard to British CW/shell developments. He would see to it.

Did he know they had captured German documents which stated that Livens drums did not always open properly and that sometimes phosgene was 'left behind'? He would talk to Livens about improving the burster charge.

Then there was Commandant Nicolardot who had given him copies of two documents:

1. The use of ammonia and its compounds in war;
2. The study of asphyxiating and other gases, of stinking, corrosive and incendiary substances made *previous to the war* in the laboratory of the Technical Section of Artillery.

'The latter,' Crossley wrote,[1] 'is an extremely interesting document, especially from a historical point of view and also that of our present knowledge of the possibilities of the use of chemical materials in war.

'I would point out that in 1900 Commandant Nicolardot suggested to the French authorities that he considered it possible, even probable that the Germans were going to make use of chlorine and bromine in warfare ... but he was not allowed to put this suggestion in his report. Further, he suggested certain protective measures against the use of these substances, among which was a mask containing sodium hyposulphite.

[1] PRO WO 142/209

'In 1905–6 a study of the subject was made and chemical substances which were thought to be of use in war were divided into the following five classes –
(a) asphyxiating gases ⎫ prohibited by the Hague
(b) deleterious gases ⎭ Convention

(c) corrosive substances⎤ not prohibited by the Hague
(d) stinking substances ⎬ Convention
(e) incendiary sub-⎦
stances

'In group (b) come chlorine, bromine, phosgene and HCN;[1] in group (c) cantharides, pepper, ethyl bromocetate (*bromo acetone?*), ethyl-iodoacetate and chloropicrin. In class (e) the first subject mentioned is thermit.'

It was a pity that more notice was not taken of the clairvoyant Nicolardot; but his superiors, the general staff, were blinded not by tear gas but the flash of bayonets. They had eyes only for 'Rosalie'[2].

---

[1] Prussic acid
[2] French novelists' name for the bayonet

CHAPTER 16

Fifty Cents Cheaper

General Pershing's sense of urgency did not always strike a sympathetic chord in Washington.

'Send at once a chemical laboratory, complete equipment and personnel, including physiological and pathological sections, for extensive investigations of gases and powders', he cabled towards the end of September, 1917.

The lab and its staff were not dispatched until January, 1918.

The raising of a regiment of 'gas and flame' troops was authorized in August, 1917, and designated the 30th Engineers. An officer was appointed to raise and command it and recruits were found from among American chemistry graduates and students. The initial enthusiasm of the War Department soon waned, however, and in December of that year Pershing's headquarters were informed that the regiment would not be available until the spring due to lack of equipment. A firm reply went off, pointing out that the 'gas troops' were not supply units but essential to the fighting efficiency of the army. They were subsequently given increased priority for shipment to France.

In recruiting the regiment the authorities had emphasized the need for 'keen, red-blooded men who wanted to fight'. Until these warriors arrived in France the officers already there manfully shouldered the burden of creating a new service.

The Americans found that life with their Allies was not all sweetness and light. References to Lafayette and the War of Independence soon wore thin. Though happy to welcome thousands of able-bodied men to replace casualties of more than three years of war, the French were tired not only of the occupation of large areas by the Germans, but also of the territorial demands of their Allies.

The peasants of the Pas de Calais were convinced, for example, that the 'English' would never go home, a sentiment shared by a lot of British troops for different reasons. The Americans were surprised by the difficulties encountered when trying to do a simple thing like finding a suitable site for an experimental establishment.

'While the French were loading millions of shells at the edge of Paris, they appeared unwilling at first to have us establish a gas experimental field except in abandoned or inaccessible spots.'

The site finally agreed on, covering twenty square miles, had one boundary only three miles from Pershing's own headquarters.

The Americans asked for six expert glassblowers to be sent to the United States to demonstrate the technique of lining shell cases with glass. They were told this was impossible but the French would happily take workmen into their factories to show them how it was done. Fifty were asked for by the US Gas Service in France, but, despite urgent pleas, none arrived.

The Americans found themselves 'pig in the middle' in old arguments between the British and French. The former said the French Vincennite gas shell was next to useless. The French had nothing but contempt for the tear-inducing properties of chloropicrin. Colonel Fries had to be tactful when he pronounced against Vincennite.

Sometimes it was like punching air. One of the first units to arrive in France was the Overseas Repair Section of 134 officers and men of the Sanitary Corps, ready to establish a plant to maintain gas masks – there were no masks to repair and the chances of getting any looked slim.

The Americans, though critical of the discomfort which had to be endured when wearing the small box respirator, had no intention of putting their troops into the line with only the M2. They considered the French mask vulnerable to dense clouds such as those created by projector atacks, which the Germans sometimes attempted. An order for 75,000 British respirators to be delivered by the end of the year was declined in London where it was understood that the United States would be supplying a model of its own. Transatlantic cables hummed before supplies from the United Kingdom were ensured.

Efforts to get the first American brigade equipped with masks from the British base at Le Havre also ran into trouble. Though officers were sent to accompany the consignment, a railway van containing 4,000 respirators of the most common size vanished in the raging snowstorms that swept the North of France and was not seen again. (What became of the escorting officer is not clear.)

The deficiency was made up by the British Second Army which released masks which had been through the mill at Passchendaele and withdrawn for 'refurbishing'. The Americans washed and disinfected them thoroughly before re-issuing them with chemical containers replenished. Even when home-produced respirators began to arrive by the hundred thousand later in the summer they were found to be in need of adjustment before they could be sent up the line. The staff of a great depot established at Châteauroux worked up to sixteen hours a day to achieve this. Fortunately, whatever else the Americans may have lacked, enthusiasm was a commodity of which there was no shortage. In the USA the development of the Chemical Warfare Service was staggering. Near Long Island City the government-run Gas Defense Plant started its existence with thirteen officers and grew swiftly into an organization employing 12,000 workers, three-quarters of whom were women. Preference was given to hiring individuals with relatives serving in the American Expeditionary Force. Employees took pride in the fact that their masks were 50 cents cheaper than those produced under contract.

At Gunpowder Neck what had been a level plain with a large tree in the centre of it was quickly covered with buildings, cooling towers and workshops. The tree vanished and so did the good old name. It became Edgewood Arsenal – 3,400 acres of installations capable of making a variety of war gases. The products were transported by the Pennsylvania Railroad to loading berths on the Bush River not far from where it flowed into Chesapeake Bay.

Immense though this effort was, it was unlikely to take effect in France until the middle of 1918 and the question which had to be answered was where the front line was likely to be by then.

Spring, 1918, brought the Central Powers increased prospects of victory. The Russians had signed an armistice on 17 December, 1917 and peace negotiations were opened at Brest Litovsk. The strain of war on two fronts was over. Immediately battalions began to embark for the training grounds in Germany to prepare for the inevitable offensive on the Western Front. Only fit and militarily mature men under 35 were selected. Ten divisions a month could be moved to France. By the end of February it was estimated that the Germans would have 185 divisions west of the Rhine and that another fifteen would arrive before the end of May. For the first time since the beginning of the war the Allies would be outnumbered. In common with the French and the Germans, the British were reducing their infantry brigades from four to three battalions to maintain the number of divisions. More automatic weapons were to make up for the shortage of men. The Americans were expected to have eight outsize divisions in the field by the end of March and thirty-three by midsummer. They would be needed.

Haig had little doubt that the destruction of the British Army would be Ludendorff's prime objective. An interesting situation had arisen vis à vis the two men. Neither of them was short of experience in handling vast armies, but the Kaiser's First Quartermaster-General had spent nearly two years on the defensive on the Western Front, a task he had carried out with great success. Haig, promoted Field-Marshal in the last days of 1916, had been directing attacks for three years, offensives which often promised success but had always ended with heavy losses. With the exception of Cambrai, Sir Douglas had been able to draw on ample reserves since summer, 1916. Ludendorff had to switch his resources from one threatened spot to the other. In 1918 it was his turn to call the tune. The British could be certain that their opponent would make not only full use of his superiority in numbers but also his exclusive possession of mustard gas. Only in February, 1918, did Sir William Pope develop a means for practical production (still based on Guthrie's formula) and the building of manufacturing plants was going to take time. Ludendorff knew nothing either of this, or that the French were nearer to making mustard gas than the British. He felt confident of being able to keep promises to his troops that the Allies would not be able to produce their own Yellow Cross before Germany gained victory.

The British soldiers by this time had an intimate acquaintance with all forms of enemy gas. It sometimes seemed as if the very soil they were fighting for was turning against them. A platoon of the 18th London Regiment who washed in water from a shell hole suffered from streaming eyes, swollen faces and, if they tried to clean their teeth, burning gums. A Blue Cross shell had poisoned the water.

Blue Cross was also suspected of causing casualties among soldiers who made a fire with wood from a wrecked house. The timber had been stained by the contents of a shell and gas was released by the flames.[1]

A detachment manning a regimental aid post welcomed the warming sun on a cool spring morning and fell victims to the mustard gas which had been drawn from the polluted soil.

The constant flow of cases had forced the authorities to take further action and late in 1917 medical officers with at least some experience

---

[1] The troops had accidentally stumbled on the best way of liberating Blue Cross.

of handling Blue Cross, Yellow Cross and other gases, were posted to all casualty clearing stations.

It was not then generally appreciated how much depended on the fit of the small box respirator. After a spell at the front certain individuals could lose weight, become drawn and gaunt, thus altering the fit of the face mask. Furthermore the nuances of gas poisoning were not properly understood. This lack of knowledge was a serious handicap to the RAMC. 'Not yet Diagnosed' centres for doubtful or unconfirmed gas casualties were set up in each Army area. According to the Official History of the medical services:

'They were of great value in the handling of light cases whose retention in the army area was necessary and who only required a period of rest in a convalescent centre.'

Such centres were also needed to identify malingerers. Foulkes, in 1917, recommended that the wound stripe which had up to then been awarded to gas casualties be discontinued. What he described as 'sterner measures' had to be taken later when excessive casualties indicated breaches of gas discipline. Courts of inquiry were held where the ratio of cases to the estimated number of shells received exceeded the norm.

The disposal of the contaminated uniforms of mustard gas patients continued to present a problem. Where clothing was only slightly affected men were sometimes sent, wearing respirators, into chambers containing chlorine gas, which acted as a neutralizing agent. Otherwise their dress was burned.

Medical staff handling patients were required to wear masks and oiled leather gloves and aprons. The transport and reception of mustard gas casualties remained a problem to the end of hostilities, especially as open warfare developed.

Bath centres with ample supplies of hot water were needed where victims could wash themselves thoroughly.

Weapons, such as the guns in bombarded battery positions, had to be examined and tons of chloride of lime were provided to neutralize contaminated equipment.

One of the gas's many unpleasant features was its potency in very small quantities. Virtually invisible, it was not identifiable easily with the nose, and there were many ideas of what it smelled like. Sometimes it seemed to strike before its odour had been detected and there were conflicting opinions as to whether or not it destroyed the sense of smell. In small amounts, which resulted in cumulative damage in victims, it was almost impossible to recognise by judicious sniffing.

'Sensors' were said to have been first used by the Germans on captured trenches. Treated metal plates were lowered into them and if, after a few minutes, the plates turned from yellow to black, the soil was known to be contaminated. A similar device which turned red was later produced in the United States. Here is a contemporary American description of Yellow Cross:

'It produces no immediate discomfort. It has a considerable delay action. It burns the body inside or out, wherever there is moisture. Eyes, lungs and soft parts of the body are readily attacked. It lingers for two or three days in the warmest weather, while in cold damp weather it is dangerous for a week or ten days, and in still colder weather may be dangerous for a month or longer. . . . It is only slowly destroyed in earth, making digging around shell holes dangerous for weeks and months.'

Brigadier-General Foulkes dubbed the contents of the Yellow Cross shells HS – 'Hun Stuff'.

It was dangerous to take the slightest risk when there was any suspicion of mustard gas being present. Lieutenant Guy Chapman, who had served with the 13th Royal Fusiliers since they landed in France in July, 1915, omitted to put on his respirator when half-a-dozen Yellow Cross shells dropped around battalion headquarters in the Ypres Salient.

'I had heard them, but since I had smelt nothing had neglected to put on my gas mask as the signallers in the next compartment had done. Now my eyes were beginning to run . . . fountains of water gushed down my cheeks.'

Despite the attention of the American medical officer, 'Doc' Toulson from Baltimore, the weeping continued and, as the battalion was out of the line soon afterwards, Chapman was sent on leave.

Back near Ypres in March, 1918, he experienced another heavy mustard gas barrage . . . after the 'faint plop' of shells the air became 'impregnated with the savour of garlic'.

Just as the shelling died down, a round fell at the entrance to a dugout where the battalion runners were sheltering.

'Ten minutes later six blind, burnt, poisoned boys . . . were being led away.' One died a few days later and none came back to the unit.

Chapman wondered whether the bombardment had been a rehearsal for the expected German offensive.

CHAPTER 17

The Deluge

Early in 1918 the British front was extended south so that Haig's four armies covered a total of 126 miles. Behind each of them stood a reserve of two divisions. Great reliance was placed on an arrangement by which Pétain would intervene if the expected German blow fell on the British and Haig would respond should the French be attacked.

Haig concentrated his strength around Arras. There General Byng had fourteen divisions to hold twenty-eight miles of strong defences. To the south, stretching beyond St Quentin to the Oise and the banks of the Ailette, Gough's Fifth Army was strung out over forty-two miles. Twelve infantry divisions with three weak cavalry divisions were located in an area which had been devastated systematically in the strategic withdrawal to the Hindenburg Line in the spring of 1917. In the north the British First and Second Armies held areas they knew well, including Armentières and Ypres,

Haig had been considering returning to the attack in Flanders but the government had instructed him to remain on the defensive. As if to compel him to obey, the supply of reinforcements dwindled.

Neither the Field-Marshal nor the Prime Minister can be said to have behaved particularly well. They did not trust each other but did nothing to resolve their differences. Haig had constantly told Lloyd George that he was destroying the German will to fight. The crushing Cambrai counter-attack on 30 November had shattered that myth.

Lloyd George regularly criticized Haig behind the scenes but at the blackest period of the Passchendaele battle he had sent a completely insincere message of congratulation. By withholding reinforcements from the B.E.F. he had given its commander a reason for resigning (as Sir William Robertson had done over a plan to create a general reserve of British, French and Italian divisions for the Allied armies). Haig simply carried on. If there were to be any reverses then it would be because the politicians had denied him men. He would not attribute it to the wastage caused by his profligate offensives in 1916 and 1917.

In any case Haig was confident his troops would not only hold the enemy but inflict heavy losses. In the north where the British had been fighting for years there was reason for his view. To the south, where Gough had extended the line to take over twenty-eight miles of front from the French, it was a different story.

The region had been quiet since an abortive attack near St Quentin made just before the opening of the Nivelle offensive almost a year earlier. The country was open, a rolling plain stretching back to Amiens with few strong natural features. Rear defences had been marked out but not built by the French. Strong belts of wire indicated where trenches should be dug but in many places only the turf had been removed.

Ordered to construct additional defence lines around Péronne on the Somme and other positions still further back, Gough estimated that 300 miles of new trench were required. Though a large labour force was built up, much of the spade work still had to be done by the combat troops.

The burden of the defence was going to rest upon the machine gun. The 'MG' companies which had been attached to each brigade were now consolidated (with a fourth added) into machine gun battalions. Each infantry battalion also had thirty-four Lewis guns – light automatics with ammunition in drums in contrast to the belt-fed Vickers Maxim guns.

The German machine-gunners had made a great impression throughout the war. Major-General Sir Oliver Nugent, who commanded the 36th (Ulster) Division when it attacked west of Bourlon during the Cambrai operations, said of them:

'It is not too much to say that the failure of our offensive to achieve the objectives laid down was entirely due to the devotion and fighting spirit of these troops of the enemy, practically unsupported by their own infantry and artillery, during the first forty-eight hours.'

'Defence in depth' was something else which had been copied from the enemy.

On the Fifth Army front brigades, generally speaking, had one of their three battalions in a Forward Zone, where they held an outpost line in front of a number of small redoubts.

Behind this was a Battle Zone occupied by the second battalion with more strongpoints linked by switch lines and communication trenches. Many of the field guns were located in this zone.

Still further back there was a Rear Zone in which the third battalion remained in reserve. There were variations on the theme but basically it relied on the successful defence of 'keeps' and redoubts.

The artillery was deployed to cover the zones and tasked to fire on enemy communications, cross-roads, possible assembly points and the opposing batteries.

Unfortunately the Fifth Army's Rear Zone in particular was seriously short of deep trenches, dugouts and pillboxes. Its divisions did their best with the means at their disposal – they were not helped by a shortage of barbed wire – but there were serious misgivings about the gaps between such redoubts as did exist. There were not enough men to hold a continuous line or even for units to maintain direct contact and it was clear that an enterprising enemy would try to penetrate between points of resistance.

Gough had been convinced at a very early stage that his troops were likely to be the target of the enemy, not the least because in January Lieutenant-General Oskar von Hutier, the victor of Riga, was identified as commanding the Eighteenth Army on the St Quentin front. The French had been so impressed by von Hutier's methods in the East that they had published a pamphlet in September, 1917, describing them. There could be no doubt that the 61-year-old general, who had commanded a Guards Division in Berlin before the war, was a bird of ill-omen. With him was his artillery adviser, Lieutenant-Colonel Georg Bruchmüller. Contemporaries said of him that he could judge the weight of shell needed to remove any obstacle merely by studying it for a few minutes through his field glasses. An amiable-looking man, who had been retired before the war, Bruchmüller was the arch-exponent of the use of gas shell. He had experimented successfully with fire directed specifically on Russian battery positions in the winter of 1916. In 1917 he had developed a system of area gassing by which a location identified by a square on a map would be saturated with Green Cross or other gas shell, thus eliminating the need to aim at specific targets.

On the Seret, in Eastern Galicia, Bruchmüller's gunners had fired gas early in order to take advantage of the damp morning air. When von Hutier swept over the Dvina, three-quarters of the fire directed on the opposing battery positions had been Blue Cross shell, nearly 120,000 rounds in all.

The German artillery expert had also used the technique of calculating ranges from meteorological and other data, rather than the system by which one gun per battery fired until it was satisfied that it was 'on target' and passed the information to its neighbours.

The new 'predicted' fire, or survey method of gun-laying, had also been tried by the British, at the suggestion of Brigadier Hugh Tudor, 47-year-old commander of the 9th Division's artillery. It had contributed largely to the initial success at Cambrai.

German staff instructions for the use of gas shell issued on 1 December, 1917, were updated in the following months. They re-emphasized the need to differentiate between the persistent gases like Yellow Cross, gases of low persistence such as Green Cross (a more potent version, Green Cross 3, was introduced in 1918), and non-persistent gases – Blue Cross and lachrymators.

Ground that had been shelled with Green Cross could be crossed by infantry within two hours of a bombardment while Blue Cross targets could be occupied the moment the gas cloud disappeared.

'The substance in the Blue Cross shell acts with extraordinary rapidity, in fact almost instantaneously, but it generally puts troops out of action for only a short time. In sufficient concentration it penetrates the French mask effectively and the English mask to a lesser degree, in which case it forces the enemy to tear off their masks. For this reason a mixture of Blue and Green Cross is recommended. In the case of an insufficient concencentration, Blue Cross at least forces the enemy to wear their masks, thereby interfering with their fighting efficiency.'

Where Yellow Cross was concerned, no area to be occupied was to be shelled within two to four days of the assault and even then some casualties were to be expected.

Mustard gas was to be used to make battery positions, assembly points and billets untenable.

The overture to the 1918 concerto for percussion instruments began softly. The doleful note of the Strombus warning horn was heard in trenches and pillboxes on many old battlefields. Yellow Cross shells belched in dull chorus at Armentières and on the gloomy Passchendaele ridge. Loos came in for special attention, and further south in the Flesquières salient officers thought they had identified a practice barrage on 8 March – not every German army commander was convinced of the virtue of 'unregistered' shoots. This was followed on the 10th by an increase in Yellow Cross shelling until on the 12th a cataract of mustard gas fell on the Third Army's position at Flesquières. One estimate put the number of shells fired at 200,000. The veteran 2nd Division, which had distinguished itself in the defence of Bourlon, suffered 3,000 casualties and the 63rd more than 2,500. It became necessary to relieve the infantry, engineers and

GERMAN GAS SHELL CONCENTRATIONS
– Spring 1918

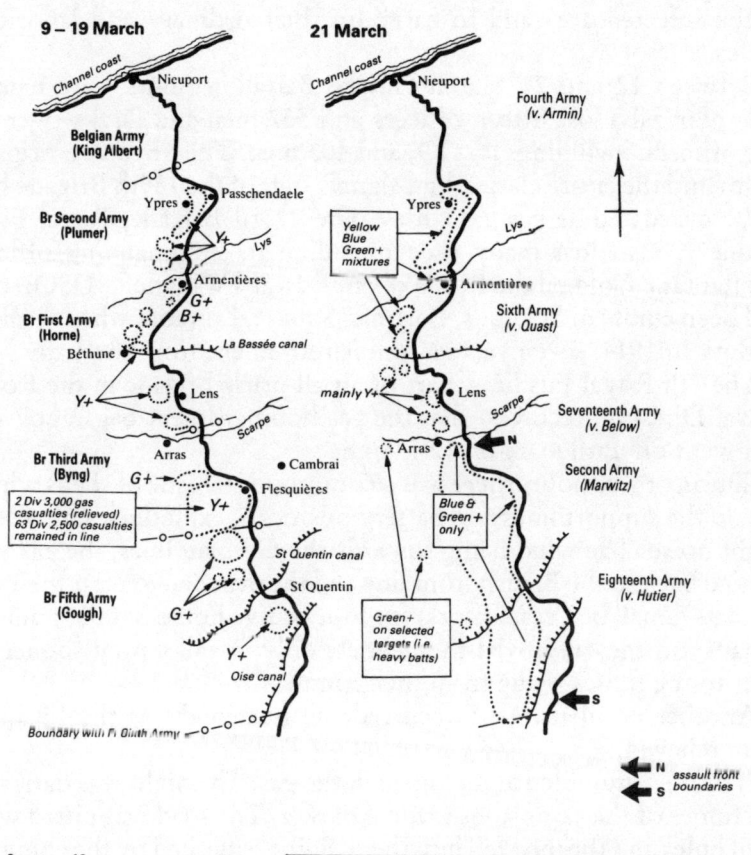

9 – 19 March

Channel coast
Nieuport

Belgian Army
(King Albert)

Ypres   Passchendaele

Br Second Army
(Plumer)   *Y+*   Lys

Armentières

G+
B+

Br First Army
(Horne)   La Bassée canal
Béthune

Y+   Lens

Scarpe

Br Third Army
(Byng)   Arras   ● Cambrai

G+   Flesquières

2 Div 3,000 gas
casualties (relieved)   *Y+*
63 Div 2,500 casualties
remained in line

St Quentin canal
St Quentin

Br Fifth Army
(Gough)   *G+*

Y+

Oise canal

Boundary with Fr Sixth Army

21 March

Channel coast
Nieuport

Fourth Army
(v. Armin)

Ypres

Yellow
Blue
Green +
mixtures   Lys

Armentières

Sixth Army
(v. Quast)

mainly *Y+*   Lens

Scarpe   Seventeenth Army
(v. Below)

Arras   ◄ N

Second Army
(Marwitz)

Blue &
Green +
only

Eighteenth Army
(v. Hutier)

Green+
on selected
targets (i.e.
heavy batts)

◄ S

N ◄
S ◄   assault front
boundaries

0   10   30   miles
|————|————|————|—————|
1 km
10   40

Based on the diagrams used by Brigadier-General H. Hartley to illustrate
his lecture to the Royal Artillery Institution, November 1919.

pioneers of the 2nd and the 47th Division replaced it between 19 and 20 March.

The 63rd remained in the line under the most difficult conditions.

'The gas ... hung round every trench, every dugout, every headquarter for an indefinite period, and no amount of gas discipline could prevent a growing casualty list among troops bound to remain in the infected area and to carry on their ordinary and laborious duties.'

Between 12 and 21 March Hawke Battalion (units were named after admirals) lost fifteen officers and 532 men and Drake twenty-one officers, includings its CO, and 403 men. The brigadier, brigade major and the entire clerical and signals staff of the 189th Brigade had to be evacuated as gas casualties. The 223rd Brigade, Royal Field Artillery, also lost many men including its commanding officer, Lieutentant-Colonel the Rev William Edward Wingfield, DSO, who had been curate of St Paul's, Portman Square, London, when recalled to duty in 1914, seven years after his retirement from the army.

The 7th Royal Fusiliers, part of an all-army brigade in the Royal Naval Division, recorded that the gas bombardment began at 7 pm and went on until 4 am on 12 March.

'During these hours there was a continuous whistle of shells which fell on the support lines and battery positions, exploding with a very slight noise. The wind being towards the German lines, the gas was carried back to the British front line and the men had to wear their gas helmets (small box respirators) for four or five hours. At the point of exhaustion they removed the helmets only to fall a prey sooner or later to the fumes rising from the ground.'

Another bombardment occurred the next night as the Fusiliers were relieved.

'The men stumbled along through the gas. The night was dark and the fumes of the explosions made it darker. The road was pitted with shell holes and the men fell into them. Some, splashed by the contents of the shells, were burned on the arms and neck.'

About 250 men were sent to hospital. Reinforcements arrived at 1 am on 21 March – 100 inexperienced young soldiers straight from England.

South of Arras, on Hutier's front, the line remained inactive, but groups of German officers with maps were seen studying the countryside opposite St Quentin. The Royal Flying Corps brought in photographs showing that shell holes a few hundred yards from the British outpost line had been prepared for use as mortar pits. From 15 March long convoys of lorries and horse transport were seen moving into St Quentin. There was no question of shelling this large town, still partly inhabited by civilians, and for years it had been a convenient concentration area for the enemy. Its many churches supplied excellent observation towers for Bruchmüller's gunners.

Two German deserters who entered the lines of the 36th Division opposite St Quentin on the 18th confirmed that assault troops were massing. Having heard of the gas ordeal of the artillery on the Third Army front, the Ulster gunners moved to new positions.

The great German offensive, code-named Michael, involved three armies. The Seventeeth, under General Otto von Below who had played a major part in defeating the Italians at Caporetto, was to strike south of Arras on one side of the Flesquières salient; the Second, under General Georg von der Marwitz, a cavalryman, was to thrust forward on the other side of the bulge. If this were pinched out the two armies would swing north to take Arras from the rear and Hutier's Eighteenth Army would drive forward to the curving line of the Somme–Crozat Canal which he could hold as a barrier protecting the flank of the others against French intervention. At the same time he would be in a position to reinforce success.

The preparations were thorough and a total of 6,400 guns were allotted to the three armies (a superiority of about five to one), Hutier getting the lion's share, including 940 heavy howitzers. Each army also had more than 1,000 mortars. In infantry the enemy opposed each British line division with three assault formations.

On the front of the stretched Fifth Army Brüchmuller's instructions were meticulous and detailed. The 1896 model 5.9s, worn by years in action, each had 300 rounds per battery to fire in the first five hours. The newer 1913 model was supplied with twice that amount.

The bombardment was to open at 4.40 am 'beginning with a crash', priority targets being communications, batteries and command posts. No mustard gas was to be fired but the barrage was to consist of nine Blue Cross to two high explosive shells for the first fifty minutes. There seem to have been some local variations as the 63rd (Frankfurt) Field Artillery fired shrapnel, Green Cross and Blue Cross alternately for the first half-hour.

After that there were to be a series of ten-minute bursts of fire, HE only on the forward infantry positions, with Blue Cross, Green Cross and tear gas directed on targets in the rear. At 7.10 the British front line was to be swept by a shell storm for two-and-a-half hours after which the infantry would attack 'without hurrahs'.

Green Cross was directed on special targets, distant gun positions in particular. Gas was omitted from the creeping barrage which preceded the storm troops but, in the event, tear gas was used in some sectors, though never less than 600 metres in front of the first waves. More than 1,000 rounds of gas shell per battery *per day* were to be supplied after that. It was a flattering if unwelcome tribute to the reputation of the men holding the thin belt of sandbagged localities bearing such names as Boadicea, Jeanne d'Arc, Racecourse Redoubts, Manchester Hill and Cooker's Quarry.

Ludendorff calculated exactly the right moment to launch the attack. The Kaiser was kept waiting in the Imperial Court train in sidings next to Operations Headquarters at Avesnes while the suitability of the wind was discussed. Taking into account the 'drift back' effect of gas shells, such as had been experienced by the 7th Royal Fusiliers in the Flesquières Salient, Ludendorff momentarily considered postponing the order to attack. Conscious of the fact that a delay would put further pressure on the keyed-up troops, he wrote later:

'And yet our artillery relied on gas for its effect, and that was dependent on the direction and strength of the wind. I had to rely on the forecast submitted to me at 11 am by my meterologist, Lieutenant Dr Schmaus. Up till the morning of the 20th strength and direction were by no means favourable; indeed it seemed almost necessary (to delay the assault).'

Dr Schmaus's report was 'not strikingly favourable' but it was good enough for Ludendorff to decide at noon that the bombardment programme would be carried out the following morning.

Prisoners taken by the 61st (2nd South Midland) Division on the evening of 20 March revealed that the attack was to be launched the next day. British howitzers fired on likely enemy assembly points for half an hour during the night, causing a number of casualties, but by then it was too late.

Winston Churchill, who had been attending a gas conference at St Omer, spent the night with his old friend Brigadier-General Tudor, advocate of the 'unregistered' artillery system. After the tornado of shells crashed upon the British lines he went to view the scene. The front line could be identified by 'a curve of leaping red flame'. When the British guns opened in reply their noise could not be distinguished in the overall sound of high explosive. If Tudor, whose father had been sub-Deacon of Exeter Cathedral, found time for a prayer, it was understandable.

CHAPTER 18

Australian Ordeal

Sister Katherine Luard, who had served in casualty clearing stations close behind the British lines at Loos, Arras and during Third Ypres, counted 102 gassed Fifth Army men in one ward on Friday 22 March, 'but only four died'.

She had not expected Marchèlépot, not far from Péronne, to be so quickly in the thick of the fighting. She had put in for leave only two days earlier but tore up her application after hearing the roar of artillery. Two days later, Palm Sunday, the commander of the 24th Division, Major-General Arthur Daly, was using her orderly room as his HQ. His units, she gathered, were 'practically napoo for the moment'. They had been in the line on the 21st. The general, son of an Indian Mutiny hero, flew his divisional flag outside the tent but controlled little else. He was grateful for the use of the phone. Eventually 1,000 wounded were evacuated by an ancient locomotive hauling fifty cattle trucks. As it pulled away Daly was still using the phone to fight his battle.

Sister Luard's records reflect an interesting aspect of the gas bombardment.

Though on the front under attack on 21 March almost a quarter of all the German shells fired were either Blue or Green Cross, *known* gas casualties were on the low side. For the week ending 23 March, when the enemy artillery was at its most active, a total of 3,378 cases were reported by the casualty clearing stations of the Third and Fifth Armies. In the same period Yellow Cross casualties exceeded that figure by more than 100 in the First and Second Army areas.

The exact number of soldiers who succumbed to the Blue/Green Cross barrage will never be known as many men fell into enemy hands or died in forward positions.

Most of the keeps and redoubts occupied by the Fifth Army had been identified by reconnaissance planes and made easy targets for Bruchmüller's gunners. Garrisons were penned in their dugouts with gas curtains drawn or forced to wear respirators while waiting for the barrage to lift. A dense ground mist blinded observers on a large stretch of the front. Waiting storm troops suffered occasionally from their own bombardment. Lieutenant Junger, watched the 'wall of fire' over the opposing lines:

'Our delight was lessened by the tears and the burning [in the nose] caused by the fumes of our own gas shells . . . the wind blew back on us. Many of the men were forced to pull off their masks when the unpleasant effects of our Blue Cross gas threw them into fits of choking and coughing. I was very uneasy, yet I felt sure that our command could not have made a miscalculation. . . .

'Meanwhile I exerted all my energy to keep the first cough back so as not to increase the irritation. After an hour we were able to take off our masks.'

In a dugout on the other side of the line, Major Deneys Reitz, a South African serving with the 1st Royal Scots Fusiliers on the Arras front near Wancourt, was convinced he heard German projectors being fired. He rushed up the staircase, ran into a cloud of gas and came back twice as fast to get his respirator.

'We were drenched with gas for 30 hours on end. . . . I was gassed twice for it was impossible to wear one's respirator continuously. The Blue Cross . . . caused eyes and throat to smart and burn, and made one violently sick, but did not otherwise incapacitate me.'

Not everyone was made of the same tough stuff as Deneys Reitz.

The surprising thing about the fighting in the Fifth Army Battle Zone on 21 March is that it went on as long as it did. Strongpoints held out until late in the day and some until the following morning. Once the enemy had penetrated between them, however, there were virtually no reserves. Haig had taken a gamble in spreading his troops thinly: for example, a single battalion of the London Regiment with a strength of 607 all ranks had to cover a sector two and a half miles wide.

Gas and fog made it particularly difficult for the British artillery. Gunners had to wear respirators for hours and banks of mist concealed possible targets. A pall of smog, dust, fumes and smoke hid SOS flares sent up by the infantry.

It was much the same on the Third Army front. The 1st Buffs, moving to their battle position, found the effort exhausting and 'recognized from the continuous and tremendous roar that the bombardment was terribly severe. The operation of getting into place was attended with great difficulty as it was dark and gas masks had to be worn on the march. By 5.45 all the forward wires were cut and there was no more telephonic communication. Gas shells were intermingled with the others.'

The rest of the story can be quickly told. Gough's divisions were consumed by non-stop battle and as they fell back, trying to maintain contact, their line shrank. The Third Army pulled back belatedly from the Flesquières salient exposing the Fifth's left. Reserves sent up to fill the gaps were too late and too few. The Haig–Pétain agreement to give mutual support in time of peril turned out to be unworkable for the simple reason that the French divisions had been dispersed behind the length of their entire line.

On Hutier's front the momentum of attack was kept up longer than in the north thanks to the use of the fleet of lorries which Ludendorff had considered to be of greater value than tanks. These ran a shuttle service – shells up and wounded back, though the casualties were so great that the medical services were hard-pressed.

Finally the attack ground to a halt in the Somme crater fields in the north while sheer exhaustion and French reserves held it up in the south.

On 28 March, when it became clear that Pétain was not prepared to commit himself to maintaining contact with the British, General Foch was appointed over his head to co-ordinate the operations of both armies and, soon afterwards, of all the Allied armies, Belgian and Italians included. Gough was relieved of his command and placed on half-pay in April. A scapegoat had to be found and none of the people really responsible was prepared to volunteer for the role.

Ludendorff considered the Great Offensive was over by 4 April. On that day troops of the Eighteenth Army reached Villers-Bretonneux, ten miles from Amiens on the long straight Roman Road that runs from St Quentin. They were severely handled by the 9th Australian Infantry Brigade, backed up by dismounted British cavalry, and went to earth.

Strategically the results of the offensive begun on 21 March had been disappointing to the Germans. The Cambrai salient had been pinched out but its defenders had managed to withdraw; in the eyes of many British officers it should never have been held in the first place. A frontal assault on Arras had been repulsed by British troops in well-established positions. The overall result had been to deflect the centre of gravity of the attack to the south. Haig's fears of trouble in Flanders were, however, soon to be realized. Colonel Brüchmüller had already been sent there to advise General Ferdinand von Quast, head of the Sixth Army. The British First Army held a 33-mile front from Gavrelle just north of Arras to Armentières which was just behind its left flank. It had Vimy Ridge in its rear, plus the Lorette Ridge, much fought over by the French earlier in the war. The First Army, commanded by General Henry Horne,[1] defended the Bethune coalfields. For this it had a total of fourteen divisions, including two Portuguese, only one of which was in the line and known to be low in morale.

It became a question of who relieved them first, British or Germans. Two of Haig's reserve divisions were earmarked for the task but as they were still recovering from their exertions in the south and needed time to absorb reinforcements the move was delayed.

Heavy mustard gas shelling began on 7 April at points ten miles apart. Armentières received 40,000 Yellow Cross shells (according to legend the gutters 'ran with mustard gas') and villages opposite Loos and Lens were also dosed liberally with the same medicine. Major-General Lothian Nicholson, commanding the 34th Division holding the line in front of Armentières, read the signs and immediately suggested withdrawing to a position behind the city to avoid being cut off. He was told to stay where he was.

On the 9th the German barrage heralding Operation Georgette I descended on a ten-mile front south of Armentières, a proportion of Blue and Green Cross being mixed with the high explosive. The attackers swept over the Portuguese division and advanced towards the base area behind Ypres. Though the Germans were held on the River Lys they shook the Allies by striking again on the 10th, this time north of Armentières – Operation Georgette II. Nicholson, son of a Victorian full general, was allowed to pull back his 34th Division. He learned later that the Germans had forbidden their troops to enter Armentières for at least a fortnight after the torrent of Yellow Cross.

Though the potential of the Georgette attacks was probably as great a threat to the Allies as the 21 March offensive, the Flanders battlefield was much more restricted than the Picardy plain and the German infantry suffered heavy losses. These were not the specially trained divisions used by Hutier but standard combat formations. Many advanced in dense masses. The British found reserves by pulling back from the hard-won Passchendaele ridge but their troops were consumed at an alarming rate. French divisions took over the

---

[1] Horne joined the Royal Artillery in 1880.

defence of the line of hills covering the approaches to Poperinghe and the bases south of Ypres.

Towards the end of April the enemy had once again accumulated large stocks of Yellow Cross shells which he proceeded to dump on Ypres and the Nieppe forest ten miles to the south, an obvious place for the concentration of Allied reserves. On the 25th he laid down a barrage which created a mustard gas 'belt' six miles long *behind* the Allied position.

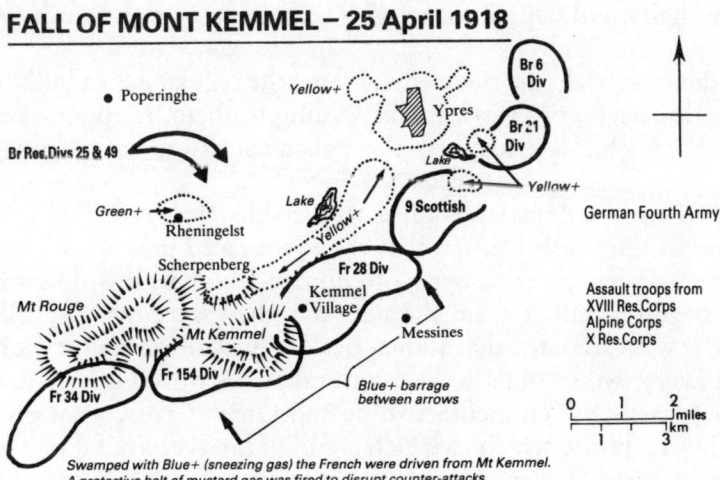

FALL OF MONT KEMMEL – 25 April 1918

Swamped with Blue+ (sneezing gas) the French were driven from Mt Kemmel.
A protective belt of mustard gas was fired to disrupt counter-attacks.

A Blue Cross barrage fell on the trenches themselves and the bastion of Mont Kemmel was overrun. The Alpine Corps crushed the French 28th and 154th Divisions within two hours and then dug in.

The loss of Kemmel, saddled with the damning description 'impregnable', caused a sensation, especially as in some quarters the French had been critical of the British fighting spirit.

All feared for the now even more important Scherpenberg height behind Mont Kemmel and there was a brief false alarm that it had fallen. Much later, when the extent of the Yellow Cross '*cordon sanitaire*' was known, it was considered that the Germans had not intended to attempt a further advance into the poisoned zone which included the Scherpenberg.

In boxing terms Ludendorff had delivered a ferocious right hook in Flanders to follow up a powerful straight left in Picardy.

War was not new to Villers-Bretonneux. In November, 1870, it had been defended vigorously by two French brigades occupying earthworks south of the little town. They had crossed bayonets with the 4th and 44th Prussian Infantry before retiring into Villers-Bretonneux itself. The houses were eventually cleared by the 1st Grenadiers (The Crown Prince's Own) who advanced with 'loud hurrahs and the beat of drum'.

In mid-April, 1918, the sector was held by the 5th Australian Division and for once the front-line soldiers experienced a modicum of comfort. Many villages had been abandoned hastily and the headquarters of the 53rd Battalion moved into the château at 'Villers-Bret' and 'drank from costly glass . . . played billiards and sat in easy chairs, and slept in sheets with beautiful eiderdown quilts over them'.

As there were almost no deep dugouts, the regular use of buildings for headquarters, the worn tracks leading to them, telephone wires and parked vehicles made them more than usually apparent from the air.

On 16 April a Bavarian soldier captured by the French who held the line to the south warned that the town faced imminent assault. There was a hasty rearranging of counter-attack troops, but when shells began to fall at 4 am the next day they were mainly Yellow Cross. It was estimated that at their peak they were arriving at the rate of one every two seconds in the town and on the woods behind it. The bombardment, which included Blue and Green Cross, went on for three hours during which two cellars full of men received direct hits. Other shelters, believed to have been proof against gas, were penetrated by fumes.

When it became obvious that the enemy intended to saturate the town with mustard gas, troops were ordered to occupy outlying trenches, but by that time many had succumbed to the menace without even knowing it. Scores of Aussies had removed their respirators when the shelling stopped and as they filed through wrecked streets they inhaled polluted air from craters. Collapsed walls, tumbled rafters and splintered doors were all impregnated with the liquid. The commander of the 53rd Battalion, which had sampled the high life in the château, tried to keep going but by the late afternoon he and his headquarters were no longer able to function. His medical officer was so badly gassed that he died later. A total of twenty-one officers, including the CO, padre and medical officer, plus 250 other ranks of the 33rd Battalion which had provided the permanent garrison of Villers-Bretonneux, became victims.

Lorry-loads of gas cases who had been picked up after making their way back from the town and the woods began to arrive at the advanced dressing station. The medical officer in charge quickly discovered that the vehicles themselves had become contaminated from contact with the clothing of the casualties. The 14th Field Ambulance promptly set up a reception centre where the patients could be given a change of clothing, rushed up from a bath unit in the rear, and washed. Their blisters were treated and eyes bathed.

Gas shelling began again that evening and the dose was repeated for three hours the next day, again from 4 am to 7 am. Though the troops were better prepared, the casualties were still high and another commanding officer, this time of the 56th Battalion, became seriously ill.

All in all the Germans had reaped a valuable harvest. Though many of their shells fell on an unoccupied switch line the others found targets. The 33rd Battalion was put out of action completely and three other battalions and a machine-gun company lost key personnel.

Soon afterwards, under previous arrangements, the Australians moved to a line north of Villers-Bretonneux which remained on their right flank. The defences were taken over by the British 8th Division, originally created from fine regular units but now composed mainly of raw recruits. Many of them were 'A-4' youths under nineteen years old who had been held back in Britain until the ravages of March required their despatch overseas. Most of them had been in France only a fortnight. Raw or not, the 8th Division was able to capture a Prussian Guard sergeant-major on 21 April and learned that forces were gathering to strike on the 23rd. As if to underline the message, the back areas were gassed that afternoon causing many casualties in an Australian battalion's horse lines.

The German field gun batteries were allocated 1,000 rounds each of high explosive and Yellow Cross shells; the field howitzer batteries had the same ration of HE with slightly fewer mustard gas shells – 750. In contrast to the usual practice, Yellow Cross was to be used on a number of objectives immediately before zero.

On the night of the 23rd the British fired heavily on possible 'jumping-off' places and an ammunition train was blown up by a Royal Air Force bomber. This did not prevent the enemy artillery opening up at 3 am, teams of gunners working in relays to maintain a high rate of fire.

At 5 am the barrage lifted to the rear and at 7 am smoke shells burst on the front trenches. Through the murk loomed thirteen German A7V tanks, clumsier than the British but well endowed with machine guns. They broke deep into the 8th Division's defences. The world's first tank v tank action was fought that morning.

No 1 Section of 'A' Company, 1st Tank Battalion, was parked in the woods behind the town, two Mark IV 'females' equipped with Lewis guns only, and a 'male' which had two six-pounder cannon in its sponsons. Lieutenant Frank Mitchell, commanding the male:

'As the wood was still thick with gas we wore our masks. While "cranking up" a third member of my crew collapsed and I had to leave him propped up against a tree trunk.'

Mitchell's first and second drivers had already become casualties and he was reduced to putting a man with only two weeks' driver training at the controls. He borrowed a soldier from one of the 'females' and went into action with a crew of six instead of the normal eight.

Despite their handicaps the section forced the crew of one enemy tank to abandon it and field guns disposed of the others if they had not already broken down. British 'whippet' tanks made a fierce counter-attack and the area became the scene of wild confusion. By evening the Germans were still in Villers-Bretonneux but a bombardment and a raid by the RAF turned the ruins into a mass of flames.

They held out until a classic counter-attack by the 13th and 15th Australian Brigades, supported by the British units, threatened to trap them inside the burning town. After that they withdrew as best they could. The 5th Guard Grenadier Regiment, occupying a wood just east of the town, complained that it reeked with the gas of their own bombardment. The 5th Foot Guards coming up to relieve them were particularly annoyed that the counter-attack was delivered as they were preparing to sample the contents of dixies unloaded from their horse-drawn cookers.

At the beginning of May, 1918, the Germans had been using Yellow Cross for ten months. It had given them a distinct tactical advantage and continued to be of major concern to the Allies, inflicting casualties, neutralizing key points and straining the medical services. There was also the question of morale. Soldiers were quick to spot that a mustard gas blister could secure their removal from the firing line and no questions asked. Good gas discipline, the quick identification of Yellow Cross and the retention of respirators until troops could get out of an infected area, was essential. But even the most reliable troops could be caught out. On 24 January men of the 1st Guards Brigade had been gassed when Yellow Cross shells fell on Fampoux where they were assembling after coming out of the line. The following month the 2nd Guards Brigade suffered ninety-one gas casualties out of a total for the month from all causes of 127.

133,702

PATENT

SPECIFICATION

Convention Date (France), Aug. 21, 1918.

Application Date (in the United Kingdom), Aug. 18, 1919. No. 24,735/19.

Complete Accepted, Jan. 22, 1920.

COMPLETE SPECIFICATION.

Improvements in Projectiles.

I, WILLIAM HOWARD LIVENS, Captain, D.S.O., M.C., of 32, Howitt Road, Hampstead, London, N.W. 3, do hereby declare the nature of this invention and in what manner the same is to be performed, to be particularly described and ascertained in and by the following statement:—

5 This invention relates to projectiles particularly to those containing liquefied gas.

According to this invention a projectile consists of a tube made in a single piece and having contracted ends, a central tube to which the ends are connected, a diaphragm dividing the tube into a rear chamber and a forward chamber a
10 hole in the tube connecting the rear chamber to the projectile, a plug for closing the rear chamber, an explosive charge in the forward chamber and a fuse closing the forward chamber.

The accompanying drawing is a sectional view of a projectile made in accordance with my invention, adapted to contain lethal gas.

15 k is a projectile or bomb formed of a tube having contracted ends welded to a central tube l which forms a stay. n is a diaphragm dividing the tube into two chambers.

The short chamber at the base end is fitted with a screw plug and has cross holes m, by which the liquid gas is introduced into the bomb, the longer end is
20 packed with the bursting charge and takes the gaine o and the fuse p. The

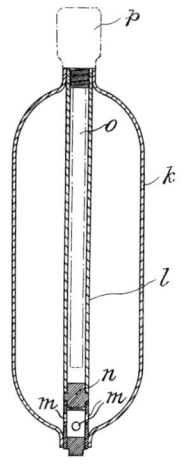

15. Facsimile of a Patent Specification applied for by Captain Livens in 1919 for a projectile containing liquefied gas. Detail left: 'k' is the bomb casing; 'l' is the central tube forming a stay; 'n' is a diaphragm dividing the tube into two chambers; 'p' is the fuse and 'o' is the gaine taking the bursting charge. The gas is inserted by the holes marked 'm'.

(Bulk contamination vehicle =

(Hush, Hush)

Chemical Mine

leads
flash head
Match head composition
Slow burning composition
Burster
2 oz. gunpowder
No. 14 electric fuse
Yellow band

$1\frac{1}{4}"$ diam. 20" high.
Contents 50 lbs mustard
Wt. empty 15 lbs
Set 10 yds. apart,
Contaminates 200 sq. yds
= approx.

Ground Bomb

-- 2 pts. o mustard
6 lbs total weight

Contaminates 20 sq. yds
approx

Cylinder (Yellow) =

70 lbs empty
70 lbs. chlorine
phosgene wi
chlorine
or chlorine

Beam and Line Methods of Using x

16. A leaf from Sapper Smith's service notebook, 1940–41. These notes were made by a member of a Royal Engineers Chemical Warfare Company in the Second World War. They show a chemical mine designed to contain 50 lbs of mustard gas.

17. From newspaper cuttings relating to gas warfare. The top two come from the *Newcastle Journal*, September, 1939. The one in the centre of the page appeared in *The War Illustrated* of 30 October, 1941, under the heading 'Gas May Yet Be Used In This War'. The last one appeared in *The Observer* in the Spring of 1986.

IN the last Great War gas was used within nine months of the opening of hostilities, but it has not yet been employed in this. It was used by the Italians in Abyssinia with the most horrible results, and from time to time there have been reports of its use in China : only the other day it was said that the Japanese were using it on the Ichang front. If it *is* used against us, then it will be probably as an accompaniment to an invasion attempt, since of all the weapons in the modern armoury gas may be credited with the most panic-raising effects.

Such panic, however, would be almost certainly the result of ignorance and unpreparedness, rather than of its lethal qualities. We know something of the effects of high explosive and incendiary bombs, but as yet gas has all the terror of the unknown. Yet, judging from past experience, gas is a far less deadly weapon than the H.E. bomb.

" Mustard gas is the most humane weapon ever invented," Mr. J. B. S. Haldane has written in one of his essays. " Of the casualties from mustard gas during the late war there were 170,000 in the British Army alone. Three per cent or less died, and less than one per cent were permanently incapacitated—a very low proportion compared with the casualties from other weapons."

This view is supported by Mr. C. W. Glover in his book, " Civil Defence." In the Great War, he tells us, while gas caused 5·7 per cent of all non-fatal battle injuries, it was responsible for only 1·32 per cent of all battle deaths. Only one casualty resulted from each 230 lb. of lung gas used ; it took 60 lb. of blister gas to cause a casualty, and 650 lb. of eye, nose and chest irritant gas ; 6,000 tons of tear gas caused not a single casualty. On an average, there was only one casualty for each 192 lb. of gas. Another point to be remembered is that in hospital gas cases recovered in about half the time that was required for other wounded.

" The judgement of future generations on the use of gas," General Hartley has written, " may well be influenced by the pathetic appeal of Sargent's picture of the first ' Mustard Gas ' casualties at Ypres, but it must not be forgotten in looking at that picture that 75 per cent of the blinded men he drew were fit for duty within three months, and that, had their limbs and nerves been shattered by the effects of high explosive, their fate would have been infinitely worse."

POISON GAS DEATH

THE body of an Iranian soldier who died from chemical gas burns in a London hospital is to be flown home to his family in Tehran today. Ibrahim Hendozadeh was one of 14 soldiers admitted last month to the private 180-bed Wellington hospital in north London. Iraq has denied using chemical weapons, but Iran claims that more than 1,000 of its soldiers have been injured in gas attacks since it began its latest offensive last month.

Doctors at the hospital are querying whether adequate medical checks are made when the soldiers arrive in Britain to ensure that the gas—believed to be mustard gas—was not still 'active' inside their bodies. 'We don't want gas around that could be absorbed by the air conditioning system,' one doctor said.

18. The 1980s gas mask and equipment to protect British troops in a chemical warfare environment are sophisticated and efficient — but they have to meet the same requirements as in the First World War. A man must be able to use his weapon (left), and/or his transport (below left). He may also have to have bullet or splinter wounds treated in a polluted location (below right). The pictures were taken by Ministry of Defence photographers of troops on exercise.

The drenching of the Flesquières salient made a serious impact. Brigadier-General Foulkes was actually on his way to attend an inquiry into the reasons for so many casualties when the offensive opened on 21 March. It was the trend that was worrying. The chief concern was that, though many of the injuries reported were slight burns or inflamed eyes, 'the number of men affected threatened at times, unless the strictest measures were taken, to amount to the equivalent of several divisions and to constitute a serious drain on the strength of the British Army'.

At this period of the war eight out of ten Yellow Cross victims were being sent to the United Kingdom for treatment. Some clearly needed to spend a long period in hospital but fatalities were few and most men could be expected to return to duty within eight weeks. Eight weeks, however, was a long time on the Western Front. As the year wore on it was possible to reduce the number of mustard gas patients evacuated to Britain to about one in four of those affected; but even mild cases spent a month away from their units.

British losses during the fighting in Picardy and in Flanders amounted to slightly more than 300,000 men, of whom 93,000 were missing or prisoners. Fifty-five divisions had been through the ordeal of battle. Only thirty-two French divisions had been engaged, losing 92,000 men, still a serious figure in view of France's enormous casualties earlier in the war. Manpower was at a premium, with munitions, clothing, chemical and ship-building industries competing for labour. The Allies looked to the United States for the next influx of fighting men.

Americans were, in fact, arriving in large numbers. Because of the emergency they had agreed to send not divisions complete with artillery and services, but thousands of infantry and machine-gunners.

Four fully-formed divisions were in France by March, 1918 – the 1st, 2nd, 26th and 42nd – and two others were training there. The 1st had taken over its own sector of front in January.

The determination of Pershing to put a 'great self-contained American army' into the field caused his hard-pressed Allies some concern, as he had neither the staffs nor organization for the various levels of command, but they took comfort in the regular arrival of troopships. All the newcomers had to be instructed in gas warfare, though this was not always given a high priority. The Americans expected to turn a man into a front-line soldier with a training programme of three months. Two days of this were allotted to learning about gas and gas masks. As the various services competed for the time available this period was whittled away to six hours, the newly formed Gas Service having no influence at all in an army highly sensitive to rank, seniority and protocol. Ludendorff, however, was on the side of the overruled on this occasion and by the time the Americans in the line had suffered gas casualties in March and the 1st Division lost nearly 900 men to mustard gas in a night after taking Cantigny, the pendulum swung the other way. The American Expeditionary Force Gas School was established with accommodation for 200 officers and a course of six weeks.

There was still opposition to the Gas Service, however, which was irritated by the way it was regarded by many simply as a defensive organization. It tried to counter this attitude by adopting the slogan of one of its lieutenant-colonels: 'Chemical Warfare Service officers have got to go out and sell gas to the Army!'

Nevertheless before one action in the Argonne, a corps staff officer refused to allow a supporting gas attack 'without an absolute guarantee in writing that it could not possibly injure a single American soldier'.

Where the renowned American drive did take effect was in the United States itself. Typical were the steps taken to provide charcoal. At first sight the production of this simple commodity, one of the essential fillings for the box or canister of a respirator, presents no problems. Quality, however, is important. The coarse material derived from red cedars was a good absorbent for chlorine and phosgene but of little value against chloropicrin. Attention then turned to the use of charcoal made from coconuts, used for more than 50 years in laboratory experiments. An 'Eat More Coconut' campaign was started by the Gas Defense authorities and by the end of the war American consumption had doubled and the charcoal manufacturers were able to lay their hands on about 150 tons a day from 'home' sources. This was not enough and other means had to be found.

Coconuts turned into charcoal lose 75 per cent of their weight so it made sense to set up a factory abroad to process raw material on the spot. Buyers scoured the Far East to buy up crops which were processed in a factory set up in the Philippines. It had 1,000 tons in hand when the war ended.

Other nuts were tried – the cohune or corozo found in Mexican and Panamanian swamps. Four thousand tons a month were ordered. Even apricot, peach and cherry stones were gathered under a scheme run by the American Red Cross with the slogan 'Help us give him the best gas mask'.

The Americans were puzzled by the ability of the Germans to produce charcoal as the blockade prevented them using anything other than conifers as raw material. Only after the war did they discover that their opponents had impregnated the wood with a chemical (zinc chloride) *before* burning it.

The blockade had other influences on the German respirator. Though the design remained the same, the facepiece was no longer of rubberized material but of heavily oiled leather. Coiled metal springs were substituted for the elastic head straps. After a time the leather tended to stretch and as the mask depended entirely on being a close fit the troops lost confidence in it. The drum containing the neutralizing chemicals remained efficient and was improved by the addition of a paper filter to keep out particles from British shells containing stannic chloride.

The French too had been obliged to alter the design of their mask, the M2 having outlived its usefulness. The ARS Mask (*Appareil Respiratoire Speciale*) was introduced which resembled the German model and worked on the same principle. Unlike the British small box respirator, it had neither nose clip nor mouthpiece.

The strain caused by wearing the SBR for long periods was constantly criticized, and it was definitely uncomfortable. The British recognized this and made sure that soldiers who might be required to wear the mask had a good set of teeth to grip the mouthpiece. A private in the Durham Light Infantry who had a number of extractions before going to France was held back at base until he had been supplied with dentures, an absence which saved him, as his original battalion was almost annihilated.

Uncomfortable or not, the SBR was efficient and, with its clip and mouthpiece, did give a man a second chance. The Italians, who had based their original respirator on the M2, were happy to switch to the British model mask after Caporetto.

After three years of gas warfare not only did every soldier have his own protection but so did most animals likely to be employed near the front line.

The horse mask produced by the Germans was a simple affair, a chemically treated nose bag which covered the nose and mouth of the animal. It was filled with wet straw and other absorbent material.

Horses were normally able to stand much greater concentrations of gas than humans. Nevertheless the British equine mask was soaked in the same solution used in the PH helmet and the bag was drawn tight over the horse's nostrils.

The Americans at first produced an 'improvement' on the British model which resulted in complete exhaustion in a trotting horse. This was modified so that animals could move at that pace for two miles without showing signs of distress. The better was often the enemy of the good in the United States Army.

Dogs, used for carrying messages and to find wounded, were also provided with masks, layers of impregnated cloth pierced with ear-holes and fitted with eyepieces. Animals were said to become quickly accustomed to respirators.

The protection of the essential carrier pigeons posed a problem and provided a puzzle. Though known to be very vulnerable to gas they nevertheless generally managed to do their job. One had even managed to bring news of the plight of Fort Vaux at the height of the battle of Verdun, though it died almost as soon as the message had been removed from its leg. The French made it a posthumous member of the Legion of Honour, stuffed it and put it in a museum.

The relative immunity of pigeons was later considered due to the speed with which they flew up through the fumes into clear air. One German device used to carry birds in safety was an otherwise sealed box into which the drum of an ordinary gas mask had been fitted to filter the air.

The bulk protection of soldiers in large dugouts was also improved. Ventilators fitted with chemical filters drew in the air and blankets treated with a mixture of lubricating and linseed oil kept the gas out. The air was expected to enter through the soil in the smaller dugouts.

Contrary to some examples cited previously, fires were forbidden in British dugouts on the principle that the flames would pull in air. Chloride of lime was sprinkled at the entrance to dressing stations, large dugouts and other important posts to neutralize mustard gas which a soldier might be carrying on his boots.

In all these matters — the identification of gases, the means of protection, when he could or could not light a fire, where to wipe his feet — the private soldier had to be instructed; at the same time he had to learn about the other lethal menaces that surrounded him. To the staff and regimental officers any chance to move to a quiet sector where they could train was welcomed. When four British divisions which had been through the mill of Picardy and Flanders heard that they were going to the Chemin des Dames it seemed too good to be true.

CHAPTER 19

To Your Kennels!

A strange piece of financial haggling took place between the French Commander-in-Chief and his Prime Minister in May, 1918. Pétain asked to be able to draw on funds in order to reward troops for the capture of prisoners opposite the Chemin des Dames. Patrols had scoured the valley of the Ailette stream without finding anyone. Yet there were increased signs of activity. Machine guns were being used more at night with bursts of harassing fire from artillery. Something was happening and Pétain wished to know what. With all the shrewdness of the Pas de Calais peasant stock from which he came, he argued that to lay on a major raid with full fire support would cost hundreds of thousands of francs. The 'incentive' method would be much cheaper. Clemenceau saw the wisdom of the argument. It was agreed that an infantryman who took a prisoner without the help of artillery would receive 1,000 francs (perhaps in 1980 terms about £100, though real comparison of values is almost impossible). A capture made with the aid of the gunners would be worth 250 francs. The equally shrewd bargainer, Clemenceau, put a ceiling on cash available to pay for prisoners of 12,000 francs per infantry company per day.

The commercial benefits of life on the Chemin des Dames had already been enjoyed by the garrison. After the battle of Malmaison, General Maistre had introduced a salvage programme under which recovered rifles and brass shell cases fetched a reward of a franc, a bayonet 50 centimes and pieces of equipment 25 centimes.

Some idea of the losses on the ridge may be gained from a letter written home by a soldier: 'I collected 338 francs for the section yesterday'.

The units occupying the *creutes* and trenches welcomed small detachments of American troops sent to them to gain experience. Some were enchanted by the generosity of the newcomers:

'Would you believe it, an ordinary soldier gets more than 200 francs a month! And they are not slow to buy a bottle of champagne.'

The average '*biffin*'[1] was sometimes startled by his ally's rations: 'They don't drink wine but tea. . . . They get very little bread. . . . I don't know how they survive.'

A number of Americans were killed either in trenches or on patrol in the sector. 'They are not yet wary enough.'

Wariness was a quality now ingrained in the British survivors of the battles in Picardy and Flanders who arrived in the Champagne at the beginning of May for a rest.

The front lay fourteen miles north of Soissons and ran some seventeen miles west to east before turning at an obtuse angle and continuing straight to Rheims. It was the blunt angle that the British IX Corps was required to occupy, the Craonne and Californie plateaux. It became part of the French Sixth Army.

The 50th (Northumbrian) Division, whose march through Ypres after the first gas attack in 1915 now seemed like ancient history, had been filled up with recruits to replace severe losses suffered when trying to cover the Fifth Army's retirement. It had been cut to pieces again trying to stem the German onrush on the Lys. The 8th Division had fought alongside the 50th on the Somme before being mangled at Villers-Bretonneux. The 21st – shades of Loos – had been reduced to the strength of one weak brigade in Picardy and had fought in the north subsequently.

All three went into the line and, because of the extended front, deployed their brigades side by side. The 50th Division held four and a half miles of trench, the 8th slightly more and the 21st about the same as the 50th. Each division was supported by its own artillery, augmented by a few batteries of French 75s. On their left, under General Renouard, was the 22nd Territorial Division, a Breton formation which had suffered severely after coming to the Fifth Army's aid on the Somme and had been further weakened by the ravages of Spanish 'flu. *La Grippe Espagnole* was as merciless as any of the other enemies the 22nd had to face. Its virulence was blamed on the evil vapours of the caves, cellars and tunnels of the Chemin des Dames ridge.

On the right of the British was the 45th Algerian Division, the very formation which had broken before the first chlorine cloud at Ypres

[1] French soldier's slang for infantryman, literal meaning 'rag man'. The term '*poilu*' lost popularity.

in April, 1915. It was well established in the outskirts of Rheims.

The incoming formations were not so confident about the position on the Chemin des Dames. Their commanders were particularly unhappy about crowding into an area with a river and canal in their rear.

'Against an attack in the grand style the Chemin des Dames was not only a bad position, as too narrow, but it was in the front line. Purely tactical considerations pointed to its occupation by a line of outposts, strong only in machine guns, the first real position being organized on the heights on the left or south bank of the Aisne.'

Lieutenant-General Sir Alexander Hamilton Gordon, commander of IX Corps, agreed with his subordinates. Sir Alexander, 59-year-old descendant of the Earls of Aberdeen, had joined the Royal Artillery in 1880, seen service in Afghanistan and South Africa, and knew a great deal about guns and their effect. The head of the Sixth Army swept his protests to one side.

Most good generals are a little mad or eccentric . . . Stonewall Jackson, Wolfe, Picton, Patton, MacArthur, Montgomery. It does not matter a great deal as long as they know their trade and are good either with the officers, who have to see that their orders are carried out, or with the troops. The best are good at all these things. General Denis Duchêne, who had been Chief of Staff in Foch's corps in 1914, was good at none. Spears, a very sensitive observer, described meeting him early in 1917:

'He meant to be pleasant and asked me to have my meals at his table. . . . I soon realized why it was that his Staff so cordially disliked him. Short, stout, sallow-complexioned and fair, his hair was almost white, he spoke with the guttural intonation of the peasants of central France. His manner, even when he was trying to be polite, was brutal. His greeting conveyed the impression that he suspected you of being a thief intent on taking advantage of his short neck and general slowness, to investigate his back pockets.'

Such was the nicest thing that the gentlemanly Spears could write of a general whose word was law on the blasted ridge of the Chemin des Dames.

Duchêne had commanded the Tenth Army during the Nivelle offensive and been sent to Italy after Caporetto. Recalled to take command of the Sixth, he had stamped his personality firmly upon it. The atmosphere in his headquarters was glacial. After dinner in the French equivalent of an officer's mess, he was apt to dismiss his staff with the remark: 'To your kennels, gentlemen'. The Chief of Staff was hardly on speaking terms with the Army Commander. At mealtimes he had been seen to swivel on one elbow so that he was almost presenting his back to '*Le Tigre*' (a description which carried with it none of the respect which attached to it when applied to Clemenceau). Under these circumstances it is not surprising that confusion arose over the interpretation of the instructions received from the *Grand Quartier Générale*.

Pétain had made it plain in his Directive No. 4 that the principles of 'elastic defence' should apply to all French armies. The front must be held by outposts while the main defences were sited out of range of the enemy's artillery. This theory, which implied giving up territory, was challenged on political grounds[1] and led to debates behind the scenes. When Duchêne argued that even temporary withdrawal from the Chemin des Dames, the Californie plateau and Malmaison, would upset public opinion, he touched a tender spot. Even more telling was his point that the possession of the ridge enabled counter-battery fire to be directed against the long-range guns then shelling Paris. It may have been that he genuinely believed there would be no attack against his front. In this he was sadly mistaken.

As ever, gas shells continued to trouble the *creutes*, woods, spurs and valleys of the tortured ridge. They disturbed the most peaceful periods. A sudden burst of Yellow Cross on 12 December, 1917, caught fifteen men and two of them died on the spot. A regiment reported an hour-long bombardment with mustard gas on 27 January and put it down to the fact that it was the Kaiser's birthday. On 1 March an estimated 5,000 gas shells fell on a three-mile stretch of country between the shattered villages of Vauclerc and Craonelle. In a five-hour bombardment in the notorious Heurtebise Farm sector another 1,500 '*toxiques*' spiced the barrage.

Whether or not it was intentional, the occasional shell storms conditioned the defenders to spending long periods in deep dugouts. Some areas were a maze of tunnels and underground shelters which a man need rarely leave.

Despite occasional violent rumblings, the Chemin des Dames had seldom been more peaceful than during the pleasant days at the beginning of May, 1918. 'Near the gun emplacements of the reserve line grew lilies of the valley, forget-me-nots, larkspur and honey-suckle.'

Such bucolic repose was unnatural and slowly suspicions grew. Three enemy ammunition dumps were blown up during a French bombardment. Strange sirens and an increase in traffic noise behind

---

[1] By General Roque who was a member of the Government.

the enemy lines were reported. Mysterious signboards had been set up at trench junctions. Even Duchêne felt some unease. He visited the 22nd Division and stared hard through binoculars at the countryside opposite.

'I've got to have prisoners,' he said, 'immediately.' It was 25 May.

The French 61st Regiment captured a soldier of the 13th Jagers. He reported that the 5th Guards Division, which had been away since losing the ridge the previous year, had returned. The Prussians were to be followed in their assault by the 197th Division. In his own unit each man had been issued with two grenades and 150 cartridges, plus two days' rations. The attack would begin at 1 am on the 27th with a gas bombardment of two and a half hours.

The information was confirmed under pressure by a German officer cadet who at first denied all knowledge of an attack. Two more prisoners told similar stories. Whether the men who captured these prisoners ever collected 'bounty money' is not recorded. It is unlikely that they lived long enough to put in a claim.

As even the American Intelligence service, working on changes identified in the enemy Order of Battle, had predicted the likelihood of an offensive on the Chemin des Dames, it is hard to understand Duchêne's scepticism. The security precautions taken by General von Boehn's Seventh Army seem to have fooled him completely. As late as the evening of the 26th a French plane reported:

'Activity nil on the routes and paths along the Ailette. The region looked deserted. Absolute calm, neither troops nor transport, no fires, no flares.'

But by then the grim truth was known. General Hamilton Gordon, who had been assured by Sixth Army headquarters two days earlier that there were 'no indications that the enemy had made preparations which would enable him to attack', received a less welcome message from the same source: 'The enemy will attack on a broad front at 0100 hours tomorrow.'

Duchêne's battle instructions to his artillery were to wait for 'the first shell of a violent enemy barrage' before beginning their counter-preparation. The British batteries interpreted this as allowing them to open up a slow harassing fire. General Naulin, commanding the Algerian division, ignored the restriction and his gunners blazed away from early evening.

The code-name for the attack was Blücher, after the tough old Prussian of Waterloo fame, 'Marshal Vorwarts'. The artillery adviser was the ubiquitous Bruchmüller.

The evening of 26 May was a bad one for Allied generals on the banks of the Aisne. The obdurate, ill-mannered Duchêne knew he was about to be put to the test. Bluster would no longer be of service. General Maud'huy waited anxiously at the command post of XI Corps. Comte Louis, who was said to have made his sons, when young, pray every night that they would grow up to be as brave as the legendary Bayard, had led an army earlier in the war. Replaced for lack of success he had swallowed his pride just so he could remain in the field. The outcome of the battle would be critical to the future of the old warrior (he was 61) who had preached the theory of '*attaque à l'outrance*' at the École de Guerre before the war. The British were on Maud'huy's right. On his left was General Chrétien's XXX Corps which, in 1916, had borne the brunt of the first attack at Verdun. There had been a slight cloud of suspicion over him since his involvement in the fall of Douaumont. His career was also in the balance.

As for the British, Hamilton Gordon had done his best. At divisional level commanders had little doubts about the fate awaiting their men.

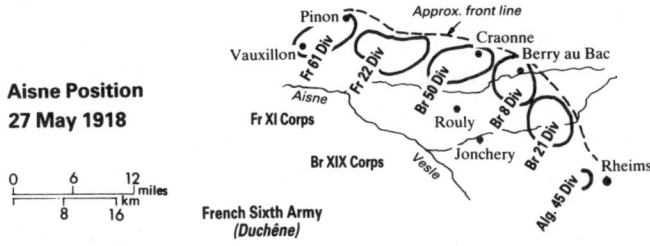

At one o'clock precisely the 'first shell' of the violent bombardment mentioned in the battle instructions arrived, accompanied by nearly 4,000 of its fellows. For ten minutes the German batteries – forty to the mile along the front of the French 22nd and British 50th Divisions – maintained the highest rate of fire over a wide spread of targets using a mixture of Yellow, Green and Blue Cross to cause the maximum confusion. Then they switched their attention to the Allied forward gun positions.

Masked and steel-helmeted, the sweating British manned their 18-pounders and blazed back but 'the enemy's shooting seemed uncannily accurate'. Shells crashed around gun pits, and into them.

In the deep dugouts and tunnels of the Chemin des Dames the heat became almost unbearable: charcoal braziers were used in some as an anti-gas precaution. Blankets were drawn tight across the entrances to the underground shelters. Breathing became agony. Where there was a suggestion that gas had percolated into a *creute* men wore their masks, sucking at the unpleasant mouthpiece of the small box respirator.

Soon after 2 am the Allied heavy batteries in the rear found themselves targets of gas and high explosive.

At 4.30 am General Anthoine, on the staff of *Grand Quartier Générale*, received a phone call from his brother-in-law, General Duchêne. The Commander of the Sixth Army asked for reserves to be sent to support his left but was not unduly worried. The bombardment was falling to a depth of eight miles behind the front with 'plenty of Yperite'. It was undoubtedly a serious attack but he thought he would be able to hold out, given the reserves. They were promised by the afternoon.

Duchêne was wasting his breath; the German guns and mortars had already obliterated his forward defences. Their storm troops had begun to advance three-quarters of an hour before he got through to Anthoine and were infiltrating the remains of the forward positions. Enemy pioneers were blowing up the entrances to the labyrinth of the Caverne du Dragon where French counter-attack troops waited. Gassed and dying men packed the fume-filled interior. A battalion of the 118th Regiment near Vassogne, many of its forty-man sections reduced to fourteen or fifteen soldiers after '*une nuit terrible dans les gaz*',[1] were glad to leave the foul atmosphere to try to recapture trenches near Heurtebise. They carried their gas-sick captain on a chair part of the way. Machine gun fire met them.

Mist had cloaked the approach of the attackers. In the Aisne valley, with its canal and river, the gas hung about much of the morning undisturbed by any breeze.

The fighting on the Chemin des Dames itself was quickly over. German tanks (the strange signboards reported earlier had been guides for them) had spearheaded the assault on the 50th Division. All three brigadiers became casualties. Two of the 8th Division's brigadiers were gassed and wounded.

Some of the forward companies were able to resist, others were trapped in deep dugouts and forced to surrender. At one point the 2nd West Yorks and 2nd Middlesex made a determined stand around a battery of French 75s which knocked out the enemy tanks (captured

[1] The Germans are reported to have used quantities of DA – diphenylcyanarsine – shells. DA was probably the most powerful irritant used in the Great War; in concentrates as low as 1 in 10,000,000 it made soldiers resort to their masks.

British Mark IVs), but in the end all were crushed. Only on the right did the line remain intact. Though eleven companies were overwhelmed in the exposed front line, the 21st Division maintained its link with the Algerians of the 45th. The latter's bombardment of the Germans in defiance of Duchêne's orders had paid dividends. The 45th formed a bastion on which others could rally.

On the left wing, beyond the smoking slopes where lay the slaughtered 50th, there was chaos. The first elements of the French 157th Division coming up in support were hurled across the Aisne on Duchêne's assumption that his second line was still intact. They were promptly hurled back. Confusion arose over responsibility for the many bridges involved. The last word was supposed to come from Sixth Army's headquarters. By the time the local commanders had decided to take matters into their own hands the Germans were across.

The self-sacrifice of some units, such as the 2nd Devons, who fought to the last in the Bois des Buttes, held up the advance, but it was on too broad a front to falter over individual efforts. A flood of men in field grey poured through the gap. Duchêne's choice of phrase to his corps commanders, 'Hang on like ringworm', did little to inspire them.

Much better if he had shown the spirit of a sergeant in the 410th Infantry Regiment who took over when his lieutenant was killed and led his men forward with: 'This way for the boys who haven't yet won the Croix de Guerre. Go and get 'em.' His section captured four machine guns before being driven back.

The 410th was in the 151st Division whose commander had been notified of the impending attack while on leave celebrating his silver wedding anniversary in Paris. General des Vallières drove back immediately to his headquarters near Juvigny where he was killed on the 28th. His car was machine-gunned by an enemy detachment firing at a range of thirty feet. While his ADC went for help, a group of pioneers recovered the body.

The highest and the lowest fell. Of a forty-two-man machine gun section of the 333rd Regiment only one survived at the end of the day and he was a prisoner. Some of his captors, whose comrades he had mown down, wanted to shoot him but a youngster managed to save him. He joined a long column of prisoners, some in *bleu horizon*, others in khaki, marching towards Germany. Bruchmüller had done it again. By 1 June the spearhead of the German thrust was at Château Thierry on the Marne, about forty miles from Paris.

Duchêne was dismissed within a matter of days. So was Maud'huy, who, after the battle, 'had the honour to report' that his 21st Division had been reduced to the strength of a battalion, while the 22nd consisted only of its general and his headquarters. The unlucky Chrétien, who had now taken part in two major disasters, was also relieved.

To stem the tide Foch sent two American divisions, both twice the size of the British or French formations, to oppose the enemy on the Marne. Since they were withdrawn from the threatened British line Haig was not at all pleased – he had not been consulted until the move took place. It seemed that his troops were going to have to make the best of it. As far as the RE Special Brigade was concerned they had every intention of doing just that.

CHAPTER 20

Express Delivery

A line of camouflaged railway trucks stood in the little town of Barlin not far from Béthune. Armed guards circled it day and night. The British were about to use a 'secret weapon'.

The 'passengers' in the train were phosgene cylinders placed upright seventy or so to a carriage and held by wooden frames. A light railway had been pushed beyond the reserve trenches and lay hidden from view. At the appointed time the infantry would be pulled back from the front and support lines, the train be driven up and the gas released. The cylinders were to be discharged electrically and simultaneously so that a dense gas cloud would roll over the enemy lines, widening as it went. The planners called it a 'beam' attack, as the cloud would broaden as it progressed like the ray of a searchlight. Four such trains were assembled along the British First Army Front at the beginning of July.

On the night of 12 July a pilot engine left Barlin and chugged along the narrow gauge track with three R.E. officers aboard. Behind came a locomotive pulling the cylinder train, a soldier with each load. By 11.30 the trucks were standing in position in the darkness with their attendants checking wires and testing circuits. The Sappers moved as quietly as possible. As they waited for the wind to settle a German bomber droned over a target on the Hulluch road and they watched the flashes and heard the explosions. More than one man swallowed hard as he looked at the long black silhouette containing 1,260 gas cylinders. If they were smashed – and they were well within range of enemy artillery – there would be little hope, respirator or no respirator. A Lewis gunner took his weapon off about 100 yards, ready to open up in an attempt to disguise the noise of the discharge.

As a favourable wind freshened tension eased. No one fancied taking the cargo back to Barlin. At 1.40 am an order was given and the Lewis rattled forth. The train was, in the contemporary vernacular, 'pooped'. Bits of detonator blew over the watchers, who had moved well away and a tremendous hissing drowned the noise of the Lewis.

A dense grey chlorine-phosgene cloud rolled away over the deserted British trenches, widening as it crossed no-man's-land. From the enemy there came not a rocket, not a flare, not a shot. The driver brought up his locomotive and attached it to the line of trucks while the pioneers made ready to depart. Second-Lieutenant Fox, commissioned the previous autumn, was responsible for seeing the train back to its depot. He was congratulating himself on a successful operation when 'there came the ominous whine of an approaching shell'. It was a dud. The next was not, but fell some distance away.

That was enough for the driver. He had already hooked up his rolling stock and a clang and a jerk announced that he was about to leave. A few startled soldiers leaped aboard trucks. Others, including Fox, were not fast enough. Train and trucks disappeared, cylinders reeking. Fortunately the handful of travellers wore their respirators on this nightmare ride.

With shells bursting all around, the rest of the company took cover. After the bombardment eased special parties examined the British trenches and warned the infantry to wait some hours before reoccupying them.

The other Special Companies had not been as lucky and had suffered some casualties, though all cylinders[1] had been discharged and reports said the gas had travelled up to eight miles behind the enemy lines, causing more than 4,000 casualties.

Despite this 'success', most Special Companies were content to return to the more arduous but less dramatic technique of firing Livens projectors. These were considered to be generally safe from anything other than a direct hit. Of one batch of 700 'guns', heavily shelled after being dug in, only seventy were put out of action and the others were discharged. Reports indicated that of all the gas weapons it was the projector the enemy feared most.

Somehow it seemed that, no matter how much experience a unit might have, it could still be caught out. At about 1 am on 18 June nearly 1,000 drums filled with phosgene were fired into and around the village of Ablainzeville, east of Arras, as the 1st Battalion of the 12th Bavarian Infantry was relieving the 3rd. There had been a warning of a possible attack three days earlier but the gas burst upon

[1] Prentiss: A total of 5,000

crowded trenches. A total of fifty-three died in the village itself, including the regimental gas officer who had served at the front since the beginning of the war. More than sixty soldiers, who had been able to march back to their rest billets, were affected as day broke. The official report of the 5th Bavarian Reserve Division recorded: 'The fatal course of the delayed illness was particularly striking.'

German projector attacks did not cause the same havoc. A total of fifteen made in the Lens area in the first five months of 1918 caused only fifty-eight British deaths. Surprise bursts of fire with Yellow Cross were more lethal. Fifty-five gunners in three siege batteries died after one bombardment towards the end of June. The message had still not been absorbed by all troops that it was essential to continue to wear respirators while in the vicinity of Yellow Cross craters.

Midsummer saw German storm troops exploit two more Bruch-müller-style barrages. The first fell on General Humbert's French Third Army on 10 June when 750,000 gas shells were fired. Though prisoners had given warning and the defending batteries caused some disruption, four corps were driven back across the Matz, an important river barrier. Humbert had failed completely to under-stand Pétain's instructions for 'elastic defence' and had been further confused by contrary orders from Foch to conduct a foot-by-foot defence. The German thrust was held by the judicious deployment of reserves and a counter-attack led by Mangin, returned to duty at the end of 1917 after his share in Nivelle's disgrace had been half forgotten.

The 17-stone General Berthelot, one of the arch-priests of the offensive before the war, had also failed to learn the changing ways of war and his Fifth Army was severely defeated west of Rheims on 15 July. The enemy crossed the Marne once more, seizing a bridgehead at Dormans. Fortunately, east of Rheims the one-armed General Gouraud had got the message. His Fourth Army had withdrawn three kilometres to prepared positions and the pungent German thunderbolt fell on empty trenches; the storm troops advanced into a moonscape of chalky craters where they ground to a halt. Some fell victim to the mustard gas with which the French had deliberately contaminated abandoned dugouts, an early, if not the first, example of Yellow Cross being used to inhibit the use of ground in a retreat.

A fortnight of fighting followed in which the French counter-attacked using large numbers of light Renault tanks. By the beginning of August the enemy had been driven from the huge salient they had created since 27 May and had retired from the Marne to the Vesle. There they dug in.

The German High Command was running out of ideas. Throughout the war it had been able to surprise the enemy with the use of the gas weapon – chlorine and phosgene in 1915, Green Cross shells in 1916, Yellow Cross and Blue Cross in 1917 and the hell's broth of a mixture of all in 1918.

They had not believed that the Allies would be able to produce a quick reply to mustard gas and it came as a nasty shock when the French fired their first Yellow Cross shells[1] on 9 June.

The Société Chemique des Usines de Rhône had been producing two to three tons of mustard oil a day since March and by July this had become twenty tons. Military labour was working round the clock to fill 75mm, 105mm and 155mm shells. Soldiers selected for this work were required to be of the quiet, phlegmatic sort! They were given two days off a week and could relax at special hostels in the mountains.

A lot of explaining had to be done behind the German lines after the first French mustard gas shells landed.

'A recent and disagreeable development is the French tendency to fire Yellow Cross gas shells into the rear areas. A few devices do exist to combat [it] . . . and they are being explained to the troops in many different kinds of regulations and orders.'

A rumour went round the trenches that 'a British officer is supposed to have been in Berlin with forged papers, gone on a gas course and thus discovered everything that was worth knowing'.[2]

In fact both French and British were in a position to make mustard gas but the French were ahead in their ability to fill shells. They made liberal use of their newly acquired asset. On 31 July the Wurttembergers of the 63rd Field artillery were holding a position 'continuously under gas'. The following day, as they withdrew to the Vesle, Lieutenant Herbert Sulzbach recorded that many men were suffering from temporary blindness and continuous vomiting. Under a barrage of high explosive and gas, his mask worked but 'this damned new gas holds on for days; it lies on the ground, you don't know it is there, you can't see it or smell it, it clings[3] to the grass like dew and does its dreadful work.'

A month earlier his battery had been under orders to fill the forests

---

[1] Between 1 April and 11 November the French filled 2,400,000 shells, mostly 75mm, with mustard gas.
[2] H. Sulzbach, *With The German Guns*, Leo Cooper, 1973.
[3] That is in low concentrations when it could burn but not be smelled.

of Villers-Cotterets with the same type of gas.

Yellow Cross was also fired by the British; stocks of captured shells were shot from batteries of captured guns.

In the meantime the R.E. Special Companies conscientiously trundled up lorry-loads of drums for Livens projectors. Hundreds of them thundered into enemy strongpoints.

Gas alone, however, was not going to win the war for either side. The Allies had switched their attention to the tank. A range of models more adaptable and mechanically reliable were coming off the production lines, some smaller, some bigger, some for direct combat and some for supply and transport. A form of open – at least less restricted –warfare lay ahead. All-arms battles were well ahead of the planning stage.

Only a few days before the opening of the Marne battle Lieutenant-General John Monash, the Australian Corps Commander, seized an important observation height on the Somme at Hamel. Using ten battalions and sixty tanks, he attacked without an extended preparation, the guns opening up eight minutes *after* zero. Within two hours he had secured his objectives, dropped 100,000 rounds of small arms ammunition from RAF planes and hauled up wire and screw pickets by tank to consolidate his gains. Added spice to the venture was given by the presence of four companies of the US 33rd Division who took part in the battle without the permission of Pershing. The date was 4 July.

The American 1st Gas Regiment suffered great frustration during this period. Two companies were all ready to launch projector attacks, a technique they had studied while attached to British units, when the French offensive on the Marne opened. The attack was not only put off but the US I Corps tried to get the engineers assigned to repairing roads. Finally their commander persuaded his superiors to let his men use their four-inch Stokes mortars to fire thermite and phosphorus on enemy machine gun nests. They did this so successfully that Pershing's headquarters performed an about-face and called for an increase in the number of chemical warfare companies from eighteen to fifty-four, to be formed into three regiments. The attitude of conventional infantry staff officers towards American gas troops remained generally suspicious. They tended to regard the specialists as interlopers. Sometimes they ignored them at their peril.

A detachment of 300 Americans was committed to a night raid on trenches overlooked by an enemy-occupied village. The ruined houses were bombarded with 75mm and 155mm gas shells during the attack and received an estimated three tons of phosgene. The distance from the objective to the village was some 700 yards and a steady breeze carried the fumes among the Americans. What with the smoke from the explosions and dust from shell bursts few of the raiders detected gas and only a few put on their masks. After marching four miles to their base 236 men went down with gas poisoning and half-a-dozen died. After this incident the chemical warfare experts were consulted more often before operations in this particular division. The Americans were learning.

Sergeant Theodore K. Jones, of Atlanta, Georgia, serving in the 320 Artillery, 82nd Division, found himself on the dispensing side on 12 September, when his battery of 75s was firing three HE to one gas shell at Saint-Mihiel. The gunners were stripped to the waist. A month later he was on the receiving end in the Argonne, thought he detected someone cooking sweet potatoes 'and took long sniffs' until he heard the gas alarm.

'I got slightly gassed but did not know it then. The only thing gas did to me was to get me sick to my stomach so that I could not eat or keep anything on my stomach for any length of time.'

The Sergeant remained on duty and the following day was back at his 75 firing HE and gas from a cold and rain-soaked emplacement.

'Doing this we discovered a way to get a little warmth. The guns would get hot . . . and we would all take turns in leaning against them.'

At the time of which Sergeant Jones was talking enemy batteries were being supplied with between 40 and 50 per cent of their ammunition as gas shell. Captured dumps on the Second Army front contained 27 per cent Blue Cross and three per cent other gas shell. In July on the Third Army front ammunition in some dumps had been equally divided into HE and gas – seven per cent of the latter being Yellow Cross. The effect of each mustard gas shell was, of course, far in excess of the others. Whereas large numbers of Blue or Green Cross had to be fired to create a toxic cloud, a slow bombardment of even 77mm Yellow Cross could have great effect. New HE mustard gas shells, which had been first used in the March offensive, had the additional benefit of being hard to distinguish from ordinary explosives. There was much to be studied in the poisoned atmosphere of the 1918 battlefield.

British troops new to the Western Front had to be constantly reminded of the dangers, especially in the divisions brought back from the Middle East where gas warfare never developed. The 52nd (Lowland) Division had reported at Gallipoli that 'a captured Turkish officer who did not like German methods' directed the 5th

Highland Light Infantry to a trench on Achi Baba where cases containing '15 long, slender, asphyxiating bombs, evidently intended to be thrown by a trench mortar' were found. On arriving in France from Palestine in May, 1918, the 52nd noted that when it began training 'special attention was paid to gas warfare'.

The 74th Division, whose Broken Spur sign denoted its Yeomanry origin, discovered on its arrival in France that 'most of the masks given out in Palestine were found to be defective, and all the containers were obsolete'. Its troops were sceptical about being lectured on the use of 'cold steel'. 'Any one platoon of the 74th Division had probably made more use of the bayonet than any one battalion in France,' but gas was 'indeed, a new experience'.

The 16th Royal Sussex, who incorporated 'Sussex Yeomanry' in their title, listened doubtfully to descriptions of gases so powerful that 'if they got into your paybook would kill your next of kin'.[1]

---

[1] In both World Wars and for some time afterwards British soldiers carried a brown book (AB64) in which were recorded such items as pay, leave periods, inoculations, trade qualifications and an abbreviated form of will; hence the next of kin reference.

CHAPTER 21

A Lot of It About!

For Sir Douglas Haig the situation 'developed more favourable for us than I, optimist though I am, had dared even to hope!' Ludendorff described it as the 'Black Day of the German Army'. General Fayolle, commander of the Groupe d'Armées de Reserve, fighting alongside the British, wrote in his diary that it was *une belle victoire*. 8 August, 1918, was in fact the beginning of three months of non-stop operations and costly battles.

The British Fourth Army, under Rawlinson, started the ball rolling on the Somme with the massed attack of the Australian, Canadian and the British III Corps. The French First Army, commanded by General Marie Eugene Debeney, supported the British right.

More than 400 tanks crawled forward and the RAF gave added vitality and extended the dimension of the assault which began at 4.20 am. Up to that time there had been some anxious moments; the enemy seemed suspicious. He made an unexpected attack on the III Corps front on 6 August, gaining some ground. Some 4,000 rounds of Yellow and Green Cross were fired into the British rear areas on the 6th and another 2,000 rounds of mustard gas caused 500 casualties late on the 7th. That night, immediately preceding the attack, 'all available (British) guns were specially authorized to open fire if the enemy began counter-preparations or opened a gas bombardment'.

It was not necessary. More than 3,500 British and French guns opened fire exactly on time on a front of twelve miles. The bombardment, which was unregistered, included a proportion of lethal gas shell (the British still did not have 'home-produced' mustard gas) and many German artillerymen were captured in their masks near their damaged weapons.

Haig did not drive his troops as relentlessly as in previous years.

Once the steam had gone out of the attack, which on the first day bit nearly seven miles into the opposing line, he paused to regroup and attack elsewhere. As battle erupted at Albert and Bapaume, as the Hindenburg Line was attacked again, the Germans used gas desperately to harass the attackers. The effect was varied. Private Richards, still with the 2nd Royal Welch Fusiliers after more than four years of war, states that 'during the last 15 months of the war, I don't believe the Battalion had 50 gas cases and very few of them were fatal'.

Perhaps through bitter experience he and his comrades had learned to be cautious for he describes a group playing cards in a barn in a sunken road near Cambrai some weeks before the Armistice with masks ready to slip on as gas shells fell nearer and nearer. Even the tough Welshman complained of feeling 'pretty rough . . . there was a lot of gas about'.

Near Albert, the 23rd Royal Fusiliers lost fourteen officers and 369 men to gas on 21 August. The next day tanks were delayed by a gas bombardment on the 12th Division's front.

On 1 September an early morning attempt by a company of the 10th Lancashire Fusiliers to carry Le Transloy cemetery on the Somme miscarried because they ran into Blue Cross shells and alerted a German sentry with their sneezing.

The 16th Royal Sussex, new to gas, took a great interest in it.

'The general consensus of opinion was that as a destroyer of one's night's rest in the line it exceeded anything else, and a bad dose of it undoubtedly had serious after-effects, but as an actual slayer of men it was not a very successful weapon against good troops provided with good gas helmets.'

Moving up to the unfinished Canal du Nord, construction having been held up since 1914, the battalion's education increased. It was doused with lachrymatory shell during its advance: 'tears streaming down one's face . . . an atmosphere heavily charged with a smell like chloroform and pineapples.'

As the men crossed, columns of multicoloured smoke shot up from heavy HE landing deafeningly in the cutting. Having dug in on their objective the Sussex men were vigorously machine-gunned by a German plane which marked their position with a smoke flare. A brisk bombardment of mixed gas and HE followed. The gas not only forced them to wear masks from time to time but fouled their cigarettes: 'A Ruby Queen is a bit of a throat twister at any time but when strongly impregnated with Phosgene the result is simply nauseating.'[1]

[1] What scientists call the 'tobacco reaction' – a flat metallic taste when smoking in the presence of phosgene. This also applied to vincennite but it could be detected by smell as well.

Food failed to arrive because the canal cutting filled with gas and ration parties got lost in the darkness and fumes.

Mustard gas was encountered later in the month and the medical officer had to be evacuated after treating a badly splashed gunner. Like many other wounded MOs at this time be was replaced by an American, Captain Robert L. Ozlin, of Dundas, Virginia. The new medico soon had ample opportunity to practise his calling. The battalion escaped lightly when it captured the notorious Templeux Quarries with 500 prisoners but lost heavily in a further attack on a strongpoint known as Quennemont Farm.

For more than three weeks the Sussex had been moving and fighting, shelled with Yellow Cross on many occasions, and when relieved, were 'hollow-eyed from lack of sleep, wearied with continued fighting and digging and croaking hoarsely from their gas-fouled throats'.[1]

Battalions with considerably more experience of gas warfare did not go unscathed. The 3rd Grenadier Guards found themselves once again near Cambrai at the beginning of September. On the night of the 5th they took over from the 1st Welsh Guards at Goat Trench. The guardsmen carried out the relief in drenching rain following a thunderstorm under cover of which the enemy fired salvoes of Blue Cross.

'For an hour the Germans bombarded the valley with sneezing gas shells, and all the officers and men kept on their masks. . . . When the gas bombardment appeared to cease and was succeeded by one of HE shells, everyone incautiously took off his mask. The new bombardment turned out to be one of mustard gas. By the time this was realized everyone was being sick, and all the officers and NCOs were casualties.'

At the end of September the British gunners were able to repay their opponents in kind. Firing home-produced mustard gas for the first time, they poured 10,000 shells into the defences of Bellenglise shortly before the Hindenburg Line was stormed for the last time.

The enemy was taken by surprise partly because the attackers advanced only two days after the bombardment: it was normal to wait up to six before venturing on to poisoned ground. On this occasion it was decided that the advantages of an early assault outweighed the disadvantages.

The Germans had also changed their tactics. They concentrated mustard gas on infantry assembly positions and at times attempted to create an impassable zone.

[1] From the description the men's masks were no longer a good fit.

The HE Yellow Cross shell, seen first in the March Offensive, was brought more and more into use. This had an upgraded explosive charge which blew the casing apart and scattered the contents as a fine spray. A whiff could be fatal and the shell had the added advantage of being hard to detect among the normal HE. A Green Cross shell with an increased bursting charge also appeared towards the end of the war and the debilitating Blue Cross was used extensively. Partly this was due to a shortage of Yellow Cross because of manufacturing and storage problems and partly due to the German's faith in *Blaukreuz*.

It was the mustard gas that did the damage, however. Deneys Reitz, posted to command the 1st Royal Scots Fusiliers after recovering from his wounds, considered his men well camouflaged in rifle pits facing the ancient town of Le Quesnoy, near Cambrai. Though they were spared direct hits from enemy shells, he had to send 207 of them to hospital. The fields were drenched in Yellow Cross.

The gas was to be encountered everywhere. A patrol sent out by Reitz failed to report and when the former Boer scout crept out to locate it he found the men lying in a sunken road. Crawling back in darkness they had entered a pocket of gas and collapsed one after the other as they struggled towards the British lines. They were evacuated only with difficulty and joined the battalion's other gas casualties in a treatment camp specially set up behind the lines. At this stage of the war only serious gas casualties were sent immediately to hospital. Reitz himself was among the sufferers and spent three days' leave at the South African Field Ambulance at Abbeville. Shortly after his return, as he was leading his men to support the Guards in the Mormal Forest, he heard a faint cheering among the troops ahead of him on the crowded road. It increased in volume. An officer threaded his way towards him and handed him a despatch: 'Hostilities will cease at 1100 hours today 11 November.'[1]

The day the war ended nine British RE chemical warfare companies were arriving in the zone of the newly-formed US Second Army which had no gas capability of its own. Had the conflict continued, the Americans would no doubt have absorbed the new units Pershing had called for and made use of the huge stock of material piling up across the Atlantic. Chemical production at Edgewood Arsenal and elsewhere had become so great that there were not enough shell cases to take it and some plants were reduced to a maintenance-only status.

The importance attached by the Americans to the gas medium had

[1] Reitz, *Trekking On*, Faber 1933.

been emphasized by the recalling of Major-General William L. Sibbert from France to be the Chemical Warfare Service's first Director.

By autumn all programmes were in full flow and whole companies of infantry were employed on the proving grounds carrying out simulated combat tasks in extensive trench systems while being deluged with gas.

In Michigan the Dow Chemical Company was given a government contract to sink seventeen brine wells capable of producing 650,000 lbs of bromine per year for tear gas, but none of it was available before the Armistice and huge quantities went into storage.

The Americans had also thrown themselves enthusiastically into the production of white phosphorus shell for smoke screens, poisonous smoke candles, signal smokes, incendiary bombs and flame throwers.

The 'Defense' Divison also flourished and after the initial faults had been eliminated more than five-and-a-half million respirators were produced, approximately 377,000 horse masks and about 200,000 dugout blankets.

The Division also experimented with anti-mustard gas protective clothing, making nearly 2,500 suits and gloves, and it produced hundreds of tons of ointment. There was even a boot to protect a horse's sensitive heel.

With the hurried development of the new industry there were bound to be accidents. From June to the end of the war 674 workers were treated for mustard gas effects at Edgewood and 251 suffered from other agents. Three people died. The Edgewood hospital had accommodation for 480 patients.

British workers also suffered and the superintendent of a large factory at Avonmouth, opened in June, 1918, reported that nearly all of his 1,100 staff suffered from mustard-gas poisoning at some time. He added that the only place that no blisters were seen was on the palms of the hands!

Despite respirators, special clothing and an elaborate ventilation system 'practically every man on the staff was more or less severely gassed . . . and many were admitted for treatment several times'.

A doctor and eight medical staff were employed in a thirty bed hospital.

'The injured returned to work again and again, notwithstanding burns, sores and ill health, being determined at all costs to produce the amount of gas required to counter-attack the enemy who had first undertaken this form of gas offensive in July, 1917.'

According to one account the problems at Avonmouth arose from a decision to conceal from the contractors who built the factory the exact nature of the raw material it would use. They were told only that it was a very poisonous liquid. As the war progressed the need for secrecy grew. Air raids became more menacing. It is significant that the British dropped a ton of bombs on the Badische works at Mannheim in March, 1918, and claimed eight direct hits. Strategic bombing was developing fast when the guns fell silent and the grey columns began the tramp back to the Rhine, followed at a distance by other columns in khaki and faded blue.

The horizon brightened as the smoke thinned over the chimneys of munitions factories in Europe and America. In the big chemical works the managers looked at the seething vats, the tall cooling towers, mountains of sulphur such as old Admiral Dundonald could not have dreamed of, and wondered what was going to happen to their products, to themselves and to hundreds of thousands of war workers.

CHAPTER 22

Gas is Good for You

From the firing of the first Yellow Cross salvoes at Ypres in July, 1917, to November, 1918, records show that 124,702 British soldiers were evacuated to hospital in France and Flanders with mustard gas blisters, burns or temporary blindness and that 2,308 of them died.

These figures are included in the total for all gas shell casualties for the period – 160,870.

Thus in round figures eight out of ten gas casualties were inflicted by Yellow Cross. Blue and Green Cross shared, about equally, responsibility for the rest.

Before the mustard gas period the total for the Western Front from April, 1915, was estimated at around 13,000. The actual figure for gas victims was even higher as the official lists refer to men passing through medical channels and does not allow for prisoners treated by the Germans or for dead left in captured trenches.

American casualties were heavier in proportion to the British. Out of 224,089 A.E.F. soldiers recorded as having been admitted to hospital for all purposes, 70,552 were suffering from gas alone and a number of others were suffering from bullet or shell wounds and gas. In addition there were nearly 1,000 U.S. Marine gas casualties listed separately. It was estimated that gas was responsible for one in three of all wounds treated, but only two in every hundred victims died.[1]

According to Churchill,[2] 'In the end many more Germans died from British gas than British from German.'

Casualties at the hands of the British were estimated at around 200,000 and with those inflicted and suffered by French, Belgian,

[1] The Americans, it must be remembered, did not face phosgene to the extent of their allies.
[2] *The World Crisis*, London, 1921.

Russian, Austrian and Italians and others, a grand total for all the belligerents in the region of 1,250,000[1] is not excessive. Casualties and tactical failures caused indirectly by the silencing of protective batteries and the interruption of communications by gas can only be guessed at, but the figure is critical when assessing its effect on the outcome of a battle.

In 1918, as far as the modern battlefied was concerned, it appeared that 'Gas is here to stay'. Certainly the men controlling the booming American chemical warfare industry thought so. Many were the innovations they would have tried had the war continued. Light-weight cylinders weighing 65 lbs when filled had been ordered for use in cloud attacks. The employment of aircraft was under consideration with the simple suggestion that a bung should be removed from a drum containing mustard gas so the contents would be atomised by the air stream. Respirators were stored in hermetically sealed boxes immediately after the war and card indexes of chemists were compiled in case they were required again.

Even before the signing of the Armistice the order had been given that, from New Year's Day, 1919, all shells were to be a quarter filled with a combat chemical.

Some British authorities were just as keen. Armour enthusiasts thought tank crews were at an advantage, riding well above contaminated ground, and, because they were sitting, able to wear heavy sophisticated masks. They foresaw tanks designed to eliminate the opposing trench garrisons (people still thought in terms of trenches) by approaching the enemy positions just behind a gas cloud and in advance of their own attacking troops.

Colonel J.F.C. 'Boney' Fuller, writing in the *Army Quarterly* of January, 1921, visualized that 'the infantry and administrative troops will be carried forward in cross-country transporters ... lightly armoured and constructed so that they may be made gas-proof.'

Another tank specialist wrote: 'Gas and tanks in combination is one of the great things of the future. Gas can be produced in such quantities nowadays that it is questionable if individuals not carried in Mechanical Vehicles will be able to cross the areas treated with persistent gas. In fact the protection to the skin, as well as the lungs, required by the soldier may well become such that he will be completely immobilized unless carried in mechanically propelled vehicles.'

---

[1] It is estimated that, despite the inefficiency of gas shells, about a tenth of a ton of chemical was expended to inflict a casualty compared to half a ton of high explosive.

One American contemplated gas projetors being carried over difficult areas on tracked vehicles.

A school emerged which argued the humanity of gas compared with other weapons. American statistics issued as late as 1937 showed the incidence of tuberculosis among gas victims of the war as being less than that among men serving in the US Army in peacetime. As far as blindness was concerned the Americans established that of 812 soldiers blinded in the war only thirty-three cases could be attributed to gas.

British statistics showed that eye injuries caused by mustard gas were generally mild enough to allow seven out of ten men to be classed as virtually fit for duty within a month. Others took up to six weeks to recover and the worst cases needed perhaps four months. In only a handful of cases was there permanent damage to a man's vision, though a number of mustard gas victims were recorded as having developed eye problems in the 1930s.

To study some of the arguments put forward it seemed almost as if 'gassing is good for you'. The public, however, was influenced by many dramatic illustrations of gas warfare in photographs and some deeply moving paintings. Gas was looked on as something particularly wicked, something unfair and cowardly, against which a 'fair fight' was impossible.

Had the public seen the clinical photographs of patients taken to Aldershot during 1916 for treatment in a surgical unit specializing in rebuilding shattered faces, it might have taken a similar view of the crude shells which caused them, photographs which 'can still disturb even a hardened surgeon'. There is nothing compromising about shrapnel or shell splinters.

The truth is that 'clean deaths' in a battle exist mainly in the imagination of those who wish to shut out reality. Bullets do not always drill neatly through the fleshy part of the shoulder as in 1930s Westerns. Blue Cross was likely to have a much less drastic effect on flesh and blood than a bayonet in the bowels or the blast caused by the detonation of tons of guncotton planted by miners under a trench.

Nevertheless the romantic idea that wars should be fought under the rules of chivalry persisted, despite the realities of four years of carnage.

The British regimental system encouraged the commissioning of young men from the upper-middle and upper classes, preferably from a family with previous military connections. It was assumed that they had learned the importance of being 'decent chaps' and knew how to 'play the game'. An officer visiting London had to be aware of the need to wear a hat and to carry gloves and an umbrella. Intellectual achievements were something to be reticent about and an addiction to sport was almost obligatory.

Not surprisingly, therefore, there was only a modest attendance at a lecture on gas warfare given at the Royal Artillery Institution late in November, 1919. It was a Wednesday afternoon – dedicated, then as now, to games. General Lord Horne, the senior officer present, who, in civilian clothes, gave the impression of a 'well- groomed gentleman farmer', underlined the feelings of the old school in a short address:

'Although gas may be an unsavoury subject in a way, and it is a thing which we [left to] ourselves would never have used you must remember you are not always going to fight people whose characteristics are the same as our own.'

He went on: 'If we fight the Germans again we must remember that they are a highly scientific race, people who have carried out their researches as regards chemistry very far, and that they will undoubtedly make use of the result of their researches and employ methods which we should consider absolutely beneath us.'

Lord Horne then warned: 'There is nothing in the world which a German will not do. . . . There is no depth, in my opinion, to which he is not capable of descending, for he covers it all, as you know, with the words "For the Sake of the Fatherland".'

He ended by conjuring up visions of 'airships' dropping large quantities of poison gas which was going to 'wipe out whole forces unless we can find some way to deal with it'.

It was an unusually strong remark coming from an officer of whom someone had said that no original contribution to or comment on the Art of War could be traced.

The lecturer on this ocasion was Brigadier-General Hartley who had returned to his Fellowship at Oxford after the war. He acknowledged the unpopularity of his subject. Nevertheless he persevered because 'gas has few friends, people are too ready to forget it, and I chose it [as a subject] from my conviction that it is one of the most serious problems we shall have to face in another war.'

As far as the artillery were concerned, gas was vital to their service. Despite the delay in producing suitable ammunition, the British artillery had made excellent use of gas shells once they got them. Much had been learned from a surprise German bombardment of the Baudimont Gate at Arras in December, 1916, when a heavy concentration had created a dense cloud which caused 100 casualties. This was a departure from the usual German tactics which, on the

Somme, had been to spread their shells over a wide area, thus making them less effective.

The British quickly realized the importance of the rate of fire in gas bombardments (strangely the Baudimont Gate affair seems to have been an exception on the part of the enemy who for a time continued to disperse his fire). Methods were devised by which short but heavy bursts could be crashed onto selected targets. Excellent results were claimed in counter-battery work.

Hartley accepted that there were many prejudices against gas, 'due to the treacherous way it was introduced by the enemy'. But he quickly made the point that the humanitarian argument against its use was unjustified, for by the end of the war the use of gas enabled many military objectives to be achieved 'with less permanent suffering . . . than by any other method'.

As he developed his theme he felt it necessary to combat the old nagging criticism that in any case the British cloud attacks had not been effective. He pointed out that there was no reason to believe that those delivered were any less deadly than those received.

After describing the enormous manufacturing effort which had enabled the Allies to reply to the enemy gas initiative, he paid tribute to German industry which was able to produce supplies of mustard and arsenic gases by 1917.

'Now all of these were complex organic substances which had never been made in quantities of more than a few grammes before the war, and their rapid production in such enormous amounts could not have been achieved without the resources of the German dye industry and the standardized plant which could be quickly transferred from one purpose to another.'

As an example he took mustard gas. The first product in its manufacture, ethylene chlorhydrin, was also the first product in making synthetic indigo. The Germans began by multiplying their synthetic indigo plant by six while the other stages of the production of Yellow Cross were carried out in the dye plant. The arsenic compounds used in other gases were made in the azo-dye sheds. Within a short time after the Armistice all these plants were back in the business of making dyes, next to no alterations being necessary.

Hartley gave statistics to show that in 1917 the Germans were producing 2,000 tons of gas for shell filling and 1,000 tons of chlorine per month, equalling the output of a million 105 mm shells a month. The need to break the peacetime German monopoly of the dye industry was self-evident.

He had no hesitation in giving Yellow Cross its due as the most effective of all battlefield gases intended to produce casualties, even though only 'a very small proportion' were fatal.

'It is effective at very low concentrations; it has a comparatively slight smell; it produces no immediate effect or discomfort, and there is nothing to suggest its danger; finally it is very persistent.'

The lecture did not spark off the discussion that so often concludes an open meeting. Sir Robert Robertson, who had been Director of Explosives Research at the Royal Arsenal, felt compelled to back up Hartley's remarks on grabbing a share of the world dye market. Not only were dyes used in the production of hundreds of millions of pounds worth of fabrics each year in Britain, but 'the field of organic chemistry provides a nursery for the training of scientific men who can turn their training . . . in many directions, not always to be foreseen.'

A rather touchy note was struck by the Chairman, Colonel William St Colum Bland, who had been President of the Ordnance Committee during the war and felt that it was not widely understood that the great delay in producing a practical British gas shell[1] was due to the considerable variation in the specific gravity of the chemicals involved.

Hartley, replying, said he feared war gases would still have to be chosen for their efficiency and not by their density.

The 'loud applause' which was recorded probably indicated the relief of the audience at being able to escape. There were ladies present and doubtless a lively evening had been planned to make up for a dull afternoon. No one took seriously the dire warnings of Lord Horne. Nor does anyone seem to have been impressed by the conviction of Brigadier-General Hartley that gas would be of 'vital importance' in any future conflict.

There was no record of the response to his revelation that when, at Ludwigshafen after the Armistice, the Germans were being pressed to give details of their mustard gas process one of them said: 'Why are you worrying about this when you know perfectly well that this is not the gas we shall use in the next war?'

As the officers and their ladies fled from the spectres raised by Brigadier-General Hartley, ex-Rifleman August Jager was looking for work. Another war was the thing farthest from his mind. A month earlier he had returned to his home town of Seebergen, in Thuringia, and counted himself lucky. His years in a French

---

[1] It is estimated that 10,000 rounds were fired experimentally before a reliable 25-pounder Yellow Cross shell was ready for production in the Second World War.

prisoner-of-war camp had not been a picnic, but at least he had survived.

Jager tried for six months to find work. In April, 1920, he applied to join the Army again. The records were checked and it was noted that he had disappeared in mysterious circumstances in 1915. In May he was interrogated at the headquarters of the 38th Infantry Division at Eisenach, and again in September. Then just as things were looking black for him an amnesty for all deserters was proclaimed. Jager left the barrack gates a free man. He was followed only by cold stares. Within a month he had the offer of a job.

In April, 1922, General Falkenhayn died at his castle in Lindstet, having published two volumes of memoirs. His account of the critical decisions of the German General Staff during his supremacy contained the plaintive phrase:

'It was years before it was possible to control gas with any certainty as a weapon.'[1]

---

[1] It may still be asked whether any weapons system is controllable 'with any certainty', modern missiles in particular.

CHAPTER 23

Dew of Death

What was claimed to be a super-gas was in preparation in the United States for the campaign of 1919. It was called Lewisite after Captain W. Lee Lewis who had carried out the research at the Catholic University branch of the American University Research Division of the US Chemical Warfare Service.

Chemically named chlorvinyl dichlorarsine, Lewisite was ready for use just before the Armistice but did not go into service. It blistered like mustard gas but because of its arsenical properties was absorbed through the skin. Three drops on the stomach of a laboratory rat killed it within three hours. The gas could also cause sneezing and had the military virtue of being persistent. It was said to smell of geraniums and, unlike mustard gas, caused permanent blindness.

The production methods were kept secret by the Americans, until two British Scientists disclosed them in the *Journal of the Chemical Society* in 1921. Its reputedly deadly powers had, however, been described in the *New York Times* in 1919 and Brigadier-General Fries is credited with describing it as 'The Dew of Death'.

Under the terms of the Armistice Treaty the Germans were obliged to reveal the secrets of the manufacture of all their war gases and it was learned that they too had experimented with a form of Lewisite but had discarded it.

Unknown to each other, both sides had also tried out a thermo-generator, a small metal box in which an arsenical solid was heated to the point where it gave off highly poisonous smoke particles which could penetrate a respirator. The Germans, once again, had used the Russian front for their experiments, which had been a failure for a variety of reasons.

The British thought their version – the M-Device – was more practical and plans were made for its use on a large scale in 1919. These were kept secret after the Armistice but gradually garbled stories leaked out and it was stated that the reason the 'Gas Box' had not been used was because no respirator was proof against it. Beverley Nichols, the popular author, (like Hartley, he was a Balliol man) wrote to this effect during the Thirties, only to be contradicted by Foulkes.

The realms of What Might Have Been flourished but briefly after the Armistice for just as the vast armies had been conjured out of nowhere so they disappeared and with them the share of national resources they demanded and the interest they created.

Congress, in the US Army Reorganization Act of 1920, provided for the continuation of a separate Chemical Warfare Service, charged with 'the investigation, development, manufacture or procurement and supply to the Army of all smoke and incendiary materials, all toxic gases, and all gas defence appliances; the research, design and experimentation connected with chemical warfare . . . the chemical projectile filling plans and proving grounds . . . the organization, equipment, training and operation of special gas troops, and such other duties as the President may from time to time prescribe'.

The rump of the establishment at Edgewood was retained, as was Porton in Britain, but as the years passed the use of gas was universally condemned, along with germ warfare.

In peacetime no one really wished to grasp the nettle. Gas was undoubtedly a practical weapon, could be produced cheaply without interfering with the demands for high-grade steel for artillery for example, and killed no one deader than anything else. What it did not have was an influential backer. There were distinguished senior officers with reputations as good infantry, good cavalry, good gunner generals; there were good defensive and good attacking generals. All were proud of their labels. No one wanted to boast of being a good gas general. Major-General Thuillier, the first Director of Chemical Warfare, had managed to obtain a posting back to command an infantry division[1] before the fighting ended.

The First World War was essentially an artillery war. Even machine guns took second place to the big guns. On the German side one of the finest exponents of the hurricane of high explosive was unquestionably Bruchmüller and he vastly increased the power of this medium by including Yellow, Blue and Green Cross shells in his

[1] The 23rd, serving in Italy.

barrages. The victors respected his methods but did not openly adopt them. Instead, as the British and American armies dwindled, the French Army fossilized and the German and Russian armies revived and concentrated on mechanization, talk of gas warfare was stifled.

The American Army was forbidden to carry out research on toxic gases for a number of years despite the immediate postwar enthusiasm. Traditionalists sat heavily on the upstarts with chemistry degrees who had no West Point class reference. In French circles, mindful of the fact that the Green Cross bombardment of Souville had nearly given the Germans victory at Verdun, the problem as applied to the new Maginot Line was carefully considered. General Sir Edmund Ironside, the British CIGS, noted after a visit that: 'The air pressure inside the fort was kept greater than the outside, so no gas could get in.'

In the rickety peace years the bogey refused to go away despite all attempts to ignore it. Large numbers of men who had been through the mustard gas period were then in their 30s and 40s and had vivid memories of their experiences. A study made of 10,000 stragglers after the March Retreat showed that 6,000 of them were not carrying arms but only 800 of them had either lost or thrown away their respirators.

'Between the wars' all British troops were trained to fight on a gas-affected battlefield. Officers were taught that the tactical objective while under chemical attack was to expose the minimum number of men and to keep their reserves intact. They were reminded that gas lingered in valleys and woods but not on high ground or in open spaces. During cloud attacks, which were not discounted, weapons had to be wrapped up where possible to prevent corrosion. Rifles and machine guns had often jammed if exposed to phosgene and chlorine in the Great War. During a gas attack they needed to be fired at intervals to keep them in working order and later to be cleaned at the first opportunity.

Against the blistering agents – mustard gas and Lewisite – special measures were devised. Increased vigilance was urged at sunrise following a night of shelling – and also during the hottest part of the day when evaporating fumes could be expected to be dangerous. A pamphlet issued ten years after Yellow Cross had first been fired in anger recommended that shell holes should be avoided and that no one should be allowed to sit or crawl on the ground. How the latter advice was to be effected under fire was not explained.

Buildings, trenches, dugouts, woods and other localities known to have been contaminated by a blistering agent were to be clearly marked so they could be avoided.

Where available, a mixture of sodium hypochlorite mixed with the humble kitchen-shelf ingredient, bicarbonate of soda, was stated to be the best destroyer of mustard gas, with chloride of lime as the next best thing. It was accepted that the availability of neutralizing chemicals would be limited, so substitutes for burying blistering agents – dry earth, sawdust and sand – were also suggested.

The treatment of almost everything which might be affected was considered; long grass, for example, was to be burned if tainted, good care being taken to stand leeward to avoid the poisonous smoke.

Decontamination squads had to remember that chloride of lime, generally referred to as bleaching powder, created a powerful reaction if put onto mustard gas liquid direct. It could cause fires and dangerous fumes. The powder had to be mixed with earth before use. In concrete emplacements floors should be cleaned with a solution of water glass.

Anyone who had ever questioned the harassing qualities of blistering gas could have no doubts about its nuisance value after the 1927 course of instruction.

For cavalry and transport units there was the added problem of the protection of mules and horses which were still in general use (infantry battalions had some horse transport until just before the 1939 war).

Though draught animals and saddle horses were not likely to be affected by tear gas and though their skins were much more resistant to blistering agents than a man's, special attention had to be paid to the heels immediately above the hoof. Contaminated ground was to be avoided and, if this was impossible, the animal's belly and legs had to be washed as soon as possible afterwards, with soap when available.

'Bags, pigeons, anti-gas' were to be indented for from ordnance depots and used to cover the birds' cages or boxes when required.

CHAPTER 24

August's Undoing . . .

In May, 1928 a few months after the War Office published revised training instructions on gas warfare, a striking example of the potential of phosgene was seen in Hamburg. More than eleven tons of the chemical was liberated in a factory explosion.[1] A dense cloud drifted through streets and over parkland leaving eleven people dead and affecting 250 in varying degrees.

The following year Belgian dignitaries attended a solemn ceremony on the banks of the Yser to unveil a monument to commemorate the events of April, 1915, and the dead of the 418th French Infantry Regiment. A relief on a stone plinth depicted a soldier clutching his throat amid dying comrades. It may not have been a great work but it told a graphic story.

Two years later the newpapers were full of something else for August and Frau Jager, whom he had married in 1921, to talk about. In July, 1930, the *Gazette de Lausanne* quoted an article from the current issue of the French *Revue des Vivants*. Written by General Ferry, who had commanded the 11th 'Iron' Division in 1915, it gave an account of the first gas attack under the title '*Ce qui s'est passé sur l'Yser*'. It went into detail.

Somewhere an old file was opened. This was not desertion. It was treason!

In May, 1931, Jager lost his job. The following month the Reichswehr reopened the case against him in the Supreme Court – Reichsgericht. On 29 December he was arrested at Erfurt, once the home of a friar called Martin Luther, and he spent New Year's Eve,

---

[1] Run by an entrepreneur called Stoltzenberg who had a contract to dismantle gas plants after the war.

1932 in a prison cell at Kassel, an important garrison town favoured by retired officers.

The preliminary investigation into the case was led by the chief provincial judge, Dr Bruno Faber. Apart from meetings with his interrogators and his own defence lawyer, Dr Hans Bucheim, Jager spent his time in solitary confinement.

For the next six months, while the Nazis were mounting a great political offensive and election fever raged, Jager remained locked up. By midsummer he was beginning to crack under the strain and appealed to the Senior State Medical Officer, Dr Otto Schutz, complaining that he was nearing a breakdown. In December, a year after his arrest, he went on trial – in semi-secret. After Kapitan sur Zee Konrad Patzig, of Military Intelligence, had outlined the case against Jager, the court sat mostly in camera, though reports did appear in the newspapers. The trial lasted a fortnight. Jager pleaded not guilty, but he did not stand a chance. His accusers claimed that by giving warning of the first gas attack he had enabled the enemy to inflict heavy losses and prevented a German victory. A number of ex-soldiers who had read brief summaries of the case wrote to the newspapers (anonymously for the most part) pointing out that the French could hardly have been unaware of what was intended, but these were ignored. Most of the witnesses were for the prosecution and few said anything in Jager's favour. Only one, a Herr Belz, who had served in the same unit, was honest enough to say that Jager could have been inspired by humane motives to warn the French. He remembered him saying that 'such a gas attack is a terrible thing' – ('*solch ein Gasangriff sei eine bose Sache*').

The court appears to have taken little notice of the ethical arguments; it was as if Jager could not possibly have had any deep feelings. What could the son of a railway ticket collector know about such things? It was all recorded: not too bright at school and far from outstanding when serving in the army from 1911 to 1913. A railway porter for a short period, Jager had obtained a driving licence in that year and had been recalled to the army as a driver. He had not been satisfactory, however, and that was why he had been sent back to his unit. There he had been disciplined a number of times. The court had heard the evidence of Rifleman Bierbebach; after finishing guard at midnight on 13 April the accused quit the trench saying he was going to the latrine. He left behind his scarf and cap and did not return. After the war he said he had been captured by the French.

It was a likely story! The man was clearly a traitor. They would

have to make an example of him: 'August Jager, you are sentenced to
ten years' penal servitude.'

The date was 17 December, 1932. Six week' later inside
Thuringen's Untermassfeld gaol, Jager heard that a former corporal
had become Chancellor of Germany.

The accelerated promotion of the ex-NCO also had repercussions on
the old Kaiser Wilhelm Institute, headed by Dr. Fritz Haber.
Attempts to have him prosecuted as a war criminal in 1919 were
quickly dropped and later his work on the synthesis of ammonia
before 1914 was rewarded with a Nobel Prize. When the Nazis came
to power the doctor wrote bluntly to the Minister of Education
refusing to accept that Jews, who had shown themselves to be as
patriotic as any other section of German society during the Great
War, were to be downgraded to second-class citizens. His resig-
nation followed and he was offered research facilities at Cambridge
by Sir William Pope, pioneer of the development of mustard gas for
use by the British. He was not made welcome by Sir Ernest
Rutherford, physicist and Nobel Prize winner (who headed the
University's Cavendish Laboratory for many years), and died in
Switzerland the following year.

In 1936 mustard gas once again appeared on a battlefield. The
previous year Italy had gone to war with Haile Selassie, Emperor of
Abyssinia. Mussolini, seeking expansion in Africa, urged the
governors of Eritrea and Italian Somaliland to pick a quarrel with
their neighbour. There were rich lands as well as desert in Abyssinia –
and the Duce also wished to avenge the humiliating defeat inflicted on
General Baratieri's army by the Emperor Menelik at Adowa in 1896.

A discreet deal was done with Laval, the French Foreign Minister,
precluding intervention from that quarter; a pointed increase in
activity by Britain's Mediterranean fleet was ignored. Mussolini
gambled that no other member of the League of Nations would do
anything to interfere with his designs and he was right. What he had
not reckoned with was the strength of Abyssinian opposition.

Converging columns crossed the frontier in October, 1935, and at
first met with easy success. A force under General de Bono, a crony
of Mussolini's, who had been police prefect of Milan, plunged boldly
on. In December, however, his troops were almost encircled and had
to fight their way out of a dangerous situation at Dembenguina. De
Bono was superseded and Marshal Badoglio took a firmer grip on the
operation.

Valuable time had now been lost and the Italians were faced with a dilemma. Unless they could speed up their campaign they would be into the rainy season, which began in May, and the war would drag on. A long conflict was something their economy could not face and prompt measures had to be taken.[1]

Mussolini also had to consider the morale of the Italian soldier. His troops lived in constant terror of being captured. Haile Selassie's regime had an unmistakeably mediaeval flavour about it. Pierre van Passen, Dutch-born columnist for a number of American papers, reported seeing in Addis a former Abyssinian Ambassador who had displeased the Emperor caged like an animal with an iron collar around his neck so that he could not rise from all fours. In 1941 a British officer serving in Abyssinia saw tribeswomen using twigs to whip the genitals of naked Italian prisoners spreadeagled in the sun. The men died in agony and he was unable to do anything to help them. The invading troops were prepared to welcome anything which might save them from a similar fate.

When the League of Nations was formed in 1919 it had the reduction of armaments as the first of the specific tasks imposed by its Covenant. A plethora of complex pacts, treaties and agreements had to be negotiated. It was an appalling task, but at least the subsequently denigrated statesmen who sponsored the League did try. After six years of frustrating talks they produced the Geneva Protocol which, though at first not in itself acceptable to, for example, Great Britain, finally led to the Locarno Negotiations and eventually to a fudge of uncertain guarantees. One thing on which all nations did agree was the following clause:

Whereas the use in war of asphyxiating, poisonous or other gases, and of all analogous liquids, materials or devices, had been justly condemned by the general opinion of the civilized world; and Whereas the prohibition of such use has been declared in treaties to which the majority of Powers of the world are parties; and to the end that this prohibition shall be universally applied.'[2]

Italy had been one of the signatories of the Protocol but the economic pressures on Mussolini to achieve a quick victory and avoid humiliation overcame diplomatic assurances and humanitarian arguments. Aircraft sprays are said to have been tried in December, 1935, at Sciri and in February, 1936, Savoia Marchetti aeroplanes dropped gas bombs on the flanks of advancing Italian columns.

---

[1] Among industries in decline were the Sicilian sulphur works noticed by Admiral Cochrane in 1811.
[2] Many countries reserved the right to use gas in retaliation if it was used against them or their allies.

Hordes of primitive tribesmen who previously had been able to raid at will were frustrated by the blister barrier. The mustard liquid vapourized quickly in the high temperatures and the lightly-clad warriors, some of whom were armed with bows and arrows, were particularly vulnerable to spray and splash.

The bombing broke organized resistance. The Abyssinians did not help themselves by rushing in crowds against troops dug in with automatic weapons and quick-firing artillery. Addis Ababa fell before the rains came, the Emperor became a refugee and his tribesmen, who were traditionally at odds with each other, either joined the victors or resorted to guerrilla tactics at which they were adept.

Before the defeat of Haile Selassie, however, all eyes had switched to another trouble spot. In March, 1936, Hitler marched into the Rhineland. Great was the indignation in the democracies; but that was all. In July Spain drifted into Civil War with General Francisco Franco sworn to oust the Republican government. Hitler and Mussolini supported their fellow fascists; Stalin backed the other side. All took the opportunity to test military equipment under battle conditions. Despite rumours, the use of gas was never substantiated. In any case the combatants had found another terror weapon – indiscriminate aerial bombing of civilian targets. The air war made a tremendous impression in Britain. People began to wonder what the skies might hold for them.

CHAPTER 25

The Budgie's Warning

Sydney Smith, a young journalist, stood on the platform at Newcastle Central Station and waved goodbye to his wife and young son. He had decided that Tyneside was a much more likely target for Hitler's bombers than Aberdeen and sent his family off to stay with Scottish relatives.

The train had been packed with women and children and he was struck by the way in which everyone had a gas mask hanging from their shoulders or round their necks.

Some of these were still in the waxed brown cardboard boxes in which they had been issued, suspended by a piece of cord. Others were concealed by cloth covers run up on mother's sewing machine and carried by a broader strap. The more well-to-do had metal containers which could be bought in the shops. Some of these resembled the German cylinder cases of 1918.

The country had been conditioned to the idea that gas bombing would be one of the natural hazards of the war about to engulf them. Cigarette cards gave tips on air-raid precautions and illustrated the best way to 'gas-proof' a cellar. Among the rows of lead soldiers in toy shop windows, where the scarlet tunic still predominated, there were sinister models of stretcher bearers clad from head to foot in protective suits for use in areas contaminated by mustard gas.

It was recalled that after the Armistice in 1918 it had been learned that the enemy had prepared a number of bombs containing phosgene but had not dropped them for fear of retaliation.

On 27 September, 1938, Neville Chamberlain said in a broadcast to the nation:

'How horrible, fantastic, incredible it is that we should be digging trenches and trying on gas masks because of a quarrel in a far away country,[1] between people of whom we know nothing.'

Fantastic indeed to the average Briton to see workmen painting strange patches on the flat tops of pillar boxes. Should invisible gases fill the streets these would change colour. Sensitive plates were also fastened to public air-raid shelters.

When the sirens sounded after Chamberlain declared war on 3 September, 1939, mothers and children took cover and sat with their masks on, fearfully waiting for the unknown terror to arrive. In Paris, where the warning had also been given, smartly dressed women ran for shelter and 'sat stifled and half fainting in their gas masks'. Berliners also took cover that day. Not a bomb fell. After the 'all clear' had been sounded people emerged blinking into the sun of a pleasant late summer Sunday. The paint patches on the pillar boxes had not changed their shade one iota. Nevertheless the fear was there. All over Europe citizens were instructed to carry their gas masks with them at all times. Only as the weeks passed without an air onslaught on the crowded cities of Britain and France did tension ease. Warsaw had been bombed but gas had not been used in Poland; perhaps the enemy did not intend to use it after all. Perhaps there would be no air raids either, though one had to be prepared for all eventualities as an advertisment in the *Newcastle Journal* indicated:

'Don't be scared to have your hair permed. If you have it done by the Superperma method you will be able to leave the chair immediately in the event of a warning.'

Another small ad offered this bargain: 'A.R.P. – Safeguard your family or staff. A pet Budgie will definitely warn you of Gas, long before your air-raid wardens can. Hardy, healthy Budgies, 6s. each, carriage paid.'

Bred in Morpeth, Northumberland, these budgies had to be hardy.

For Britain's firemen the delivery of anti-mustard gas ointment struck a more ominous note. Already equipped with heavy oiled protective clothing to be worn if necessary, their eyebrows went up when they saw the size of the drums in which the ointment came. Leading Fireman Stanley Rogers, who later went through the Blitz on Portsmouth, took pride in being able to heave the things about: 'They weighed about a hundredweight each.'

Nevertheless politicians and public remained sceptical. By October, 1939, Churchill, recalled from the political wilderness to become First Lord of the Admiralty, was writing to the Prime

[1] Czechoslovakia

Minister to urge that gas masks should be carried permanently in 'target areas' such as London. In seven-eighths of the country they could be kept at home. It was not perhaps really his concern but he had never hesitated to meddle in the affairs of other ministries.

Air Raid Wardens carried out a spot check in Leeds the following month and found that, despite notices urging the population to 'Carry your gas mask with you at all times', only a third of people actually had a respirator in the box on their shoulders. The others were using them to carry sandwiches and personal belongings.

This casual attitude could not be allowed to apply to the fighting troops. A 1939 photograph of Field-Marshal Lord Gort, Commander-in-Chief of the British Expeditionary Force, with Lieutenant-General Alan Brooke, then a corps commander, shows them greeting the War Minister, Mr Hore-Belisha, in France, with the straps of their respirator satchels passing smartly across their chests at the same angle. No doubt the Generals, both of whom had experienced gas in the trenches, wished to set an example to the troops. There were no signs of a mask on Hore-Belisha.

Another news photograph of kilted highlanders outside a Maginot Line blockhouse shows a section being inspected with respirators at the ready position.

General Ironside, 12 October, 1939: 'News this morning looks as if the Germans were really about to mount an attack through Luxembourg, and also along most of the front of the Maginot Line. . . . Reports are being circulated of a new gas in large quantities and the French are in a thoroughly nervous state. I wonder.'

Britain's ally had learned that the enemy mask provided protection against arsenical smokes, the product of the celebrated 'gas box' with which the Germans were to have been given the coup de grâce in the proposed 1919 offensive. On the strength of this information, modification of Service respirators took place on a large scale.[1]

The jumpiness noted by Ironside was not helped by German accusations that the Poles had used gas in the campaign of 1939 and that the British had supplied it. Shades of 1915!

Though gas was not used during the Nazi invasion of the Low Countries and France there were scares. Lieutenant Airey Neave, R.E., who was wounded and captured at Calais: 'A heavy artillery bombardment fell on all the Rifle Brigade and Q.V.R. (Queen Victoria Rifles) positions. . . . At the Cellulose factory shells burst in the yard and yellow acrid smoke drifted towards the ramparts. There

---

[1] Hinsley, *British Intelligence in the Second World War*, Vol II.

were cries of "Gas!" and respirators were hurriedly put on.' Minutes later it was realized that the smoke was from burning cordite. Neave reports several false alarms on 25 May, 1940, but probably the only gas weapon used in earnest that year was the Panzerbusche Model 1938 anti-tank rifle issued to the German infantry.

'The bullet had a tungsten carbide core; at the base was a tracer element, and between that and the tungsten carbide, marvellous to relate, was a small pellet of tear gas!' The pellet was supposed to puff a little cloud of eye irritant into the confines of a pierced tank. 'Since the pellet was hardly bigger than an aspirin, the size of the cloud was not likely to be noticed at all. Nor was it; it was only when captured ammunition was broken down that it was discovered.'

So runs a passage in *Men Against Tanks*, published in 1975, which exemplifies military misunderstanding of chemical warfare even when the writer is a highly professional soldier such as the late Colonel John Weeks. It was not 'the size of the cloud' or the minuteness of the pellet which counted but the reaction of the agent when exposed to the atmosphere. A single gram of diphenyl-cyanarsine (a Blue Cross derivative) would have made a tank with a volume of, say, ten cubic metres, uninhabitable very quickly if the crew were unprotected. Just a drop of DA (another Blue Cross version) tried almost absentmindedly by an inquisitive member of Foulkes's staff cleared the headquarters building in seconds at St Omer in 1917.

By the time France fell, military intelligence (which had already suggested that if the Nazis did resort to chemical warfare the main agents would once again be mustard gas and phosgene delivered by bomb,shell or spray) had intercepted and compiled references to anti-gas officers being appointed in German units and to troops being sent on CW courses. The Germans, on their part, went through the harvest of captured documents they had reaped. Both sides were aware of their opponents' capability to employ CW based on Great War experience. Neither knew what new products may have arisen during research. Vesicants were still held in high regard.

In October Mr Churchill, who had become Prime Minister, was inquiring about the 2,000 tons of mustard gas ordered by the Chamberlain government: 'The latest information . . . shows that the bulk stockof mustard gas on December 9 (the previous year) was 1,485 tons. I was also informed . . . that 650 tons of new storage was to have become available last week, and that production was being increased accordingly. Was this promise fulfilled?'[1]

[1] See letters reproduced in the Appendices to Churchill, *The Second World War* Vol II.

Throughout the autumn and winter of 1940 the Prime Minister concerned himself with the possibility of poison gas being used in the event of an invasion in the New Year. He comforted himself with the knowledge that British 'progress in this sphere' was considerable. He informed the Chiefs of Staff Committee on Boxing Day, 1940, that he was deeply anxious that chemical warfare should not be introduced and for that very reason feared the enemy might turn to it. He had even considered whether the enemy might be deterred if the British announced that they would never be the first to use gas, though they had ample stocks in the necessary containers. On balance he thought it better to say nothing as there would be 'too much bluff' in such a statement. A few days earlier he had been concerned to note that, because of air-raid damage to factories, the production of gas bombs had fallen 'noticeably'. Only fifty-two had been produced, nine of which were of the largest variety – one thousand pounders. (There was nothing, of course, to prevent bomb cases being stored on or near airfields ready to be filled with mustard agent, albeit at some risk, and dropped quickly.)

As early as July, 1940, Churchill had ordered the nation's gas masks to be checked in case Hitler launched chemical warfare. Though Britain might not initiate such a thing, the country had to be prepared to retaliate against the German civil population should the need arise.

For the use of whatever stocks were available, Mr Churchill could draw on expert advice. Apart from the scientific experts at Porton the old hands were still available. Charles Foulkes had retired as a major-general in 1930 after spending four years as Chief Engineer, Aldershot Command. He wrote *Commonsense and ARP* in 1938; up to that time some 90 per cent of air raid precautions activity had concerned anti-gas procedures; later the emphasis switched to combating HE and incendiary bombs.

Foulkes's erstwhile superior, Henry Fleetwood Thuillier, had also served until 1930, retiring as a major-general after three years in command of the 52nd (Lowland) Division TA. In 1939 he published *Gas in the Next War* and the following year, though 70, left the comfort of his Cheltenham home and disappeared into the Ministry of Supply with the rank of major. (From 1942 until the end of hostilities he served in the information and record section at Porton.)

Brigadier-General Hartley, whose lecture had been received with 'loud applause' at the Royal Artillery Institution in 1919, was also at hand. Having become, appropriately, a director of the Gas, Light and Coke Company in 1922, he had pursued a dazzling business

career, been knighted and become Chairman of the Hartley
Technical Sub-Committee assessing Axis oil reserves (originally the
Lloyd Committee) and Chairman of the Fuel Research Board.

Livens was still available and so was Barcroft (knighted in 1935) of
the celebrated gas chamber experiment. Barcroft was to spend two
more years at Porton before returning to Cambridge and agricultural
research.

Mr Churchill could also rely on the assistance of the young
journalist. Sydney Smith had been nominated 'late sub' in the spring
of 1940 which meant going on duty at midnight to await news of a
German offensive. It was just his luck that he was on holiday when
the panzers roared into Belgium. Soon afterwards, however, he was
called up and had to explain to an elderly major just what a newspaper
sub-editor actually did. The old warrior nodded sagely, not understanding a word, and declared, 'I'll put you down for Signals.'

Conscientiously he invested in a booklet, *How to Learn the Morse
Code in Thirty Minutes*, and practised assiduously in the wire room
of the *Newcastle Journal* during his late vigil. When his call-up papers
arrived he found himself posted to the Royal Engineers. In Hut 50 at
Barton Stacey camp just outside Andover, Hants, ten minutes' drive
from Porton, 200 Sapper Smith joined schoolteachers, Oxford
graduates, chemists and a sprinkling of manual workers. They
formed part of a force of 10,000 chemical warfare troops and were
told not to bother to apply for postings abroad as they were specialist
personnel. In peacetime the Army gas course lasted eighteen months.
In 1940 this was condensed to sixteen weeks.

'Our main task, it was impressed on us, was as a last line of defence
in the event of an invasion . . . to spread a carpet of gas in the way of
the Jerries, thus holding up their advance until reinforcements
arrived.'

The means of laying the carpet was to be an improved version of the
Livens Projector. Eleven groups of three companies plus a headquarters staff were raised ready to be deployed by lorry. The groups
were equipped with 240 projectors weighing 112 lbs each. The
drums, when full, weighed up to 65 lbs. As Corporal Fox had
discovered in 1915, the skills of the navvy were soon recognized as
more useful than those of a chemist. Sapper Smith found: 'The barrels
[projectors] were often slippery with mud and the main feat was in
heaving one of them onto your shoulder. Often the most adept at this
task were not the rugger-playing types but the smaller hard men from
the North. Despite special exercises devised by PT sadists, men still
suffered hernias from struggling with the damned barrels, though

successful experiments were being carried out using mortars and rockets. The mortars in particular combined a high rate of fire with a good gas capacity.'

Unlike the original Livens projector, the new model was not dug into the ground but propped against a metal rest. The range was similar – up to 1,800 yards. After firing, all barrels had to be heaved from the ground into which the recoil had thrust them and carried back to the waiting lorries.

The men of the 'CW' companies had no illusions about their fate should the Nazis land: 'Old Jerry would simply blow us to pieces as we humped the projectors back to the lorries!'

They had no moral reservations, however, about discharging their drums of mustard gas[1]. Any Germans they encountered would not be in Britain by invitation or for the good of their health.

[1] Mr Smith says no mustard gas was actually fired in training.

CHAPTER 26

Awful Arthur!

The British sappers were instructed in the nature of all gases encountered in the Great War and some which had been improved or developed afterwards. These were split into four classes:

> *Choking –* including phosgene and di-phosgene (as in the 1917/18 Green Cross Shells), chlorine and chloro-picrin.
>
> *Nose –* DM or Adamsite (a solid which gave off poisonous smoke); DA (a version of Blue Cross) and DC which had a similar effect.
>
> *Tear –* CAP, which could cause spasms in the eyelid; KSK, which smelled of pear drops and BBC, which had the scent of 'sour fruit'.
>
> *Blister –* Mustard gas and Lewisite.

Even hydrocyanic gas, which had been tried unsuccessfully in 1916, and the relatively useless sulphuretted hydrogen were on the curriculum.

The troops were also warned to look out for Arthur, a sinister German product sent over as a grey powder which, on contact with water, gave off arsenical fumes. Not a few eyebrows were raised when it was revealed that any water passed by victims of 'Arthur' after a few hours would be red and that later it would be impossible to urinate at all.

The troops took comfort in the knowledge that their respirators were proof against all known gases.

Training in the New Forest as the Luftwaffe pounded South-ampton, they applied themselves enthusiastically to the science of planting fields of mines containing mustard gas which could be blown electrically when entered by the enemy.

Throughout the winter of 1940/41 the preparation for battle went on and Smith's company was moved from the New Forest to Exmoor and later to Ayrshire and the North-East coast. Wearing a pink and green shoulder flash, a throwback to the armbands worn at Loos, they were for some reason frequently mistaken by the public for 'Free Belgians' or 'Free something or other'. It made no difference. Wherever they went they found themselves made welcome.

As late as October, 1941, *The War Illustrated* was urging the public to carry their gas masks. An article entitled 'Gas May Yet Be Used In This War' stated:

'Nearly two years have passed since we published (Vol.1,p.534) an article in which it was stated that expert opinion was then almost unanimous in believing that it was very unlikely that gas would be used in this war. That view has not yet been falsified by experience; but, in view of the many warnings issued by Government spokesmen, it is obvious that the possibility – some would say the probability – still exists.'

Gas, it was emphasized, was mainly a means of causing panic and was most likely to be used 'as an accompaniment to an invasion attempt'.

The writer insisted that, despite its reputation, mustard gas was far less deadly than high explosive bombs. Professor Haldane, C.W. Glover in his book *Civil Defence*, and Brigadier-General Hartley were all quoted in support of this contention.

There was one belated gas casualty. On 8 May, 1941, the Germans blew up the monument on the Yser. Various reasons were given. The Belgians believed it was because of the wording which stated that the Germans were the first to use poison gas as a weapon. Strangely the Canadian memorial to an estimated 2,000 men who died in 'The First German Gas Attacks' was untouched.

The absence of any firm intelligence that the Axis powers had used gas against the Allies (though there were reports of it being identified in China during fighting at Ichang in Hupeh Province in 1941) had led to a noticeable lowering of fears and expectations. The training of soldiers to be prepared to meet gas continued, nevertheless. Though it was still made quite clear that it was not British policy to initiate chemical warfare, every fighting man had to be prepared. Gas had to be regarded as a weapon on a par with bombs, bullets and shells. Individuals could not make it an excuse for not carrying on with a battle. Training manuals made it plain that though non-persistent gases might be encountered, the greatest danger still lay with mustard gas or its equivalent which might well be sprayed from aircraft. In this case the first duty of every man in a unit under attack was to fire on the plane until his commander gave the alarm 'Spray', whereupon men might take cover. It was laid down that every officer and man was responsible for his own preservation to which end he had been highly equipped.

Apart from the mask itself, the soldier carried in the respirator satchel two pairs of goggles, detectors to be worn on the sleeves, tins or jars of ointment, a camouflaged chemically-treated cape and an ounce of cotton waste to be used in applying the ointment. A wallet to protect a man's paybook (AB 64) was also issued (*not* to be carried in the respirator haversack), giving new life to the old joke about gasses so strong that they would poison the next-of-kin.

Lightweight protective suits were available for motorcyclists and the crews of the Bren gun carriers. Some suits of battledress had also been treated (marked 'A/V'), which gave some protection against mustard gas vapour but not against liquid splashes. The manual emphasized that the strong-smelling serge of the A/V was no more resistant to lice than normal uniform cloth. New types of clothing apart, anti-gas drill was much as outlined in the 1927 manual, with warning rattles of 1918 vintage still in use.

One lesson drummed home was that because new gases might be odourless and invisible, any inexplicable feeling of nausea, choking or tightness of chest must be treated suspiciously, along with strange liquids or smoke encountered, and respirators had to be worn until the cause had been identified.

Metal plates covered with detector paint were issued for use in and around camps and field locations: a spot of mustard gas or Lewisite would show up red or brown. Sensitive paint could also be applied to the bonnets of lorries so that the driver could see whether or not he was driving through a contaminated area.

Troops were told that the Germans had gas shells, bombs and projectors and that the tactics to be expected would be similar to those of the previous war with emphasis on a mixture of gas and high explosive in bombardments.

Litre pots of mustard gas were issued for training[1] so that troops,

---

[1] The theft of a number of jars from a private house led to urgent warnings being issued by the police in North-West Britain in July, 1985. The thieves were warned that one whiff of the contents would kill them. It took twenty-four hours to discover the jars were harmless training aids . . . souvenirs!

suitably protected, could recognize the effect of Yellow Cross on their sleeve detectors, smell it from a distance and identify concrete, earth and cloth tainted with it. A drop of the liquid was dabbed on the arm of each man who was required to rub in ointment vigorously for thirty seconds. Any blister would be his own fault.

Tank crews were also trained to combat choking and blister gases. With thunderflashes tied to their turrets to simulate hits by shells or bombs, the umpire (during an exercise) had suddenly to sprinkle the 'tankies' with a specially concocted training mixture. Methods of decontaminating vehicles were also rehearsed. The British soldier of the 1940s was well-trained to deal with a Western Front-style gas attack, and to deliver one.

The Russians, too, took precautions. Stalin feared the Germans would unleash mustard gas when they resumed the offensive in the spring of 1942 and wrote to Churchill. The British Prime Minister replied that, 'We shall treat any such outrage as if directed upon us, and will retaliate without limit.' This, Churchill claimed, we were in a good position to do. In March he told Stalin that Britain had been building up 'immense stores' of bombs and was ready to drop them if need be.

The possibility of using gas in other theatres of war was not neglected. By June, 1942, No. 1 Chemical Warfare Group, with the 58th, 62nd and 67th Companies under command, was in India with its headquarters eventually in Poona.

The Americans, too, were still producing 'Y' shell for possible use and in December, 1943, an ammunition ship, the *John Harvey*, blew up in Bari harbour during an air raid. Gallons of liquid mustard gas gushed into the water in which sailors were swimming for their lives and the docks area was severely contaminated. The death roll was eighty-three and about 500 victims were treated in hospital. Everything was done to hush up the incident. Medical officers were at first unable to identify injuries because the gas dissolved in the oil spillage from the wreck.

For the average soldier, however, the threat of gas had become unreal. As the war dragged on gas capes came to be regarded more and more as essential adjuncts for romantic rather than military pursuits. Some disreputable troopers in the 9th Lancers, slogging their way up Italy, discovered that the ointment in their battered respirator satchels made an excellent substitute for hair cream . . . even though they did 'smell of carbolic a bit'.

Still the Royal Artillery continued to fire gas shell in practise shoots. An officer who took part in an exercise in the Sperrin

Mountains in Northern Ireland in 1943 recalls seeing an accumulation of pink fumes but could not remember the nature of the gas.

'The British Government has no intention of initiating the use of gas,' said a contemporary artillery training manual. 'The British Army must, however, be prepared to protect itself against the use of gas by an enemy.' The manual emphasized that the decision to use chemical shells 'must be made by the highest headquarters possible; i.e. seldom lower than divisional headquarters'.

Once gas warfare had started all troops in the open would wear eye shields. Any British shells would be fired to burst in the air to spray their contents. By then, however, it was clear that offensive gas warfare would become the responsibility of the Royal Air Force.

The R.E. Chemical Warfare companies were transferred to other tasks at which they were not so expert. Sergeant Smith, as he had become, stood with his comrades fascinated as a bridge they had built slowly subsided into the Humber carrying their officer with it. They had to snap into action to save him from drowning. Many CW sappers went into assault engineer units in preparation for the Normandy landings. Some found themselves building roads in Assam. Other units were converted into conventional field companies. Sergeant Smith considered himself lucky to end up in Calcutta doing his civilian job as a sub-editor on the Forces newspaper, *SEAC*.

CHAPTER 27

Mein Kampf Clue

Immediately after the war the Allied experts found themselves once more going through the pockets, so to speak, of German scientists. While some spirited away the rocket designers, others scurried back to their laboratories with strangely marked shells – what did GA or GB stand for?

The chemists made the sobering discovery that the enemy had identified a series of agents which acted on the human nervous system, robbing victims of all control of their normal bodily functions. One of these, Tabun, had been stumbled on before the war by a scientist working on insecticides. The gas had been put into production and used for bomb and shell filling; large quantities were found in reserve ammunition dumps. There was nothing to indicate that the enemy had been preparing to use them, but Tabun was considered to be much more deadly than any known gas and the factory which made it, at Dyhernfurth on the Oder, fell into Russian hands.

Nerve gases credited with properties even grimmer than Tabun were traced – Sarin and Soman – but these had remained at the experimental stage, production in bulk being technically difficult. Others may have been located by countries who decided it was in their best interests to keep them to themselves.

Tabun was certainly one of the most potent secret weapons available to Hitler and the question why he did not use it still remains unanswered . . . as does the explanation for the non-use of gas by any of the belligerents in the 1939-45 war. Even today war gases are regarded as 'an unsavoury subject', to quote General Lord Horne's 1919 description. A sense of outrage, even guilt, is invoked by mention of them in some quarters.

A report published in February, 1985, by the Stockholm Inter-national Peace Research Institute (an organization described by the *Daily Telegraph* as 'respected') was regarded as worthy of headlines by 'revealing' 45 years afterwards that the British had 6,000 mustard gas bombs available to be dropped on the beaches should the Nazis invade. The newspaper's Defence Correspondent at the time, Major-General Edward Fursdon, a retired sapper officer, com-mented that Churchill was determined to go to any lengths 'even to using poisoned gas' to stop an invasion. The sub-editor who put the headline on the story was equally apologetic: 'Last Resort Measures'.

A plan to use military aircraft to spray the beaches with blister gas and, even stranger, one to use Tiger Moths to do the same with an insecticide containing an arsenic compound, was recalled. Consider-ing the vulnerability of the lumbering Lysanders, which were to play the lead role in the first instance, and the flimsy Tiger Moths, in the second, the term 'Last Resort' may have applied more readily to them.

But if Churchill thought the use of mustard gas was justified for the sake of preserving the British Empire in which he believed, along with the majority of his countrymen, why should Hitler not have been prepared to go any lengths to defend the Thousand Year Reich he envisaged?

The moral, political, religious and economic arguments had been exhausted by the time mustard gas made its appearance in 1917. An appeal by Pope Benedict XV and the International Red Cross for the end of gas warfare had been rejected as late as 1918. The Entente thought it was well meant but to the advantage of their enemy.

No new fundamental arguments emerged between the wars, despite the signing of the Geneva Convention of 1925. Though solemn condemnation of poison gas came from every side, the belligerents were all prepared for it in 1939. What they did not anticipate was the speed of modern warfare. With one or two exceptions most generals on both sides were surprised by the success of the Blitzkrieg. Fuller's vision of tanks and gas being used together did not materialize because the enemy lines could be broken without resorting to chemical warfare. A persistent gas attack on Dunkirk might have written a different ending to the story but by then Hitler was enchanted by the war of manoeuvre ... which mustard gas hinders.

The absence of gas bombs from the rain of high explosives dropped on Britain in 1940 is more of a puzzle. Ian Hogg, in his study *Gas*, attributes the general reluctance to the proposition that 'no nation was willing to be the first to use gas, partly because of the stigma of being the first to breach the (Geneva) Protocol, and partly because the other side might reveal a considerable superiority.'

It is a commonsense view but over looks the fact that Italy had already breached the Convention. With regard to world opinion, the destroyer of Warsaw and Rotterdam was unlikely to have qualms about that. As to the British, standing alone after the fall of France, whatever chemical agents they might possess they had scant means of delivering them. The RAF's strike capacity was severely limited. Day raids over the German coast had proved too costly and night flying raids were in their infancy. Even if the British had been in a position to riposte, they were hardly likely to drop deadly gas bombs on enemy bases in conquered territory.

Conversely the Luftwaffe could have inflicted critical wounds on Britain's defences. Had airfields and radar stations been attacked with bombs containing a vesicant, the cratering of runways would have posed extra problems and a heavy strain on the men required to repair them. In the lovely summer weather, ground crews and pilots would have operated in a constantly suspect atmosphere. Underground control rooms equipped with filters would have protected the personnel but their job would not have been made any easier. The possibility of such attacks had not been ignored. Sensor plates were fixed to airfield buildings and detector panels painted on aircraft. Mercifully they remained as unresponsive as those on the pillar boxes.

Was it because German stocks of Yellow Cross were relatively low, though the overall supplies of chemical agents was large? This, coupled with Goering's confidence that the Luftwaffe would do the job with high explosive, is the most likely explanation.

It has also been suggested that there was an 'emotional factor' behind the non-use of gas throughout more than five and a half years of war – that Hitler developed an aversion to the weapon after being blinded by it while serving in the 16th Bavarian Reserve Infantry Regiment in 1918. He was in hospital when the Armistice was signed. The 'aversion' theory was put forward by General Thuillier before the war and repeated later. However, it is clear that the Führer did not have any reservations about making chemical war on those he considered to be his enemies. The following passage appears in *Mein Kampf*, published in the 1920s:

'If at the beginning and during the war someone had only subjected about twelve or fifteen thousand of these Hebrew enemies of the people to poison gas – as was suffered by hundreds of thousands of

our best workers from all walks of life and callings on the battlefield –
then the sacrifice of millions at the front would not have been in vain.'

The logic behind this passage is unfathomable, as is the way in
which it attracted so little comment as Hitler rose to power.
Throughout his dictatorship great importance was attached to the
study of chemical warfare. The experimental establishment at
Raubkammer in North-West Germany was kept well staffed and
equipped and its scientists worked on a variety of agents, including
the nerve gases.

However, from the beginning of the Nazi era there were doubts in
high places about the viability of chemical warfare. Under the terms
of the Versailles Treaty, Germany was forbidden to retain or replace
her war gases, a restriction which the Weimar Republic broadly
adhered to, though there was nothing to stop her chemists and
soldiers theorizing and recording and studying foreign developments. When practical research began again there were those who
wondered whether the scientists could ever make up for the lost
years. They were, they considered, years behind their potential
opponents. According to one American writer, the Germans suffered
a severe crisis of confidence: 'The gap appeared unsurmountable.'[1]

German concern over the imagined technological gap and Allied
fears that Hitler might commit some 'mad dog act'[2] out of frustration
or desperation made the subject particularly sensitive.

When in the summer of 1942 the Red Army reported signs that the
enemy was about to resort to chemical warfare, Churchill was faced
with a delicate situation. Were the Russians genuinely worried or
were they preparing the way for a bogus claim that they had suffered a
gas attack? Was the Bear crying Wolf? Stalin might be trying to
induce his allies to carry out their earlier promise to help him with
retaliation in kind if subjected to chemical warfare. Gas bombing of
Germany might be as good as the Second Front for which he was for
ever pleading. Churchill responded by repeating his assurances of
CW retaliation in the appropriate circumstances and made a broadcast to this effect on 10 May. Another agitated Soviet report in 1943
said that new filters had been fitted to the respirators which German
soldiers carried and led to the Prime Minister repeating his earlier
declaration.[3]

In their turn, the Germans became alarmed at intercepted signals

[1] F.J. Brown, *Chemical Warfare, a Study in Restraints*, Princeton, 1968.
[2] Hinsley, *British Intelligence in the Second World War*, Vol III.
[3] Hinsley, Vol III

which appeared to indicate that the British were likely to use chemical warfare in the Middle East and had sent an anti-gas team to Benghazi in 1942. In 1943 they alerted *Panzerarmee Afrika* to the dangers of a gas attack. Chemical shells, perhaps sent out for a riposte, were found in dumps overrun when the Axis forces capitulated in North Africa. Similar finds, along with CW equipment, were made in Russia. There was a certain irony in the alarm expressed by Stalin. It was to Berlin that the Russians had turned when they set up a central CW headquarters at Volsk, near Kuibyschev, in 1928. The establishment was conveniently near factories producing toxic substances and German advisers got a clear impression that the Soviet forces were keen on the development of new weapons.

By 1935 the Red Army had not only three chemical warfare regiments on its Western frontier but eleven independent battalions 'for an arm on which the Soviet command placed the greatest importance not only because it was relatively inexpensive but also it seemed to combine the advantage with that of considerable effectiveness'.[1]

In the chaos which followed the German invasion of June, 1941, an event which took the Red Army by surprise despite repeated indications that it was imminent, these troops seem to have been swept away without deploying their special weapons. Once again the Blitzkrieg tactics invalidated the need for gas to neutralize the Russian masses who were captured in huge encirclement battles. Until the crack Sixth Army was trapped at Stalingrad and forced to surrender in January, 1943, the Führer could still hope to achieve 'Final Victory' by conventional means. This prospect vanished the following July with the failure of the panzers to pinch out the fortified Kursk salient, where vesicants might have been employed to good effect. Hitler was thus restricted to a survival strategy which meant yielding large tracts of territory,and of this he was psychologically incapable. From then on his salvation lay in developing devastating new weapons, employing powerful old ones, and divine intervention. As his prayers were unlikely to be answered, he chose to rely on 'Secret Weapons'.

Allied intelligence kept a close check on the concrete emplacements being built by Todt workers only a few miles from Cherbourg, one near the handsome château of Martinvast (just off the D900) and the other between the village of Sottevast and the little town of Bricquebec (where a blacksmith still uses one of the storage bunkers

[1] Erickson, *The Soviet High Command*

as a workshop). Towards the end of 1943 reports were received that Hitler had ordered experiments to be made with rockets filled with gas. It was also understood that Field-Marshal Milch, Goering's right-hand man, had been told to prepare 2,000 aircraft for a gas attack on England, but had been obliged to reply that he could not assemble the planes.

Rockets with yellow crosses on their sides, aerial armadas drenching the South Coast with vesicants ... in some respect Hitler's plans resemble the instant-victory hopes placed on the chlorine cloud at Loos by Haig and Falkenhayn's faith in the Green Cross barrage at Verdun. Yet, at a lower level, there were occasions when limited use of CW might have served him well. One opportunity arose when the Allies were restricted to the bridgeheads on the Normandy coast on and just after D-Day, particularly in the American sector at Omaha Beach.The possibility of meeting chemical opposition had been foreseen and for that reason a complete set of protective equipment had been produced, including a new gas cape and respirator. A mask without the familiar 'elephant's trunk' had superseded the old small box respirator; the tube got in the way of a man in a hurry to fire his rifle or Bren. The new Cromwell tanks of the Guards Armoured Division had little yellow detector patches painted on their frontal plate.

General Omar Bradley speculated later on what might have happened if the beaches had been contaminated with a persistent gas. The six-barreled nebelwerfer would have made an excellent delivery system. Consideration for the population of, say, Caen would have prevented or at least hindered retaliation on the spot. For the Allies to have replied by gas bombing the Reich would have invited some sort of reprisal and the rocket sites (which were flourishing in the Pas de Calais and near Le Havre) were still something of an unknown quantity. One-fifth of the US artillery shells landed in Normandy during the invasion were chemical rounds (and there is no reason to suggest the British were any less well armed) so the capability to retaliate was there. But the decision to open fire was a political one. By introducing a new factor Hitler might have gained time.

On the Eastern front the river bridgeheads seized by the Russians proved to be a constant source of trouble. It took tremendous efforts to shift them, as General Mellenthin relates in his book *Panzer Battles*, writing with a feeling bred from bitter experience. Yet these bridgeheads, which absorbed the Wehrmacht's invaluable armour in the closing stages of the war when skilled infantry were scarce, were very vulnerable to attack with blister gas, especially as most Soviet troops were indifferently trained and equipped for chemical warfare.

Hitler might have also used vesicants to good effect in the gloomy, dripping rides of the Reichswald as the British and Canadians cleared the west bank of the Rhine in February, 1945. Veterans of the earlier war said the landscape reminded them of Ypres; only the Yellow Cross was missing. By that time Hitler can have had little concern about the results of retaliation. Defeat meant that the German people had let him down, had failed to fulfil their destiny and deserved whatever might befall them. Ultimately he ordered the destruction of all public utilities and factories, an act of insanity that was thwarted by the Armaments Minister, Albert Speer. If all he intended to leave the victors was a smouldering desert, what can it have mattered if the sands reeked of toxic chemicals?

In the event, Hitler clung to his faith in his other secret weapons – rockets, jet fighters and new submarines. He may no longer have had the specialist troops or means to use gas, or to attempt it could have overloaded the cracking war machine. As it was, the grim products of the laboratories were inflicted only on the helpless inmates of concentration camps.

The reluctance of the democracies to indulge in chemical warfare against Nazi Germany must have baffled Hitler as much as his reticence to turn to it puzzled them; especially as, unlike him, they could not point early in the war to victories gained without it. Britain and France had shown themselves capable of ferocious retaliation in the Great War. It was common knowledge that in 1919 the 'gas box' was to have been used against the Kaiser's army on a large scale. Foulkes said so in his book and also mentioned that a special respirator had been designed to protect the Allied troops against arsenical smokes (though this may have been a belated bluff). The results might have been dramatic ('might' because what happens on a battlefield usually differs considerably from the experiences of the trial grounds). Churchill wrote in 1921 of his job at the Ministry of Munitions: 'It astonished me to read in these after-years the diabolical schemes for killing men on a vast scale by machinery or chemistry to which we passionately devoted ourselves. "*Les bons pères de famille sont capable de tout*".'[1]

Churchill himself was a strange mixture of romancer and realist. The man who had ridden in a cavalry charge in the Sudan and who felt it his duty to serve in the trenches while in political disgrace in 1916

[1] *The World Crisis*

did not hesitate to order attacks on the French fleet in 1940, despite his love of France, or to prepare all manner of 'diabolical' welcomes for potential invaders the same year. Some eighteen months later he was paying a compliment in the Commons to Rommel 'across the havoc of war'.

Mindful of the panoply of his funeral and the simplicity of his grave, it may be that he never really realized that chivalry has always been a relative commodity. There was nothing chivalrous about the Trojan Horse; the Vikings admired nothing more than cunning and treachery – Harold Hardrada gained access to a subborn fortress in Sicily after his men asked the inhabitants to give their 'dead' leader a Christian burial.

More than 500 years before the Third Battle of Ypres reached its soggy climax solemn deliberations took place within bow-shot of Passchendaele. Young Charles VI of France had to decide whether or not to unfurl the crimson Oriflamme, a sacred banner which had been 'sent from Heaven' to inspire an earlier king. According to legend it was so potent that it had never been displayed previously against Christian foes; that would have been cheating. Besides, no one wished to put the Bon Dieu in the awkward position of having to choose between one god-fearing side or the other. The principle applied well enough when kings fought kings but Charles was faced with a well-organized army of beefy Flemish artisans carrying lead maces and pikes, resentful of the oppression of the Count of Flanders. Their leader, Philip van Artevelde, was 'in trade', though his life style was regal enough. After considerable thought it was decided that the Flemings did not qualify for normal exemptions. There were two popes at that time and, as the Flemings supported Urban against the French-sponsored Clement, they were declared unbelievers and outside the Faith.

Sir Pierre de Villiers raised the Oriflamme, the mists which had been hanging about disappeared, and the French prepared to meet the serried ranks of burghers who tramped stolidly forward after unleashing a few salvoes from their bombards and cannon. The dense formation of the citizen army proved to be its undoing. Many of them were unable to use their weapons in the press and at the end of the day their dead lay in heaps on the Goudberg spur where hundreds of New Zealand, Canadian, British and Australian troops found their graves in 1917. The Oriflamme got the lion's share of the credit for Charles's smashing victory, entered in the history books as the battle of Westroosebeke. On his return to Paris, where the tradesmen had been making ominous noises, Charles was able to give a meaningful nod metaphorically in the direction of the magic banner and there was a respectful silence. It was a classic example of principle bowing to policy. Asking himself the question: 'What do we stand to gain? What do we stand to lose?' Charles decided against taking any risks.

Required to consider the same proposition in 1940, Churchill reckoned there was nothing to lose by laying mustard gas mines in the path of the enemy, or by motorizing CW companies armed with Livens projectors. Fear of the consequences of defeat overcame any doubts about offending international opinion or of overriding humanitarian scruples.[1]

The same attitude seems to have been adopted by the Iraqis in their long-drawn-out struggle with the Iranians. Not relishing the prospect of being submerged by waves of religious fanatics, they have resorted to chemical warfare. The result: a stabilization of the front, an indignant outcry from the mullahs in Tcheran, and a guarded reaction from the rest of the world. In May, 1985, the United Nations Security Council condemned the use of toxic gas against Iranian soliders during an abortive offensive. The 1925 Geneva Protocol was cited and strict compliance urged. Mr Ali Akbar Hashemi Rafsanjani, a spokesman for Iran's Supreme Defence Council, asked crowds gathered for Friday prayers why the Iraqis were 'so cowardly'? The Iranian Foreign Minister, Mr Ahkbar Velayati, told the United Nations Conference on Disarmament that Iran had suffered 4,600 casualties from Iraqi chemical weapons. Eight of these soldiers were flown to Britain for treatment in private hospitals; others had been cared for elsewhere in Europe previously.

The Iraqis having maintained a stolid silence on the subject, rather as the Germans omitted mention of the use of chlorine immediately after employing gas at Ypres in 1915, exactly seventy years earlier, the Iranians sought confirmation of their allegations from British doctors. Dr Allister Vale, director of the West Midlands poison unit, who examined some of the Iranians, confirmed that the blisters were consistent with vesicant gas injuries. When an inquest was held on an 18-year-old soldier, Dr. Iain West, a pathologist at Guy's Hospital, told the court that the patient had died of bronchial pneumonia attributable to skin burns consistent with exposure to mustard or some other blister gas.

[1] The French knight Bayard, often held up as the epitome of ancient chivalry, was famed for his part in the fairest of fights in which a dozen German knights met a dozen French. After the introduction of firearms, he showed his disapproval of this type of weapon,which enabled a humble foot soldier with a gun to kill a mounted lord with a sword, by torturing and putting to death captured musketeers.

The Westminster coroner, Dr Paul Knapman, accepted that 18-year-old Golm Shivilico received his injuries during fighting at Magnoon Island, but refused to be drawn on whether or not there had been, in his opinion, a breach of international law. He recorded a verdict that Shivilico had died as a result of enemy action.

Came the spring of 1986 and the Iranians launched another furious assault on their opponents. According to *The Observer* the Iraqis still denied using chemical weapons, while the attackers claimed that more than 1,000 of their men had been 'injured in gas attacks'. Fourteen Iranians were reported to have been admitted to North London's Wellington Hospital (a private concern), one of whom had died there. The body of Ibrahim Hendozadeh was flown back to Teheran. As a curious footnote to the report, indicating the mystery which still surrounds vesicants, a doctor was quoted as saying that checks ought to be made to ensure what was believed to be mustard gas was not 'still active' inside the bodies of patients flown into the country.

'We don't want gas around that could be absorbed by the air conditioning system,' said one of them.

In the sixtieth anniversary year of the unleashing of the chlorine cloud at Ypres, Dr Lutz Haber, son of the originator of gas attacks, gave an absorbing lecture at Bedford College, London.[1] In it he stated that, allowing for minor exceptions, 'As far as I know gas has been the only instance where a weapon introduced in one war was not employed in the next.'

He could well have drawn attention to the role forecast for it in 1919 by a committee of scientists and soldiers who had been most concerned with the medium.[2] Its findings included the statement: 'In no case has a weapon which had proved itself to be successful in war ever been abandoned by nations fighting for existence, therefore the study of Chemical Warfare must be carried out in a wholehearted and energetic manner, in order that the safety of the Empire shall not be left to chance. A nation unprepared for gas warfare lays itself open to sudden and irretrievable disaster. The scale and quality of our preparations in peace must be adequate. It is impossible to divorce the study of defence against gas from offence.'

Dr Haber, a member of the faculty of Surrey University, gave one reason why Britain and the United States failed to reach the desired 'scale and quality' of preparations between the wars as the widening

---

[1] 'Gas Warfare 1915-1945, The Legend and the Facts'
[2] The Holland Committee or the Committee on Chemical Warfare Organization.

of the gap between 'chemists and soldiers'. The commanders in the Second World War had been regimental officers in the First and this, he believed, led to their negative attitude: 'Their dislike of specialists being so well documented that we can, in retrospect, take it as widespread among senior officers in France, Britain and the US as well as Germany.'[1] Those who were of a 'bookish turn of mind' could consult official histories, but these he criticized for attaching 'little significance' to chemical warfare [though not everyone would agree with him]. They might also read 'published reminiscences' which he classed generally as 'hostile'. Whereas a topic such as the use of tanks might inspire changes in the conventional approach, 'the low intellectual level of the textbooks on chemical warfare and the dreary content of the specialist articles were powerful disincentives to tactical thinking. The military establishment was anti-gas.'

In Haber's view the attitude of the undefined military 'establishment' had the specific effect of 'downgrading the preparations for offensive gas warfare'. Thus in 1939 German stocks stood at 10,000 tons of poison gas, ten times more than the British and Americans possessed.

By contrast, the precautions for *defending* the United Kingdom were well advanced and 38,000,000 masks had been distributed by the autumn of 1938, enough, to all intents and purposes, for the whole population. Even in 1939 the Germans had issued only 9,000,000 to the public, though the population was much larger, and eventually concentrated on collective protection, gas-proofing shelters and buildings. Both sides, it would seem, had good reason for not embarking on indiscriminate chemical warfare during the early months of hostilities.[2]

Even accepting Haber's argument, when the crisis arose in 1940 the campaign was over so quickly that, had the Allies wished to use a blister agent in their defence, it is unlikely that the command structure could have organized or controlled the necessary measures. Poor communications and a lack of reliable signals and radio equipment were an important factor in the collapse of French resistance. Thanks to the speed with which the rear areas were overrun, British files were among those which fell into enemy hands at Le Bouchet, the French equivalent of Porton. Perhaps the Nazis read more into them than was necessary. They seemed to be left in no

[1] Montgomery's employment of specialist armour on D-Day appears to make him an exception.
[2] In a later publication Haber states that the British civilian masks, though plentiful, were not proof against arsenical gases at first.

doubt as to Britain's interest in chemical warfare and they already knew of her defensive preparedness.

Having conquered much of Europe without the aid of CW, the enemy felt no need for gas when the panzers swept first into the Balkans and then deep into Russia. There, in the autumn of 1941, the problem was not so much how to destroy the Red hordes but the mundane business of supply and transport, plus a growing shortage of trained troops.

Hitler's personal dislike of gas provided an 'emotional factor' according to Haber: 'His explicitness on the matter undoubtedly contributed to the slowing down of research and development, particularly on nerve gases.' Not until 1944, says Haber, did the Führer change his mind.

Hitler was not the only person to have second thoughts. In 1943 President Roosevelt said in a speech: 'I state categorically that we shall not resort to the use of such weapons unless they are first used by our enemies.'

In 1944 chemical shells were ready for *retaliation* in Normandy, but the stocks which were accumulated during preparations for the proposed invasion of Japan, Operation Olympic, indicate an *aggressive* attitude. The Japanese had let it be known that they were dismantling their CW capability (thus contradicting the Holland Committee's proposition that a nation would never abandon gas as a weapon if its survival was threatened). Perhaps they were seeking a quid pro quo. Truman, who took over the Presidency when Roosevelt died, had been a gunner in France in the First World War and did not have the same reservations as his predecessor. He was not likely to accept that heavy losses, such as had been suffered in the Pacific must be inevitable when the mainlaind was assaulted. Like it or not, gas would at least be available to American commanders to whom, with rare exceptions, the possession of the atomic bomb was unknown.

Earlier in the Second World War the Japanese had indicated through diplomatic channels (the Mexican Embassy in Tokyo) that they would be guided by the Spirit of Bushido where chemical warfare was concerned and would not be the first to use it. The Samurai warrior was not happy in a gas mask, it seems.

Did a similar leaning to 'chivalry', fostered by regimental tradition, influence the British Army during the '20s and '30s or was the 'military establishment' opposed to gas weapons, as Haber claims, because they were dull dogs whose eyes glazed at the sight of a bunsen burner?

The evidence is that the military and civil authorities involved did their best under successive governments facing severe economic problems, but CW had to be fitted into the general picture along with other weapons. Politicians were not blind to its existence. As early as 1922 Mr. Balfour, at a meeting of the International Committee on the Limitation of Armaments, accepted the desirability of outlawing the use of poison gas in war, but repeated an argument already heard at the League of Nations: 'It is impossible to prevent a nation bent on chemical warfare from making preparations in peacetime, no matter what the rules might be.'

Britain was no more in a position to abandon a vital weapon than any other major power, and trained its Army to fight on battlefields where CW would be encountered. If preparations for offensive chemical warfare were inadequate so were those for the other arms and services. Under the Government's Ten Year Rule, military forward planning had to be based on the assumption that Britain would not be involved in a major war for a decade, the base date being advanced from time to time until the restriction was limited in 1933. By then the damage had been done.

'Thus in 1939,' Dr Haber told his audience in 1975, 'the technical aspects of gas were in no way different from those in 1918, and in this respect differed profoundly from the tank, the only other innovation in Land Warfare of the First World War which had been greatly developed during the 1930s.'

'Greatly developed' the tank had been, but, when war broke out the armoured fighting vehicles of the opposing nations were about on a par with the quality of their equipment (though the Russian T-34 was a rod in pickle). German tanks were neither better nor more numerous than those of the Allies, they were simply better handled. Despite the Experimental Brigade manoeuvres on Salisbury Plain there was no recognizable new armour policy and not a single tank division existed in Britain in 1939.

As regards equipment, the Royal Artillery, cornerstone of the whole khaki complex, was worse off. As one of the most penetrating military studies of recent years put it:

'In the upshot the Royal Artillery had to fight the earlier battles of the Second World War with the first Mark of 25-pounder, the retubed 18-pounder on an improved carriage . . . and obsolete First World War equipments, which included the 18-pounder Mark I and the 60-pounder which dated back to 1914.'[1]

[1] Bidwell and Graham, *Fire-Power, British Army Weapons and Theories of War 1904–1945*, Allen and Unwin, 1982

If the experts could not agree on whether to have a 5-inch or 5.5-inch medium gun what chance was there to design effective chemical ammunition for it, the ballistic problems being as difficult as ever?

The implications in Haber's lecture that chemical weapons suffered more than others from the conflict of interest between scientists, soldiers and politicians must be seen in the context of the general malaise which traditionally surrounded arms development in peace-time (before military hardware became a vital cog in the earning capacity of so many national economies). It took years after Waterloo for the percussion cap to replace the flintlock on a musket.

Policies with weaknesses and weapons with drawbacks which in retrospect should have been glaringly obvious were overlooked in the period 1918-39. To give one simple instance, the Royal Navy, which had lost three battlecruisers in spectacular explosions at Jutland in 1916 failed in twenty years to devise adequate protection for HMS *Hood* which in 1941 met a similar fate. On a different level, the Germans did not realize the value of the heavy bomber until it was too late. So there was no special reason why potential chemical weapons should have been exempt from the morass of muddled thinking, particularly as pacifists and their opponents twisted the legends and the facts to suit their own ends, a point which Haber makes very forcefully.

Avoiding 'all mention of the moral issues raised by the intro-duction of poison gas,' Haber said that sixty years after the event it was difficult for the modern generation to appreciate 'the intense passion' they had generated and he did not expand on the subject, though accepting that it left a large gap in his lecture. Inevitably in a talk many things had to be omitted but fortunately for students of the subject Dr Haber continued his research and after another ten years or so published *The Poisonous Cloud*, in which he goes into great detail on the use of chemical warfare, mainly in the 1915-18 period. He was able to draw largely on personal contact with the long-lived Sir Harold Hartley and veterans of the Great War. It is fascinating to conjure up the picture of the son of the instigator of the Ypres chlorine cloud asking scarlet-coated pensioners at the Royal Hospital, Chelsea, what it was like to wear a small box respirator.

In his book Haber poses an important question: 'Was gas a failure?' and gives the answer 'Yes!' From the mass of facts and opinions he has gathered it is possible, however, to draw other conclusions. He says himself that the 'statistical approach leads to a dead end'.

Had Foulkes lived to read the book he would have been surprised, perhaps, to see that the individual operations of the companies of the

Special Brigade earned the comment: 'It cannot be claimed they had any effect on the war . . . but they vexed the Germans and caused them losses.' In the Doctor's opinion the role of gas in the two to two and a half years after the Second Battle of Ypres 'was to act as a special psychological weapon to wear down the enemy'.

In partial agreement with Haber is Squadron Leader A.F. Graveley, of the Royal Air Force Regiment, who, in an article in the *Army Quarterly and Defence Journal* in October, 1980, concluded that, from medical statistics gas was a failure in the war of attrition on the Western Front as a means of permanently reducing the strength of an opponent.

This gives further food for thought. Though the recovery period of gas casualties was relatively short – one estimate puts the average at forty-two days – the overall reduction in the ability of gassed units to carry out their missions was of major importance. On occasions whole formations (brigades and divisions) had to be withdrawn, such as at Ypres in July, 1917, and in the Flesquières Salient in March, 1918. These could be replaced only from reserves and the erosion of reserves *at a critical time* is what attrition aims at.

Foulkes maintained after the war that 'The reduction of the enemy's manpower was our main preoccupation'.

In this respect, and in contrast to Haber, Graveley credits the Special Brigade's cloud attacks with obtaining 'significant results up to the end of the war'.

The Squadron Leader insists that much is to be learned even today from Great War experience and lists the stocks of war gases known to be held by the Red Army. They include many of those proved in action by 1918, plus nerve gases found in Germany in 1945. 'If there is such a thing as fashion in world military thinking, then Chemical Warfare (CW) may be said to be in vogue again.'

Allowing for the fact that modern agents are many times more powerful than those of 1915–18 and that means of delivery have been improved (so that fired from multi-barrelled rocket launchers the once suspect and criticized Vincennite would be a much nastier proposition) the writing-down of an opponent's manpower would again be one of the main objectives of chemical warfare. Essentially a surprise weapon – attacked troops have only seconds to don their masks – it would be used to create confusion and provide opportunities for other arms to exploit. The scale may be related in the case of the Red Army to the estimate that there are at least 100,000 CW troops[1] (VKhV units) and possibly as many as 130,000. They would

[1] Valerie Adams, *RUSI Journal* article, 1985

clearly not act in isolation but deliver their assault as an invaluable contribution to the overall plan designed to dislocate the NATO defence structure.

Rocket projectors à la Livens, spray, shell and bomb could be among the means adopted to deliver the chemical, and there is no real reason to rule out cloud attacks. To be prepared simply for defence under such circumstances requires serious and specialist training under realistic conditions. The NATO generals cannot afford to adopt the attitude that the simulation of chemical attack during manoeuvres holds everything up, restricts movement of tanks, artillery and infantry and 'spoils a good exercise'.

Squadron Leader Graveley summed up the situation by stating that the vital ingredient required in training was 'the determination to think clearly and honestly about the problems of fighting in a chemical environment'.

A future conflict would not necessarily last long enough for a gradual conversion of attitudes.

Clear and honest thinking must also apply to the politicians, who might well ponder Mr Balfour's words on the subject: 'It is impossible to divorce the study of defence against gas from offence.'

Does Mrs Thatcher's statement in the House of Commons in January, 1985, really reflect clear thinking? 'Britain abandoned its chemical warfare capability in the late 1950s. There has been no change in government policy since then nor is any change proposed, but as a responsible government we have a duty to keep defence policy under review in the light of the massive Soviet capability in CW.'

Or does it supply evidence for the criticism implied in a statement of the views of General Bernard Rogers, Supreme Allied Commander Europe, made the same year? 'The discussion of chemical weapons is so sensitive here in Western Europe that the role the political authorities wish to play has become too tough to handle. I find it is put in the too-sensitive/too-tough box and it just reposes there.

'We, the military authorities, have submitted a series of questions which we want them to answer. One of the paradoxes of this last half of the century is that if deterrence is your mission, you have to convey that you are prepared to use every system in your inventory in order to defend – otherwise your deterrent isn't credible, and that includes chemical weapons.'[1]

---

[1] Interview by Bob Hutchinson for *Jane's Defence Weekly*

CHAPTER 28

August Jager Again

With the re-emergence of chemical weapons in the Middle East, along with a remarkable reticence on the part of anyone but the Iranians to say so openly, renewed efforts have begun to outlaw CW.[1] If talk of the immorality of using blister agents and the like is muted, it could be because of the complexity of the cultures concerned. Muslims, Jews, Christians and atheists, to name but a few, have different rules for distinguishing right from wrong. All of them fear surprise but, as Henry Stanhope pointed out in *The Times* in March, 1985, the 1925 Protocol which still applies: 'prohibits use of chemical munitions only in wartime, leaving countries free to produce and stockpile them out of mutual distrust'. He added that the United States had considerable quantities of chemical weapons in Europe but said none had been manufactured since 1969.

Mr George Schultz, the American Secretary of State, told an audience of scientists in Washington that thirteen countries were capable of making chemical warfare, though he did not name them. In 1963 only five nations had possessed such weapons. Clearly there had to be some new thinking and a United States commission led by Walter Stoessel, a former ambassador in Moscow, Bonn and Warsaw, sounded out European opinion. British officials were said to have indicated they would not oppose the US plan to make new chemical weapons, but hoped that a worldwide ban would be worked out at Geneva. The *New Scientist* magazine hinted darkly that there were already commitments to accept the storage of nerve gas bombs at nuclear bases in East Anglia. Someone pointed out that the newest

[1] A comprehensive international treaty outlawing micro-biological (germ) weapons was signed in 1972.

monstrosity, the 'Bigeye' bomb, would not be ready until 1989 so there was no immediate reason to enter into a commitment.

Interest in the subject had received a grisly fillip from the Bhopal disaster in December, 1984, when a huge cloud of gas from a pesticides factory fell on an unprotected populace. Two thousand Indians died. Volumes have yet to be written on this particular incident but one point is clear – even in a peaceful world there is an abundance of chemicals which could be converted rapidly and simply to military uses. Agents which are harmless on their own can quickly be mixed to make a variety of evil concoctions. In the First World War the German chemists switched from making dyes to mustard gas and back again with extraordinary rapidity.

Though opposed to the idea of aggressive chemical warfare, British politicians have recognized the threat posed by the Soviet Union in this field. Every soldier is now trained to fight in what is referred to popularly as a Noddy Suit. Men and vehicles are clothed or designed to defy gases, powders, potions and radiation. During exercises many spend days cooped up in armoured personnel carriers or tanks sealed off against a supposedly poisoned atmosphere. It is generally accepted that, should the East launch a sudden strike against the West, the Warsaw Pact forces would attack initially with conventional arms and chemical weapons while Britain's highly professional little army would do the decent thing and defend itself with only the former. Soldiers may well ask if there is any logical reason behind the ban which prevents the use of the proven defensive qualities of even old-fashioned mustard gas to stem an attempt to overrun Europe? It can hardly be on humanitarian grounds. Modern high-velocity weapons deliver bullets at such a speed that instead of passing through or making a hole in an individual they destroy the body tissue: hence the change in the venerable RAMC terminology from GSW or gunshot wound to 'bullet trauma'. The choice between the impact of a projectile from an Armalite or SLR (self-loading rifle) and a splash of blister gas is not a pleasant one but it is fairly easy to guess which most people, including the unfortunate Iranian infantrymen, would opt for.

Is the ban then a matter of cost? This seems unlikely. Chemical weapons are as cheap as they are nasty. A cynic might even take the view that for that very reason the makers of sophisticated conventional arms – minimum cost of a medium HE shell about £100 – could be opposed to some other sector of industry getting a cut of the astronomical arms budget.

Are there religious objections? Not from the evidence. There is nothing to indicate that the Russian chemical warfare troops are all atheists, while recruits with Orthodox connections finish up in rifle platoons. From the Middle East struggle it is clear that the Iranian objections are concerned with the 'cowardly' nature of the weapon; the Iraqis are content with its efficiency, a point which may have been noted by the vast Moslem population of the USSR.

What about possible 'knock-on' effects should Britain arm troops with chemical weapons? Successive British governments have been at one in dealing with the threat to the 'innocent civilian', as far as potential attacks on the home islands are concerned. With scrupulous fairness they have provided no protection for any of *us* (as apart from *them*, that is). In some of the gloomier corners of Europe tunnels have been burrowed into the mountains; the Russians have beavered away at a civil defence system in the past, and the Chinese too. Unlike the British they do not seem to be confident that it will be all right on the night.

The supposition, of course, is that if someone is fool enough to start or provoke a hot war in Europe that people will see sense (the 'over by Christmas' syndrome) before it escalates to the nuclear stage. NATO soldiers with tanks, guns, aeroplanes and the usual rifles, rockets and grenades, will hold the Warsaw Pact armed with tanks, guns, planes and the usual rifles, rockets and grenades *and* gas/chemical weapons.

If the line breaks and T-72 tanks with snorkels blob in and out of the Rhine and head for the Channel, unspeakable things are likely to fill the sky and Noddy Suits (do the Prime Minister and Leader of the Opposition each get one?) will be at a premium, along with sets of 1938 ARP cigarette cards.

Nobody in his right mind wishes to add to the collection of nightmares packed into concrete silos and underground bunkers, but, if the theory of deterrence holds good, there just could be something to be said for putting NATO on a par with the Warsaw Pact where chemical weapons are concerned. It is at least time to remove the humbug which surrounds the subject.

All need to argue about the use or non-use of gas might have been scotched in 1915 *if* the French generals had read the intelligence reports properly; *if* the reports of the Belgian agents had been correctly interpreted; *if* the sergeant who found the cylinders on Hill 60 had been believed; *if* the pilot of the ramshackle plane from 6 Squadron RFC had spotted something. A violent bombardment of the enemy positions before the wind changed could have caused havoc by unleashing the gas in the opposite direction. There might have been no Second Battle of Ypres as we know it. After such a spectacular failure the Germans might well have written off gas as an over-estimated weapon and gone on with the familiar old business of blowing people to pieces with high explosive.

If only the deserters had been believed . . . *if* only August Jager had been more convincing.

Poor August! If ever there was a 20th century martyr it was the ticket inspector's son from Seebergen, by ancient Gotha in the shadows of the green hills of Thuringia.

Many of the actors in this tragedy enjoyed long lives, particularly the British. General Thuillier, who preferred commanding infantry-men to deploying gas cylinders, lived to be 85. Foulkes made 94 and Sir Harold Hartley (whose later business career included the chairmanship of British European Airways and BOAC) was 96 when he died in 1972. Eight years earlier he had written the obituary notice published in *The Times* recording the career of W.H. Livens. Even the 'Mad Major' reached the age of 75. If Fritz Haber was still in his sixties when he faded away in exile at least he was honoured by his own scientific contemporaries. His son's book, among others, will perpetuate his memory. But who will spare a thought for August Jager? It is doubtful if he even got to know his own children.

Not quite a year after Jager was gaoled a letter went from No 8 Prinz-Albrecht-Strasse, Berlin, headquarters of the Geheimes Staatspolizeiamt, the national HQ of the Secret State Police (merged into the Gestapo later). It instructed the Prussian Minister of Justice to 'ensure that after completing their sentences traitors are taken into protective custody'. In July, 1941, as the panzers thundered towards Smolensk, Jager's case came up for review. He seems to have been due for release; his long period of detention awaiting trial may have been taken into consideration. Once more his dossier made its appearance. Jager was clearly a 'security risk', just the sort of person for whom the special arrangements had been made. In 1938 Himmler, as Chief of the German Police, had ordered that all protective custody prisoners should be sent to a camp near Weimar (once known as the Athens of Germany because of its tradition of philosophers and poets). And so August Jager arrived at Buchen-wald.

Buchenwald, in 1941, was classified as a Grade II camp for protective custody prisoners whose conduct record was 'less good' than it might have been but 'who are likely to benefit from education and reform'. After a period there Jager succeeded in getting himself transferred to a Grade III camp, Mauthausen, designed to take prisoners with bad records and who could not be 're-educated'. The granite quarries there were owned and managed by the SS whose policy was to work the prisoners to death.

How Jager survived is not known, but survive he did. As the Red Army drew nearer, the whole bureaucracy of evil dissolved into chaos and Himmler ordered the removal of the inmates of camps in the east to camps in the west. In the last winter of the war hundreds of thousands took to the roads or were crammed into insanitary unheated trains which crept to their destinations. Jager left Mauthausen near Linz, in Austria, and became one of 30,000 souls slowly starving at Dachau, near Munich. The sounds of war drew ever nearer.

On 24 April, 1945, a few months before his 54th birthday, at the time of the 30th anniversary of the Ypres gas attacks, August emerged cautiously into a strange world dominated by tanks marked with a white star controlled by foreign soldiers who were forever chewing. Technically he was still an 'enemy' and therefore likely to be questioned more closely by the occupation authorities than non-Germans drifting through the countryside. Nevertheless for the first time in fourteen years he was on the right side of the barbed wire. As he made his way to wherever he thought was home he could see long columns of prisoners heading for captivity. White flags were flying from the buildings. Around Munich there was scant evidence of fighting but he began to hear tales of widespread devastation. He trudged on and into obscurity. Germany was once again well and truly defeated, but at least they couldn't blame it on him this time.

The first issue of a glossy technological defence magazine[1] launched in the spring of 1986 had a flavour of 1915 about it. An Iraqi general is quoted as accusing the Iranians of using mustard gas bombs in mortars. Another feature showed coloured photographs of Iranian victims of what was once called 'Yellow Cross'. There were pictures of Afghan villagers posing beside fragments of Russian-made chemical warfare bomb casings – and details of a United Nations team's claim that Tabun had been identified on battlefields of the Gulf War. With 1987 starting with an attack on Basra, it looks as though there is going to be no shortage of material for the new publication, a hint perhaps for the West to start looking for the key to what General Rogers calls the 'too tough box'.

[1] *Nuclear, Biological and Chemical Defense and Technology International*, published in New York.

Appendix 'A'

Colour Code for British gas cylinders 1914–18

Red Star	Chlorine
Two Red stars	Sulphuretted hydrogen with 12 per cent carbon disulphide intended to increase density. It was highly inflammable. German flares set fumes ablaze during a 1,600 cylinder discharge at Monchy in July, 1916.
White Star	50 per cent phosgene/50 per cent chlorine (in general use from summer, 1916).
Yellow Star	30 per cent chloropicrin/70 per cent chlorine.
Green Star	65 per cent chloropicrin/35 per cent sulphuretted hydrogen (quickly discarded).
Blue Star	80 per cent chlorine/20 per cent sulphur chloride. The latter was to help keep the cloud close to the ground. Its use was discontinued because dangerous pools of poisonous liquid were apt to linger at the end of the parapet discharge pipes.

Appendix 'B'

Gas Shell Colour Code 1914–18

British Army
All chemical shells were painted grey and, as the variety increased, colour bands were added for easy identification.

One Red Band	CBR I = 50 per cent phosgene/50 per cent arsenic trichloride. (lethal) CBR II = 60 per cent phosgene/40 per cent stannic chloride. (lethal). (Arsenic trichloride was identified as BR, stannic chloride as KJ.)
Two Red Bands	JL mixture – primarily a prussic acid gas mixture. JL = Jellite. (lethal)
Three Red Bands	JBR – another mixture containing arsenic trichloride. (lethal)
One White Band	PS shell containing chloropicrin, a tear gas which was toxic in certain quantities. 'PS' from Port Sunlight where Lever Brothers first investigated its possibilities, though it was produced elsewhere.
Two White Bands	PG = 75 per cent chloropicrin/25 per cent 'Collongite' (see below). (lethal)
Three White Bands	AK = 85 per cent hydrogen cyanide/15 per cent SK. (lethal)
One Red, one White, one Red	CG, phosgene produced at Coulogne, near Calais. (lethal)
One White, one Red	VN or 'Vincennite' = 50 per cent hydrogen cyanide or prussic acid gas/30 per cent arsenic

trichloride/15 per cent stannic chloride/5 per cent chloroform. (lethal)

One White, one
Red, one White   NC mixture = 80 per cent chloropicrin, 20 per cent stannic chloride. (lethal)

No Bands   KSK = 100 per cent ethyl iodoacetate
                      SK = 75 per cent ethyl iodoacetate/25 per cent alcohol or ethyl acetate (Tear gases – researched at 'SK' South Kensington Imperial College of Science).

So much artillery work was done at night that from 1917 onwards shells were stamped with letters corresponding to colour bands so the gunners could identify them by touch, eg WRW on a shell painted with One White, one Red, one White band. KSK and SK were stamped NB meaning 'No Bands'. Mustard gas shells were marked BB – from ßß-dichlor-ethyl-sulphide.

United States Army

The Americans used colour to indicate the nature of the shell and the number of bands its 'strength'. White bands denoted non-persistent gases, red persistent.

One White   Diphenylchlorarsine. (similar to the German Blue Cross filling)

Two White   Phosgene.

One White,
one Red   Chloropicrin.

One White, one
Red, one White   75 per cent chloropicrin/25 per cent phosgene.

One White, one
Red, one Yellow   80 per cent chloropicrin/20 per cent stannic chloride.

One Red   Bromacetone. (tear gas)

Two Red   Bromobenzylcyanide. (a toxic lachrymator)

Three Red   Mustard gas.

Yellow bands denoted smoke in a US shell and purple bands marked incendiary shells.

German Army

White B or BM   B Stoff = Bromo methyl ketones. (tear gas)

Black or Green T   T Stoff = Xylyl bromide/or benzyl bromide or a mixture. (tear gas)

Blue Cross	Diphenyl-chlorarsine/diphenyl-cyanarsine/ mixed or with N ethyl carbazol.
White C	C Stoff or K2 Stoff - Trichlormethyl-chloro-formate. (lethal)
White D	Phosgene. (lethal)
Green Cross	Called diphosgene by British, Surpalite by French, Superpalite by Americans = trich-lormethyl-chloroformate; or bromo-methyl-ethyl-ketones, or, in 1917, phenyl-carbyl-amine chloride. (lethal)
Green Cross 1	65 per cent trichlormethyl-chloroformate/35 per cent chloropicrin. (lethal)
Green Cross 2	Mixture of phosgene, trichlormethyl-chloro-formate and diphenyl-chlorarsine. (lethal)
Green Cross 3	From July 1918 contained ethyl-dichlorarsine plus either dichlor-methyl ether or ethyl-dibrom-arsine. (lethal)
Yellow Cross 1	Up to July 1918 this was the designation of Green Cross 3 (see above). (lethal)
Yellow Cross	Mustard gas – about 80 per cent dichlor-ethyl-sulphide with solvents added.

A Lorraine Cross on a mustard-gas shell meant that it contained an enhanced explosive charge. A green Lorraine Cross denoted a phosgene shell with a large HE content.

Appendix 'C'

Appendix II (to Instructions on the use of lethal and lachrymatory shell) (March, 1918) SS 134
Typical Programmes of Gas Shoots
  No 1
Target – Central battery of a group of 5 hostile batteries which were causing inconvenience.
  Velocity of wind: 2 mph
  Guns employed: Three 60-pounder batteries (18 guns)
  Zero Hour – 11 pm June 16th [1917]
  Programme –

0.0 – 0.2	50 C.B.R.	(Two minutes' intensive lethal fire to catch the enemy before he can protect himself.)
0.2 – 4.2	576 S.K.	(Four hours' slow bombardment to saturate battery positions and force the enemy to use up his drum.) (drum-respirator filling)
4.2 – 4.12	99 C.B.R. 129 P.S.	(Ten minutes' intensive lethal fire with P.S. and C.B.R. – P.S. to pass through the drum after four hours' wearing and cause coughing, and C.B.R. for added lethal effect.)

Result:
  The [German] batteries in the group did not open fire until the following times –
  1. 8.36 pm .... June 19th
  2. 9.15 pm
  3. 11.20 pm
  4. 11.40 pm

The central battery did not open fire until 11.29 am on June 24th though it had not moved.

Note: Had they been available considerably greater effect would have been obtained by substituting C.G. for C.B.R. and N.C. for P.S.

Appendix 'D'

The following summary and extracts are from a report[1]
'Casualties due to Gas Poisoning resulting from German Cloud Gas Attacks December, 1915–August, 1916,' by Major Thomas Renton Elliot, FRS, and Captain Claude Gordon Douglas. Six attacks in all were delivered and it was assumed – the report says there was 'little doubt' – that phosgene had been added to the chlorine cloud. The enemy was said to have obtained high concentrations of gas by liberating the agent 'very rapidly'. Estimated casualties in relation to the number of British troops under attack

Date	No of Troops in sector	Total gas casualities	Total gas deaths	Casualities as percentage of sector troops	Deaths as percentage of sector
12 Dec	25,000	1,069	116	4.3	0.4
27 Apr	29,379	1,260	338	4.3	1.2
29 Apr					
30 Apr	13,964	512	89	3.7	0.6

On 17 June there were 562 casualties resulting in 95 deaths, a fatality rate of 17 per 100 gas casualties. Of 804 gas casualties on 8 August 371 died, a rate of 46 men per 100 affected.

Estimated length of discharge on 19 December was half an hour; on 30 April it lasted 10 to 15 minutes; on 8 August the discharge also lasted some 15 minutes.

[1] PRO WO 142/209)

Appendix 'E'

TWO MEN WHO WOULD NOT GIVE IN TO GAS

German failure to exploit the gas advantage at Ypres in 1915 was due, among other factors, to the courage of individual ordinary soldiers.

On 1 May, Private Edward Warner, No 7602, 1st Bedfordshire and Hertfordshire Regiment, took over and defended single-handed a trench near Hill 60 when its garrison had been driven out by a chlorine cloud. This quotation comes from his Victoria Cross citation:

'Reinforcements were sent to Private Warner, but could not reach him owing to the gas. He then came back and brought up more men, by which time he was completely exhausted, but the trench was held.'

That was on May 1. The next day Private John Lynn, No 1272 2nd Lancashire Fusiliers, also won the Victoria Cross:

'When the Germans were advancing behind their wave of asphyxiating gas, Private Lynn, although almost overcome ... handled his machine-gun with great effect against the enemy, and when he could not see he moved his gun higher up on the parapet, which enabled him to bring even more effective fire to bear, and eventually checked any further advance.'

Both men died soon after their exploit. Lynn, who was born at Forest Hill, then in Kent, enlisted in the army at New Cross, London, before the war and had won the Distinguished Conduct Medal at Ypres in December, 1914, once again manning a machine-gun. His medals are on display in the Regimental Museum, Wellington Barracks, Bury, Lancashire.

Bibliography

Books and publications and unpublished sources consulted –
Official Histories World War I
Bean, C.E.W., *The Australian Imperial Forces in France*, Angus and
   Robertson, Sydney, 1937
Duguid, A.F., *History of the Canadian Forces, 1914–19*, Ottawa,
   1938
Edmonds, Sir James E., *Military Operations, France and Belgium:*
   1915, Vol I; *1916*, Vols I and II; *1917*, Vols I and II; *1918*, Vols I
   and II, HMSO.
Hinsley F.H. et al, *British Intelligence in the Second World War*, (3
   Vols), HMSO
Macpherson, Sir W.G. et al, *Medical Services – Diseases of the War*,
   Vol II, HMSO
Miles, Wilfred, *Military Operations, France and Belgium 1917*, Vol
   III, HMSO
Nicholson, G.W.L., *Canadian Expeditionary Force 1914–19*,
   Ottawa 1964.

Unpublished material
Handwritten letters from Mr Asquith, the Prime Minister, to King
George V relating to Cabinet Meetings in 1915 are taken from
photographic copies in the Public Record Office, Kew, of original
letters preserved in the Royal Archives and made available by the
gracious permission of Her Majesty the Queen.
   Public Record Office file CAB 37/127/40 and 43, (April); and in
October PRO CAB 37/131/34.
   Other PRO references.
   Washington Embassy report on German threat to withhold from

the U.S. essential dye-stuffs in April, 1915 – PRO CAB 37/127/49; Military situation appreciation given to Dardanelles Committee October, 1915 – PRO CAB 42/4/2; Churchill's memorandum on the potential for gas at Gallipoli – PRO CAB 42/4/4; Smuts's request for gas to be used in East Africa – PRO CAB 42/21/14; Porton reports various – PRO WO 142/209.

Also Fox, Martin S, *Corporals All*, typescript diary in the Ministry of Defence Library, Old War Office Building; Smith, Sydney, notebook compiled as a sapper in a chemical warfare company in World War II.

Lectures with limited circulation
Hartley, Brigadier-General Harold, 'A General Comparison of British and German Methods of Gas Warfare,' published in *Journal of the Royal Artillery*, XLVII, No 11. February, 1920;
Haber, Dr. Lutz F., 'Gas Warfare 1915–1945, the Legend and the Facts,' Bedford College, University of London

Chemical warfare histories
Brown, F.J., *Chemical Warfare, A Study in Restraint*, Princeton, 1968
Foulkes, C.H., *Gas! The Story of the Special Brigade*, Blackwood, 1934
Fries and West, *Chemical Warfare*, McGraw-Hill, 1921
Haber, L.F., *The Poisonous Cloud, Chemical Warfare in the First World War*, Clarendon Press, 1986
Haldane, J.B.S., *Callinicus*, Keegan Paul, 1925
Hogg, Ian, *Gas*, Pan Ballantine, 1975
Prentiss, A.M., *Chemicals in War*,McGraw-Hill, 1937
Thuillier, H.F., *Gas in the Next War*, London, 1939

Campaign Histories
Blaxland, Gregory, *Amiens 1918*, Muller, 1968
Clark, Alan, *The Donkeys*, Hutchinson, 1961
Essame, Hubert, *The Battle for Europe 1918*, Batsford, 1972
Goodspeed, D.J, *The Road Past Vimy*, Macmillan, Toronto, 1969
Horne, Alastair, *The Price of Glory*, Macmillan, 1962
    To Lose a Battle, Macmillan, 1969
Moore, William, *See How They Ran*, Leo Cooper, 1970
Pitt, Barrie, *The Last Act*, Cassell, 1962
Seth, Ronald, *Caporetto, The Scapegoat Battle*, Macdonald, 1965
Spears, E.L., *Prelude to Victory*, Cape, 1933

Divisional histories

Boraston, J.H., *The History of the Eighth Division*, Medici Society, London, 1926

Falls, Cyril, *The History of the 36th (Ulster) Division*, Belfast, 1922

Gillon, Stair, *The Story of the 29th Division*, Nelson, 1925

Headlam, Cuthbert, *The Guards Division in the Great War*, Murray, 1924

Jerrold, Douglas, *The Royal Naval Division*, Hutchinson, 1923

Sandilands, H.R., *The Twenty-Third Division, 1914–19*, Blackwood, 1925

Scott and Brumwell, *The History of the 12th (Eastern) Division*, Nisbet, 1923

Thompson, R.R., *The 52nd (Lowland) Division 1914–1918*, Maclehose, 1923

Wyrall, Everard, *The History of the 62nd (West Riding) Division, 1914–1919* (Vol I), Bodley Head

Regimental and Unit Histories

Atkinson, C.T., *The South Wales Borderers 1914–19*, Medici Society

Cook, Hugh, *The North Staffordshire Regiment*, Leo Cooper, 1970

Goold Walker, G, *The Honourable Artillery Company in the Great War*, Seeley Service, 1930

McLaughlin, R., *The Royal Army Medical Corps*, Leo Cooper, 1972

McLellan, Edwin, *The United States Marine Corps in the World War*, Washington, 1920

Moody, R.S.H., *Historical Records of the Buffs, 1914–19*, Medici Society

O'Neill, H.C., *The Royal Fusiliers in the Great War*, Heinemann, 1922

Popham, Hugh, *The Dorset Regiment*, Leo Cooper, 1970

Sheppard, E.W., *The Ninth Queen's Royal Lancers*, Gale and Polden, 1933

Wylly, H.C., *The Green Howards 1914–19*, Richmond, Yorks, 1925

Wyrall, Everard, *The Duke of Cornwall's Light Infantry, 1914–19*, Methuen, 1932

Various, *The 23rd London Regiment, 1914–19*, Times Publishing Co, 1936

Biographical

Blake, Robert (Ed.), *The Private Papers of Douglas Haig*, Eyre and Spottiswoode, 1952

Chapman, Guy, *A Passionate Prodigality*, MacGibbon and Kee, 1965

Churchill, Winston S., *The World Crisis*, Butterworth, 1921; *The Second World War*, Cassell, 1948

Farrar-Hockley, A., *Goughie*, Hart-Davies, 1975

Gough, Hubert, *The Fifth Army*, Hodder 1931; *Soldiering On*, Barker, 1954

Graves, Robert, *Goodbye to All That*, Cape, 1929

Harrington, C., *Plumer of Messines*, Murray, 1935

Liddell Hart, Basil, *Foch, Man of Orleans*, London, 1931

Neave, Airey, *The Flames of Calais*, Hodder, 1972

Reitz, Deneys, *Trekking On*, Faber, 1933

Richards, Frank, *Old Soldiers Never Die*, Faber

Robertson, Sir William, *From Private to Field-Marshal*, Constable, 1921

Rogers, Sydney, *Twelve Days*, Arthur Barker, 1935

French references

Becker, Jean-Jaques, *Les Français dans La Grande Guerre*, Laffont, 1980

Botti, Louis, *Avec Les Zouaves*, Paris, 1922

Cartier, Raymond, *Histoire d'Une Victoire*, serialised in *Match*, Paris, 1968

Chevallier, Gabriel, *La Peur*, Paris, 1930

Fayolle, Maréchal M-E., *Cahiers Secrets de la Grande Guerre*, Plon, 1964

Genevoix, Maurice et al, *Vie et Mort des Français 1914–1918*, Hachette, 1962

Isorni, Jacques, *Histoire Verédique de la Grande Guerre*, Vol III, Paris, 1970

Micquel, Pierre, *La Grande Guerre*, Paris, 1983

Mordacq, General, *Le Drame de l'Yser, Surprise des Gaz 1915*, Paris, 1933

Nobecourt, R-G., *Les Fantassins du Chemin des Dames*, Laffont, 1975

Belgian reference

Wanty, Emile, *L'Art de la Guerre*, Gerrard, 1967

German references

Binding, Rudolph, *A Fatalist at War*, Allen and Unwin, 1929

Falkenhayn, Erich von, *General Headquarters 1914–1916, and its critical decisions*, Hutchinson, 1920

Groehler, Olaf, *Der lautlose Tod*, East Berlin, 1978

Hanslian, R., *Der chemische Krieg*
Junger, Ernst, *Storm of Steel*, Chatto, 1929
Ludendorff, Erich, *My War Memoirs*, Hutchinson, 1921
Renn, Ludwig, *War*, Martin Secker, 1929
Remarque, E.M., *All Quiet on the Western Front*, Putnam, 1929
Sulzbach, Herbert, *With the German Guns*, Leo Cooper, 1973

War Office publications consulted
SS16 *Defensive Measures Against Gas Attack* published 1916; SS134
Instructions on the Use of Lethal and Lachrymatory Shell, published
March, 1918; *Defence Against Gas 1927*; *Artillery Training* Vol III –
Field Gunnery Pamphlet No 5, 1943; *The Handbook of Land Service
Ammunition*, Historical Section, 1971.

Also consulted
Adams, Valerie, *RUSI Journal* article, 1985
Bidwell and Graham, *Fire-Power – British Army Weapons and
    Theories of War 1904–1945*, Allen and Unwin, 1980
Erickson, J., *The Soviet High Command*, Macmillan, 1962
Froissart, *Chronicles*, trans. by G. Brereton, Penguin Edition, 1968
Fuller, J.F.C., 'Problems of Mechanical Warfare,' *Army Quarterly*,
    October, 1921
Graveley, A.F., Article in *Army Quarterly and Defence Journal*,
    October, 1980
Kitchen, M, *The German Officer Corps 1890–1914*, Clarendon
    Press, 1968
Liddell Hart, B, *The Tanks*, Cassell
Luard, K.E. *Unknown Warriors*, Chatto, 1930
Macleod and Kelly, eds, *The Ironside Diaries 1937–1940*, Constable,
    1962
Trumpner, Ulrich, *The Road to Ypres*, Journal of Modern History,
    USA, 1975
Williams, Trevor, *A Biographical Dictionary of Scientists*, Black,
    1969

Index

The index is divided into four parts – General, People, Locations and Military Formations

MILITARY FORMATIONS

BRITISH EMPIRE